D1452403

AUTONOMY AFTER AUSCHWITZ

AUTONOMY AFTER AUSCHWITZ

Adorno, German Idealism, and Modernity

MARTIN SHUSTER

THE UNIVERSITY OF CHICAGO PRESS

CHICAGO AND LONDON

MARTIN SHUSTER is chair of the Department of Philosophy and Religious Studies at Avila University in Kansas City, Missouri, and is cofounder of the Association for Adorno Studies.

The University of Chicago Press, Chicago 60637
The University of Chicago Press, Ltd., London
© 2014 by The University of Chicago
All rights reserved. Published 2014.
Printed in the United States of America

23 22 21 20 19 18 17 16 15 14   1 2 3 4 5

ISBN-13: 978-0-226-15548-7 (cloth)
ISBN-13: 978-0-226-15551-7 (e-book)
DOI: 10.7208/chicago/9780226155517.001.0001

Library of Congress Cataloging-in-Publication Data

Shuster, Martin, author.
  Autonomy after Auschwitz: Adorno, German idealism, and modernity / Martin Shuster.
      pages cm
  Includes bibliographical references and index.
  ISBN 978-0-226-15548-7 (cloth : alkaline paper)—
  ISBN 978-0-226-15551-7 (ebook)   1. Autonomy (Philosophy) 2. Adorno, Theodor W., 1903–1969. 3. Philosophy, German.   I. Title.
  B808.67.S58 2014
  141—dc23   2014005521

♾ This paper meets the requirements of ANSI/NISO Z39.48-1992 (Permanence of Paper).

For my parents

When man is for once overcome by the horror of alienation and the world fills him with anxiety, he looks up and sees a picture. Then he sees that the I is contained in the world, and that there really is no I, and thus the world cannot harm the I, and he calms down; or he sees that the world is contained in the I, and that there really is no world, and thus the world cannot harm the I, and he calms down. And when man is overcome again by the horror of alienation and the I fills him with anxiety, he looks up and sees a picture; and whichever he sees, it does not matter, either the empty I is stuffed full of world or it is submerged in the flood of the world, and he calms down. But the moment will come, and it is near, when man, overcome by horror, looks up and in a flash sees both pictures at once. And he is seized by a deeper horror.
—Martin Buber, *I and Thou*

The relation of history to reason remains constitutive for the discourse of modernity—for better or worse.
—Jürgen Habermas, *The Philosophical Discourse of Modernity*

The earthquake of Lisbon sufficed to cure Voltaire of the theodicy of Leibniz, and the visible disaster of the first nature was insignificant in comparison with the second, social one, which defies human imagination as it distills real hell from human evil.
—Theodor W. Adorno, *Negative Dialectics*

CONTENTS

ACKNOWLEDGMENTS

The basic questions in this book, in one way or another, can be traced back to interests I had as an undergraduate. For that I have to thank Stephen Vicchio, who first introduced me to the philosophical problem of evil. I probably wouldn't be writing about German philosophy, however, if it weren't for Jim Kreines, who hooked me on Hegel during my first foray into graduate school at Yale. At that time Richard Swinburne also proved an important interlocutor. However, this book, and the questions that animate it, began as a project at the Humanities Center at Johns Hopkins University. Since then, especially through my years at Hamilton College, I have incurred many debts, and I have no doubt that this book has benefited greatly from the individuals I will cite. Any mistakes or errors remain my own.

This book wouldn't have been possible without the intellectual climate and rigor provided by my graduate training at the Humanities Center. Those who have visited the center know there is a kind of magic in the air (and it's not just the special Baltimore pollen). The center offered me an opportunity to pursue diverse interests, while also allowing for my own philosophical voice. Hent de Vries and Paola Marrati continue to be inspirations. Eckart Förster, Dean Moyar, and Terry Pinkard (at Georgetown) contributed immensely to my knowledge of Kant and Hegel. While at Johns Hopkins, conversations with Jenny Astin (née Bautz), Donald Clark, Tarek Dika, Josh Gold (may his name be a blessing), Espen Hammer, Sandra Laugier, Giorgi Lebadnize, Christoph Menke, Ken and Anne Moss, Joyce Tsai, and Cara Weber proved helpful at one point or another. Thanks also to Marva Philip for her help, and a special thanks to Daniela Ginsburg and Xandy Frisch. Xandy tirelessly read earlier pieces of this book and generally has been a wonderful *chavruta* throughout the years.

The first chapter of this book was written under the auspices of a Diane and Howard Wohl fellowship at the Center for Advanced Holocaust Studies at the United States Holocaust Memorial Museum in Washington, DC. I was fortunate to be in residence at the museum from 2007 to 2008; special thanks to Lisa Yavnai for her support while I was there. I also benefited greatly from the scholarship of and discussions with Michal Aharony, Ferzina Banaji, Donald Bloxham, Michael Brenner, Jennifer Cazenave, Jehanne Dubrow, Devin Pendas, and Mark Roseman. Jennifer, Don, and Devin were especially helpful (and I will always look back fondly on our *Wire* marathon). I also have to thank Oxford University Press, which published some of the first chapter as part of my entry in the *Oxford Handbook of Genocide Studies*, and which kindly gave me permission to use that material here.

With my first job at Hamilton College, I stumbled into a little mecca of philosophy that proved an amazing and ever-renewing inspiration for the writing and rewriting of this book. I am especially grateful to Todd Franklin for reading very early drafts of some sections, and to Marianne Janack and Katheryn Doran for hearing parts of the third chapter. I also profited from conversations with Russell Marcus, David Pereplyotchik, Bob Simon, and Rick Werner. Outside the philosophy department, Virginia Clark (née Gutierrez-Berner) was an invaluable conversation partner during the initial phases of this book, as was Jeremy Skipper. Also invaluable were the students in my Ethics After Auschwitz seminar during my first semester at Hamilton, and those in my seminar on Hannah Arendt this past year. In this vein I thank Taylor Coe, Mercy Corredor, Robbie Fagan, Stephanie "Philostepher" Hudon, Dan Knishkowy, and Cara Quigley. I am also especially grateful to Alex Host and Chelsea Wahl, who journeyed intellectually with me as I wrote this book. Thanks to Allison Eck, who copyedited an earlier version of chapter 3 and the introduction (since scrapped, through no fault of hers).

In the past couple of years, Kathy Kiloh and I established the Association for Adorno Studies, and the first two meetings have proved extremely rewarding. Questions about parts of my first chapter from Gordon Finlayson, Robert Kaufman, Iain Macdonald, Brian O'Connor, and Max Pensky were very useful. Above all, though, I am grateful to Kathy, without whom the organization undoubtedly wouldn't exist.

Thanks to the interlibrary loan staff at Johns Hopkins and Hamilton College; they were both dear to the book's completion. Thanks also to Jennie Rathbun and Susan Halpert at the Houghton Library of Harvard

University for locating an Adorno letter and sending me a copy, and thanks to Christoph Gödde for tracking down an Adorno source for me.

Elizabeth Branch Dyson at the University of Chicago Press supported the project from the beginning, and I am grateful for her patience and wisdom in guiding the book toward completion. Thanks also to Russ Damian at Chicago and to Alice Bennett for her copyediting. I am also grateful to the anonymous reviewers at Chicago, who without doubt made this a stronger, clearer, and overall better manuscript.

My friends Reuben and Ian provided the nonacademic adventures and conversations necessary to sustain a philosophical life in academia. I am forever grateful to them and look forward to future adventures.

The love of my life, Robin, observed the various changes in this book over the years (and in me along the way) and provided constant love and support through them all. I am grateful almost beyond words for our life together and the prospects it makes possible for me.

Above all, I thank my parents. Without their courage, their sacrifices, and their encouragement throughout the years, I wouldn't have had the same opportunities or thought to take advantage of half of them. Their heroism and resilience are a daily inspiration, and it is to them that I dedicate this book.

These abbreviations are employed in the body of the text. If only a non-English source is cited, the translation is my own.

ADORNO

AGS   *Gesammelte Schriften*. 20 vols. Frankfurt am Main: Suhrkamp, 1984.

CM   *Critical Models: Interventions and Catchwords*. Translated by Henry W. Pickford. New York: Columbia University Press, 1998.

DE   *Dialectic of Enlightenment: Philosophical Fragments*. Translated by Edmund Jephcott. Palo Alto, CA: Stanford University Press, 2002.

H3S   *Hegel: Three Studies*. Cambridge, MA: MIT Press, 1993.

HF   *History and Freedom*. Edited by Rolf Tiedemann. Translated by Rodney Livingstone. Cambridge: Polity Press, 2006.

    Zur Lehre von der Geschichte und von der Freiheit. Edited by Rolf Tiedemann. Frankfurt am Main: Suhrkamp, 2001.

LND   *Lectures on Negative Dialectics*. Edited by Rolf Tiedemann. Translated by Rodney Livingstone. Cambridge: Polity Press, 2008.

    Vorlesung über Negative Dialektik. Edited by Rolf Tiedemann. Frankfurt am Main: Suhrkamp, 2003.

M   *Metaphysics*. Edited by Rolf Tiedemann. Translated by Edmund Jephcott. Stanford, CA: Stanford University Press, 2000.

    Metaphysik: Begriff und Probleme. Edited by Rolf Tiedemann. Frankfurt am Main: Suhrkamp, 2006.

MM   *Minima Moralia*. Translated by Edmund Jephcott. London: Verso, 2005.

ND   *Negative Dialectics*. Translated by E. B. Ashton. New York: Continuum, 1973.

PMP   *Problems of Moral Philosophy*. Translated by Rodney Livingstone.
           Stanford, CA: Stanford University Press, 2000.
           Probleme der Moralphilosophie. Edited by Thomas Schröder.
           Frankfurt am Main: Suhrkamp, 1996.

TLP   "Theses on the Language of the Philosopher." In *Adorno and the
           Need in Thinking: Critical Essays*, ed. Donald A. Burke, Colin J.
           Campbell, Kathy Kiloh, Michael K. Palamarek, and Jonathan Short,
           35–39. Toronto: University of Toronto Press, 2007.

The German edition of Adorno's writings cited is Theodor W. Adorno, *Gesammelte Schriften*, 20 vols. (Frankfurt am Main: Suhrkamp, 1984). Citations are of the format English/German. Since the edition of *Dialectic of Enlightenment* in the Adorno corpus is not a critical edition, the German version cited is volume 5 of Max Horkheimer, *Gesammelte Schriften*, 19 vols. (Frankfurt am Main: S. Fischer, 1987). Finally, although I have consulted the German in the case of the lectures, I have cited page numbers of the English only.

KANT

1C   *Critique of Pure Reason*. Translated by Paul Guyer and Allen W.
           Wood. Cambridge: Cambridge University Press, 1998.

2C   *Critique of Practical Reason*. Translated by Lewis White Beck.
           Indianapolis, IN: Bobbs-Merrill, 1956.

3C   *Critique of the Power of Judgment*. Translated by Paul Guyer
           and Eric Matthews. Cambridge: Cambridge University Press,
           2000.

G   *"Foundations of the Metaphysics of Morals" and "What Is
           Enlightenment?"* Translated by Lewis White Beck. 2nd ed. Upper
           Saddle River, NJ: Prentice Hall, 1997.

LE   *Lectures on Ethics*. Translated by Peter Heath. Cambridge:
           Cambridge University Press, 1997.

MOM   "The Metaphysics of Morals." In *Practical Philosophy*, edited and
           translated by Mary J. Gregor, 353–605. Cambridge: Cambridge
           University Press, 1996.

R   *Religion within the Boundaries of Mere Reason*. Edited by Allen
           Wood and George di Giovanni. Cambridge: Cambridge University
           Press, 1998.

The German corpus cited is Immanuel Kant, *Gesammelte Schriften*, edited by Preussischen Akademie der Wissenschaften, 29 vols. (Berlin: Walter de Gruyter, 1912). If my reference is not to one of the texts above, then only the German pagination is cited. When citing the first critique, I use the accepted standard of citing A/B editions. I also throughout refer to the *Foundations of the Metaphysics of Morals* simply as the *Groundwork*.

HEGEL

E   *The Encyclopedia Logic*. Translated by T. F. Geraets, W. A. Suchting, and H. S. Harris. Indianapolis, IN: Hackett, 1991.

LA   *Hegel's Aesthetics: Lectures on Fine Art*. Translated by T. M. Knox. Oxford: Oxford University Press, 1975.

PR   *Elements of the Philosophy of Right*. Translated by H. B. Nisbet. Cambridge: Cambridge University Press, 1991.

PS   *Phenomenology of Spirit*. Translated by A. V. Miller. Oxford: Oxford University Press, 1977.

The German edition of Hegel's writings cited is G. W. F. Hegel, *Werke* (Frankfurt am Main: Suhrkamp, 1970). Where possible, I cite only the section. The *Philosophy of Right*'s preface is cited by English/German page numbers.

OTHERS

I   Anscombe, G. E. M. *Intention*. Cambridge, MA: Harvard University Press, 2000.

CR   Cavell, Stanley. *The Claim of Reason: Wittgenstein, Skepticism, Morality, and Tragedy*. Oxford: Oxford University Press, 1979.

CHU   Cavell, Stanley. *Conditions Handsome and Unhandsome*. Chicago: University of Chicago Press, 1990.

UA   Cavell, Stanley. *This New Yet Unapproachable America: Lectures after Emerson after Wittgenstein*. Albuquerque, NM: Living Batch Press, 1989.

CW   Cavell, Stanley. *Cities of Words: Pedagogical Letters on a Register of the Moral Life*. Cambridge, MA: Harvard University Press, 2004.

BPP   Horkheimer, Max. *Between Philosophy and Social Science*. Translated by G. Frederick Hunter, Matthew S. Kramer, and John Torpey. Cambridge, MA: MIT Press, 1993.

          Horkheimer, Max. *Gesammelte Schriften*. 19 vols. Frankfurt am Main: S. Fischer, 1987. References are English/German, by volume and page number.

PI   Wittgenstein, Ludwig. *Philosophical Investigations*. Translated by G. E. M. Anscombe. Upper Saddle River, NJ: Prentice Hall, 1973.

This book is about Adorno's assessment of the notion of autonomy, and of freedom more broadly, especially as the concept is developed by Adorno's two greatest interlocutors, Kant and Hegel. That notion famously made its way into the German tradition through Rousseau,[1] for whom freedom consists in a thoroughgoing independence, in obeying "no one but oneself."[2] That this issue forms the lifeblood of a large part of modern German philosophical thought can be surmised from passages like the following from the *Philosophy of Right* (1820), where Hegel writes that it is a "great hardheadedness [*Eigensinn*], the sort of hardheadedness that *does honor* to human beings, that they are unwilling to acknowledge in their attitudes what has not been justified by thought" (PR 22/27; translation modified and emphasis added). Hegel reinforces this point when he summarizes things with the claim that "this hardheadedness is the characteristic property of the modern age." In turn, this can be seen as a variation or extension of Kant's claim in "What Is Enlightenment?" that modern enlightenment ought to be characterized by "man's release from his self-incurred tutelage," where the chief problem is that we have failed or refused to use our reason *"without direction from another"* (G 7:35; emphasis added).

1. For Rousseau's influence on Kant, see Susan Meld Shell, *Kant and the Limits of Autonomy* (Cambridge, MA: Harvard University Press, 2009), 34ff., especially note 18. For Rousseau's influence on Hegel, see Frederick Neuhouser, *Foundations of Hegel's Social Theory: Actualizing Freedom* (Cambridge, MA: Harvard University Press, 2003), 55ff.

2. Jean-Jacques Rousseau, *The Social Contract*, trans. Maurice Cranston (New York: Penguin, 1968).

Commenting on Kant's claim in a radio discussion, Adorno points out that Kant's conception remains "extraordinarily up-to-date."[3] In the same broadcast, however, Adorno also voices concern about whether, like Kant, we can say that although we do not live in an "enlightened" age, we do live in an "age of enlightenment." Viewed from a high-enough altitude, it might seem that Adorno is just another figure in a long line of philosophers voicing hesitations and worries about the possibility of autonomy as self-legislation.[4] In many ways, especially to the extent that he is familiar with Hegel (as a critic of Kant), Nietzsche (as a critic of the German philosophical tradition), Heidegger (as a critic of modernity), and others (notably Kierkegaard, Marx, and Husserl, as critics in their own right), such an assessment is not entirely wrong. Nonetheless, it would miss the fact that for Adorno the most interesting and pressing issue is not so much that autonomy is somehow "impossible," "implausible," or "unsatisfying" (although he also surveys and frequently proposes these ideas), but rather that autonomy may well be satisfying but ultimately is dangerous or destructive. Although this point will become fully apparent only in chapter 1, I can emphasize now that Adorno will claim that Kant's notion of autonomy, if adopted as a norm, dissolves our capacity for reason, especially practical reason, and thereby our very standing as agents, and it is in *this sense* that Kantian autonomy proves "dangerous" or "destructive." So far as modern social, economic, and political configurations are repressive, a commitment to autonomy exacerbates these problems by producing agents incapable of resisting such conditions, even through thought.[5] (And I should note that while I cannot here offer an exhaustive justification of the former claim—the charge that modern institutions or configurations may be repressive—Adorno's point will stand even if this is not true: Kantian autonomy destroys our status as *agents*, and this would remain a conceptual issue even if we lived in utopia; that said, I will return to the issue in more detail in chapters 1 and 3.) What is striking, however, is that Adorno nonetheless maintains an attraction to autonomy,[6] just no longer Kantian autonomy.

3. Theodor W. Adorno and Helmut Becker, "Education for Maturity and Responsibility," *History of the Human Sciences* 12, no. 3 (1999): 21.

4. For such an account, see Robert B. Pippin, *Modernism as a Philosophical Problem: On the Dissatisfaction of European High Culture*, 2nd ed. (Oxford: Blackwell, 1999).

5. Hannah Arendt diagnoses an analogous worry. See Martin Shuster, "Loneliness and Language: Arendt, Cavell, and Modernity," *International Journal of Philosophical Studies* 20, no. 4 (2012): 473–97.

6. Cf. Iain Macdonald, "Cold, Cold, Warm: Autonomy, Intimacy and Maturity in Adorno," *Philosophy and Social Criticism* 37, no. 6 (2011): 669–89.

Insofar as talk of "committing" oneself to autonomy sounds peculiar, my way of framing the issues may already strike some as inappropriate or outright wrong. After all, either we are autonomous or we are not. For Adorno, however, the issues involved are not fundamentally metaphysical or ontological ones, say, whether we *are* free or whether we are the sorts of natural beings that can initiate novel causal chains (issues I pursue in detail in chapter 3). Instead, for Adorno, like others in the German philosophical tradition, the issues center on norms, on *normativity*. In this tradition, when I self-legislate, it is not that I create the law in question from thin air, but that I come to *regard* the law as my own, as if it *had been* authored by me. I must thereby come to understand my legislation as expressive of myself as a rational agent, that is, as expressive of my innermost commitments as a rational human. (From here, at least according to Kant, it is also an important step that freedom and morality come to be intertwined.)[7] As interpreters suggest, for Kant this picture amounts to valuing our very capacity to set ends,[8] that is, to valuing our *humanity* (otherwise Kant is subject to a "paradox" around self-legislation: I cannot legislate the law to myself unless I do so lawfully, but to do so lawfully, I must have already legislated the law to myself, and so on).[9]

Adorno's worries in response to this picture cluster around two interrelated sets of issues. First, Adorno, like Hegel, is convinced that *what* counts as "valuing humanity" can be elaborated only in concrete social and historical circumstances (there is more to be said here, both for the charge and in Kant's defense; both are taken up in chapters 2 and 3). On this picture, morality is thereby just one feature of a larger, complex web of normative commitments and cannot be understood apart from it—that is, apart from an entire form of life. Second, because of the embedded nature of our practical reason, and because of worries about our commitment to autonomy and our socioeconomic and sociopolitical configurations, Adorno questions whether freedom, especially understood as Kantian morality or as reflective self-legislation, is any longer possible *as* a norm. He will frame this claim as the thought that in modern life "original sin has been secularized" (ND 243/6:241). This is so much so that whatever we might do, we are

7. In this context, see chapter 2, note 5, on the "Reciprocity Thesis."
8. See especially Christine M. Korsgaard, *The Sources of Normativity* (Cambridge: Cambridge University Press, 1996). See also chapter 3, section 10.
9. For the formulation of the paradox, see Terry Pinkard, *German Philosophy, 1760–1780: The Legacy of Idealism* (Cambridge: Cambridge University Press, 2002), 59, and Robert B. Pippin, "The Actualization of Freedom," in *The Cambridge Companion to German Idealism*, ed. Karl Ameriks (Cambridge: Cambridge University Press, 2000).

allegedly already "infected [*angesteckt*] by evil . . . and no less infected" when we do "nothing at all" (ND 243/6:241). Whether such pessimism can be harnessed toward any positive program depends in large part on whether we can produce a notion of freedom as reflective self-legislation that is nonetheless responsive to such issues (the "after Auschwitz" element of my title—a topic I pursue in chapter 3).

Because Adorno is seen as occupying a place in the German philosophical tradition of thinking about freedom, I grant considerable space to the tradition itself. Before presenting Adorno's own notion of freedom, I present Kant's notion of autonomy in detail (chapter 2), as well as Adorno's criticism of that notion (chapter 1). Thus, although Adorno is in many ways the central figure, this book is not solely about him; it is equally about Kant and Hegel and a certain tradition of thinking about freedom. Again, this is apparent as much from Kant's rejoinder to Adorno's critique (chapter 2) as from a consideration of the way Adorno's own notion of freedom might benefit from Hegel's conception of the same (chapter 4). Furthermore, given Adorno's own diverse intellectual interests, this book does not present anything like a unified or systematic or even complete view of Adorno's thought. My aim has been to follow one thread from Adorno's corpus (his thinking about freedom) in order to situate him as an important interlocutor within a German philosophical tradition that is witnessing a recent revival and that still has many insights to offer. To the extent that Kantian autonomy remains important (both historically and conceptually), Adorno's criticisms of that notion and his alleged improvements on it are also important.

Throughout, I engage with recent philosophy, both European and Anglo-American. I am convinced, in light of the breadth and originality of his thought, that Adorno has much to offer to a variety of traditions (and vice versa). In this vein, Stanley Cavell is a frequent voice in this book as I explore the parallels between his conception of morality and Adorno's (a point introduced briefly in chapter 1 and expanded in chapter 3 and the conclusion). Cavell conceives his brand of "moral perfectionism" as addressing a moment "in which a crisis forces an examination of one's life that calls for a transformation or reorienting of it" (CW 11). While the types and aspects of crisis that demand their attention are distinct (although not always, and never are they unrelated), the sensitivity, earnestness, and care with which they probe the contours of a moral life makes the comparison fruitful, indeed, synergistic.

Finally, with an eye toward the textual resources I marshal, I note that in addition to Adorno's various published works, I make extensive use of his lecture courses. While it is true that with the publication of some of his lectures in 1962 Adorno claimed that "nothing spoken . . . could meet the demands . . . placed on a text," he also frequently used his lectures as early drafts for published work (AGS 20.1:360). Furthermore, some of the published material (e.g., the discussion of "the addendum" in *Negative Dialectics*) is impenetrable without the lectures. I have done my best to cross-reference them with the written text.

To summarize what follows, the book begins with an overview of Adorno's critique of Kantian autonomy. In chapter 1, I provide a new reading of the first essay of Horkheimer and Adorno's *Dialectic of Enlightenment* (1947), demonstrating that interpreters have failed to notice that Kant and his notion of autonomy constitute the centerpiece of this text. As already mentioned, Horkheimer and Adorno illustrate how far a commitment to Kantian autonomy dissolves our capacities for practical reason, and thereby our standing as agents. With this first chapter, it ought already to be apparent that Adorno is a profitable interlocutor within the Kantian and German idealist tradition. In chapter 2, following Adorno's own estimation of Kant's aspirations after the first *Critique*, I present Kant's potential rejoinder to Horkheimer and Adorno. With this rejoinder we see that Kant's rational theology (based on the highest good) not only is an essential component of his notion of autonomy but also potentially responds to Horkheimer and Adorno's critique. To move beyond this standstill, the next chapter focuses on Adorno's mature thought, especially as found in *Negative Dialectics* (1966). Adorno's own anti-voluntarist notion of freedom is presented and explicitly opposed to Kant's rational theology. In Adorno's view, our agency is intertwined with our capacities for action and expression (and it is this latter concept that allows him to retain a notion of reflective self-legislation). Furthermore, in that such capacities are ultimately "drawn out of us" by our environment, our understanding of freedom must be intimately concerned with social and historical configurations. Here it becomes apparent that Adorno's conception of freedom, like Kant's (albeit in a very different way), is wedded to a conception of morality (and Adorno's "new categorical imperative" is thereby elaborated). Chapter 3 suggests that we can tease out Adorno's philosophy of action (taken as an account about the mechanics of action) to see how those mechanics are tied to a theory of moral action (and thereby morality). At the conclusion of chapter 3, Adorno's worries about Kant's rational theology are explicitly hashed out. Chapter 4, in response to a worry encountered with Adorno's own notion of freedom, presents Hegel as a necessary interlocutor, with a discussion of the *Phenomenology of*

Spirit (1807). In this way the favor between Adorno and the German philosophical tradition is returned when it is shown how Adorno's account of agency can benefit from Hegel's own. In the conclusion, I suggest that all of this presents us with a formal conception of freedom while its actualization remains a practical task.

And a crucial one at that.

I Against I:
Stressing the Dialectic in the
Dialectic of Enlightenment

1. INTRODUCTION

The *Dialectic of Enlightenment*, Adorno's cooperative effort with Max Horkheimer, serves as the backdrop to all of Adorno's subsequent thinking about freedom. For this reason it is essential to understand Horkheimer and Adorno's aspirations with this text, especially the critique of modernity found there. Unfortunately this is no easy task—the *Dialectic of Enlightenment* has been read alternatively as elaborating an "'excess' Enlightenment,"[1] as a "'retrogressive anthropogenesis,'"[2] as approximating a "traditional form of cultural criticism,"[3] as a work that "is not a historical treatise but a collection of haphazardly chosen and unexplained examples to illustrate various forms of the debasement of 'enlightened' ideals,"[4] as an attack "essentially in line with the romantic tradition,"[5] as a "deliberately discontinuous work,"[6] as an attempt to "dismantle the myth of history

Parts of this chapter were written under the auspices of a Diane and Howard Wohl fellowship at the Center for Advanced Holocaust Studies, United States Holocaust Memorial Museum, from 2007 to 2008. Parts of the chapter also appeared in Martin Shuster, "Philosophy and Genocide," in *The Oxford Handbook of Genocide Studies*, ed. Donald Bloxham and A. Dirk Moses (Oxford: Oxford University Press, 2010), 217–35.

1. Robert B. Pippin, *The Persistence of Subjectivity: On the Kantian Aftermath* (Cambridge: Cambridge University Press, 2005), 102.

2. Axel Honneth, *The Critique of Power: Reflective Stages in a Critical Social Theory*, trans. Kenneth Baynes (Cambridge, MA: MIT Press, 1991), 43.

3. Ibid., 42.

4. Leszek Kolakowski, *Main Currents of Marxism: Its Rise, Growth and Dissolution*, trans. P. S. Falla, 3 vols. (Oxford: Oxford University Press, 1978), 3:373.

5. Ibid., 3:376.

6. Fredric Jameson, *Late Marxism: Adorno, or The Persistence of the Dialectic* (London: Verso, 1990), 15.

as progress,"[7] as a "radical and sweeping critique of Western society and thought,"[8] as unmasking "as reification all attempts to demonstrate the possibility of the full realization of man's humanity,"[9] as "a bewildering book,"[10] as what looks "like a series of wild generalizations barely susceptible to empirical confirmation,"[11] as a "reconstruction of the prehistory of subjectivity as the dialectic of myth and enlightenment,"[12] as a "series of hit-or-miss aphorisms rather than a sustained argument,"[13] and as rejecting the "conceptual dualism of enlightenment and myth."[14] In short, there is neither a scholarly consensus about the text nor a consensus about its alleged contents (and thereby about the actual nature of the critique).

My goal in this chapter will be to propose yet another reading of this text, with an eye to making sense of its critique of modernity. Crucial to such a task is understanding the centrality of the first essay, "The Concept of Enlightenment," to any reading of the book and recognizing the way a serious engagement with Kant animates the argument of the text (points I argue, respectively, in section 4 and sections 8–10 below). In my view, Kantian autonomy drives the dialectic of enlightenment and thereby, insofar as such autonomy constitutes human agency and potentially underwrites the fabric our lives, the scope of the argument is meant, ambitiously, to extend to the entirety of human life. All of this is still at a high level of generality and requires significant contextualization and elaboration, but in broad outline the story will turn out to be that, in Horkheimer and Adorno's view, and insofar as Kantian autonomous agency cannot allow for any standpoint that grounds its stance in something external to itself, this drive toward self-grounding will be what fuels the dialectic of enlightenment and underwrites their critique of modernity. My procedure comprises three steps: I will argue that the dialectic of enlightenment, in scope, can apply to every

7. Susan Buck-Morss, *The Origin of Negative Dialectics: Theodor W. Adorno, Walter Benjamin, and the Frankfurt Insitute* (New York: Free Press, 1977), 60.

8. Martin Jay, *The Dialectical Imagination: A History of the Frankfurt School and the Institute of Social Research, 1923–1950* (Berkeley: University of California Press, 1973), 256.

9. Bernard Yack, *The Longing for Total Revolution: Philosophic Sources of Social Discontent from Rousseau to Marx and Nietzsche* (Princeton, NJ: Princeton University Press, 1986), 129–30.

10. Simon Jarvis, *Adorno: A Critical Introduction* (Cambridge: Polity Press, 1998), 20.

11. Ibid.

12. Anke Thyen, *Negative Dialektik und Erfahrung: zur Rationalität des Nichtidentischen bei Adorno* (Frankfurt am Main: Suhrkamp, 1989), 109.

13. Richard Rorty, "The Overphilosophication of Politics," *Constellations* 7, no. 1 (2000): 128.

14. J. M. Bernstein, *Adorno: Disenchantment and Ethics* (Cambridge: Cambridge University Press, 2001), 87.

facet of human life (the claim to totality); then I will show that the dialectic of enlightenment does apply to every facet of human life (the claim of necessity); and finally it will become apparent that the dialectic of enlightenment dissolves the possibility of practical reason (the claim about practical reason). Furthermore, in that all these claims can be demonstrated, *Dialectic of Enlightenment* is shown to be not a bloated mess or merely an assemblage of possibly related, possibly unrelated non sequiturs, but rather an intentionally fragmentary[15] but nonetheless philosophically sophisticated thesis about the possibility of autonomous reason.

2. THE TEXT OF THE *DIALECTIC OF ENLIGHTENMENT*

Before moving to this discussion, however, I want to get some historical details on the table. Doing so requires retreating from philosophical issues all the way to the most basic historical details about the text and its composition. A retreat at this point allows for a focus explicitly on the text, thereby raising these issues organically, from the ground up. In this way I hope to make the case for my proposed reading more forceful. I will defer the discussion of autonomy and Kant until we have a clear understanding of how these issues arise from the more explicit and traditionally discussed themes of the text, especially the notions of enlightenment and myth. But before we get there, a few textual points.

The most important, and obvious, point is that *Dialectic of Enlightenment* was written jointly.[16] Its joint authorship might be accounted for in a variety of ways: we can examine the trajectory of both Adorno's and Horkheimer's later works for clues about how to understand *Dialectic of Enlightenment*,[17] the various pieces of the work can be attributed to different authors,[18] certain features of the text, whether positive or negative, can

---

15. Such a style is justified roughly a decade later in Theodor W. Adorno, "The Essay as Form," *New German Critique* 32 (1984): 151–71.

16. The best overview of issues of composition is G. S. Noerr's "Die Stellung der 'Dialektik der Aufklärung' in der Entwicklung der Kritischen Theorie," in Max Horkheimer, *Gesammelte Schriften*, 19 vols. (Frankfurt am Main: S. Fischer, 1987), 5:423–52. See also Anson Rabinbach, *In the Shadow of Catastrophe* (Berkeley: University of California Press, 1997), 166–74; Rolf Wiggerhaus, *The Frankfurt School*, trans. Michael Robertson (Cambridge, MA: MIT Press, 1994), 302–44.

17. Cf. Robert Hullot-Kentor, "Back to Adorno," *Telos* 81 (1989): 7–8.

18. For G. S. Noerr's theories about the composition of various parts of *Dialectic of Enlightenment*, see Horkheimer, *Gesammelte Schriften*, 5:427–29. Cf. Rabinbach, *In the Shadow of Catastrophe*, 167. Robert Hullot-Kentor has pointed out that such "positivistic philology is not of great use here because . . . the essays were the result of collective dictation and intensive

be explained as by-products of collaboration,[19] or we can use some combination of these methods. By my lights, employing all these methods sparingly is appropriate. The final text is a single unit, and there is not sufficient reason to discard sections of it. Furthermore, the prospects for determining the authorship of "The Concept of Enlightenment" are not promising; arguments for joint authorship or for sole authorship by Horkheimer or by Adorno have equal currency. Short of new evidence, there is simply no good way to adjudicate such debates.

A few other details about composition are worth noting. First, as Gretel Adorno and Leo Löwenthal have pointed out, many passages were dictated together by Adorno and Horkheimer, so certain types of philological inquiry will not help with questions of authorship. Horkheimer and Adorno refer to something like this when they write in the preface to *Dialectic of Enlightenment*: "No one who was not involved in the writing could easily understand to what extent we both feel responsible for every sentence. We dictated long stretches together; the *Dialectic* derives its vital energy from the tension between the two intellectual temperaments which came together in writing it" (DE xi/5:13). Second, the text was originally "published" in 1944, in a limited mimeograph edition in honor of Friedrich Pollock's fiftieth birthday. The original title was simply "Philosophical Fragments." Then in 1947 the text was revised and reprinted by a professional publisher (Querido). The title of the original lead essay, "Dialectic of Enlightenment," became the new title, while the original title became a subtitle.[20] Finally, note that in June 1941 Hannah Arendt delivered to Adorno a stack of papers by Walter Benjamin. This collection was Benjamin's last work, the "Theses on the Philosophy of History."[21] Benjamin committed suicide in 1940 after unsuccessfully attempting to escape to Portugal through Spain. Both the manuscript and Benjamin's death had a profound effect on Horkheimer and Adorno, personally and philosophically.

---

conversation. The typescripts Noerr examined are mediated documents." See Hullot-Kentor, "Back to Adorno," 7. Hullot-Kentor instead stresses the importance of "stylistic comparisons."

19. Cf. Christopher Rocco, "Between Modernity and Postmodernity: Reading *Dialectic of Enlightenment* against the Grain," *Political Theory* 22, no. 1 (1994): 85, 91.

20. There was also a subsequent version published in 1969. For some of the textual variants between the 1944 and 1947 versions, see "The Disappearance of Class History in 'Dialectic of Enlightenment,'" in *Dialectic of Enlightenment*, 248–52. I will say more about the textual variations shortly.

21. Walter Benjamin, *Illuminations* (New York: Schocken Books, 1968), 253–65. On this point, see Adorno's June 12, 1942, letter to Horkheimer in Horkheimer, *Gesammelte Schriften*, 17:59.

3. ENLIGHTENMENT AS A HISTORICAL CATEGORY?

Indeed, Benjamin's influence is present in the opening words of the preface, where Horkheimer and Adorno write that they "had set out to . . . explain why humanity, instead of arriving at a truly human condition, is sinking into a new type of barbarism" (DE xiv/5:16; translation modified). To avoid vacuity, such an inquiry must be tempered by Benjamin's claim in the *Theses* that "the current amazement that the things we are experiencing are "'still'" possible in the twentieth century is *not* philosophical. This amazement is not the beginning of knowledge—unless it is the knowledge that the view of history which gives rise to it is untenable (Thesis 8)."

And something like Benjamin's point is evident when Horkheimer and Adorno immediately reframe their intent as "merely" inquiring about the "self-destruction of enlightenment" (DE xvi/5:18). This raises the issue of how to understand the way Horkheimer and Adorno use "enlightenment." We are urged to see "enlightenment" as a process, not as designating a historical period (DE 1/5:25). A process, however, also has a history, and thereby a beginning and perhaps also a goal, or at least a conclusion. The distinction, then, between period and process, which is important and without which *Dialectic of Enlightenment* would become an assortment of "wild generalizations barely susceptible to empirical confirmation," is difficult to negotiate (DE 1/5:25).

One way to cope with this difficulty is to read *Dialectic of Enlightenment* as a cultural critique akin to other writings from the period (for example, those of Huxley, Jaspers, Jung, Klages, and others). In this way, if one is sympathetic to the argument, "enlightenment" might refer to something like "a linear historical narrative of enlightenment,"[22] taken broadly to designate either disenchantment with the world, instrumental thinking, scientistic rationalism, or some combination of these. If one is unsympathetic to the argument, then "enlightenment" might just be an essentially "fanciful, unhistorical hybrid composed of everything" that Adorno and Horkheimer "dislike."[23] Neither reading need imply conservatism, since either is compatible with seeing *Dialectic of Enlightenment*'s chief task as revealing the pitfalls of particular practices, without also insisting on a return to some real or imagined past.

---

22. Morton Schoolman, *Reason and Horror: Critical Theory, Democracy, and Aesthetic Rationality* (London: Routledge, 2001), 7.

23. Kolakowski, *Main Currents of Marxism*, 3:376.

While I am sympathetic to these approaches, I think they minimize an important feature of the text. Such readings frequently forget that *Dialectic of Enlightenment*'s impulse was not solely negative, and thereby pessimistic in nature.[24] While the text's bleakness is undeniable, Horkheimer and Adorno also refer to a "secret utopia harbored within the concept of reason" (DE 66/5:107) and explicitly claim that the "critique of enlightenment given . . . is intended to prepare a positive concept of enlightenment" (DE xviii/5:21). At the same time, they do not help themselves here, since such a positive program never appears. Nonetheless, this aspiration is important not only for understanding the aims of their critique (which is meant to be part of a larger project), but especially for a proper understanding of the trajectory of Adorno's later thinking. Such an aspiration also suggests that the critique is philosophical in nature, concerned neither merely with a historical process, nor with any particular cultural failing. Some cultural critiques, of course, call into question the whole gamut of Western civilization; in this sense they overlap with Horkheimer and Adorno's approach. Their differences lie in something like the level at which the critique is pitched. To put my cards on the table, I do not take Horkheimer and Adorno to aspire "just" to comment on some ill-defined "Enlightenment project,"[25] even one that stretches across multiple historical periods. Their aspiration is rather to comment on the status of reason itself. To the extent that they view reason itself as an achievement, any such commentary will have a historical component. Everything hinges, however, on where the historical details enter the account, whether they serve as the justification for the critique (for example, crassly, as in "had this not happened, we would not be in this mess"), or whether they instead serve as its historical basis (as in "because this *happened*, we now *cannot but* understand that so-and-so"; i.e., because we have certain concepts, we must deal with certain issues). Stanley Cavell's suggestion about how to understand the difference between Spengler and Wittgenstein is relevant in this context. He proposes that Wittgenstein's uniqueness "comes from the sense that he is joining the fate of philosophy as such with that of the philosophy or criticism of culture, thus displacing both" (UA 73). I think the same can be said of Horkheimer and Adorno (however, it is not my aim to analyze contemporaneous cultural critiques

24. The classic statement of *Dialectic of Enlightenment*'s pessimism is Jürgen Habermas, "The Entwinement of Myth and Enlightenment: Max Horkheimer and Theodor Adorno," in *The Philosophical Discourse of Modernity* (Cambridge, MA: MIT Press, 1987), 106–31.

25. James Schmidt, "What Enlightenment Project?," *Political Theory* 28, no. 6 (2000): 734–57.

with this point in mind, nor do I think much hinges philosophically on such a task). Horkheimer and Adorno—in this sense, like Wittgenstein—are concerned with more than "just" a critique of culture. At the same time, they refuse to criticize "reason" (taken here as our practice of "giving and taking reasons") without a sensitivity to historical detail, or without insight into the origins of reason as well as possible alternatives.

4. THE *CONCEPT* OF ENLIGHTENMENT, AND ENLIGHTENMENT AND MYTH

Dialectic of Enlightenment, then, is a philosophical critique, dealing with the most basic elements of any thinking that aims to enlighten, where such thinking is taken in the broadest possible terms.[26] As Horkheimer and Adorno write, "Enlightenment understood in the widest sense as the advance of thought, has always aimed at liberating human beings from fear and installing them as masters" (DE 1/5:25). "Enlightenment," then, designates an outlook that spans temporal and spatial boundaries. As Adorno will later write, "*As far back as we can trace it*, the history of thought has been a dialectic of enlightenment" (ND 118/6:124; emphasis added). In this spirit I want to highlight an important change between the two editions of *Dialectic of Enlightenment*.[27] In the original 1944 printing, the first chapter was titled "Dialectic of Enlightenment." In subsequent printings, however, the same chapter appears as "Concept [*Begriff*] of Enlightenment." This revision is important and gives us two clues for reading the text. First, most of the revisions to *Dialectic of Enlightenment* primarily toned down the Marxist language of the first edition (in part, surely, to avoid censorship and in part perhaps because of the changing political orientation of the authors themselves).[28] Revisions that do not serve this goal, then, should be

26. Cf. Hent de Vries, *Minimal Theologies: Critiques of Secular Reason in Adorno and Levinas*, trans. Geoffrey Hale (Baltimore: Johns Hopkins University Press, 2005), 191.

27. Cf. James Schmidt, "Language, Mythology, and Enlightenment: Historical Notes on Horkheimer and Adorno's *Dialectic of Enlightenment*," *Social Research* 65, no. 4 (1998): 807–38.

28. There is debate about to what extent *Dialectic of Enlightenment* is a Marxist text. Martin Jay has argued that by this point the Frankfurt school was moving away from Marxism; see Jay, *Dialectical Imagination*, 255–61. For an opposite view, see Buck-Morss, *Origin of Negative Dialectics*, 61–62. More broadly, for an argument for Adorno as a Marxist thinker, see Jameson, *Late Marxism*. For an opposite view, see Jameson, *Marxism and Form* (Princeton, NJ: Princeton University Press, 1971), 3–60. For an overview of the issues, see Espen Hammer, *Adorno and the Political* (London: Routledge, 2006), 26–49.

carefully examined. Second, although *Dialectic of Enlightenment* is fragmentary, this revision highlights an obvious organizational scheme, making it explicit that "The Concept of Enlightenment" somehow anchors the essays following it. As Horkheimer and Adorno clearly point out in the preface, this essay is the "theoretical basis of those which follow" (DE xviii/5:21). Designating the first essay as the "concept" of enlightenment expressly invites speculation about the nature of this concept, especially its coherency and actualization. Not shying away from such a task, the remaining chapters serve as applications, extensions, or implications of the concept of enlightenment thinking, focusing on its various elements (so, "Myth *and Enlightenment*," "*Enlightenment* and Morality," "*Enlightenment* as Mass Deception," and "Limits of *Enlightenment*"). Therefore, though it is a collection of "philosophical fragments," the 1947 version of *Dialectic of Enlightenment* is quite unitary. In fact "enlightenment" is here exactly a conceptual category as opposed to a historical one.

To understand enlightenment in this way, we must understand the relation between enlightenment and myth. Adorno and Horkheimer write: "Enlightenment has always regarded anthropomorphism, the projection of subjective properties onto nature, as the basis of myth. The supernatural, spirits and demons, are taken to be reflections of human beings who allow themselves to be frightened by natural phenomena. According to enlightened thinking, the multiplicity of mythical figures can be reduced to a single common denominator, the subject" (DE 4/5:28).

Furthermore, they propose that "enlightenment . . . wanted to dispel myths, to overthrow fantasy with knowledge" (DE 1/5:25). In this sense the idea seems to be that "the mind, conquering superstition, is to rule over disenchanted nature" (DE 2/5:26). Knowledge is power. Not only that, it is a power that "knows no limits, either in its enslavement of creation or in its deference to worldly masters" (DE 2/5:26). If unchecked, enlightenment turns on everything, including what it holds dear. All ideas, but most disturbingly ideas like rights or freedom, become suspect and take on a mythical light. Every "definite theoretical view is subjected to the annihilating criticism that it is only a belief, until even the concepts of mind, truth, and, indeed, enlightenment itself have been reduced to animistic magic" (DE 7/5:33). Horkheimer and Adorno point out that "in the authority of universal concepts enlightenment detected a fear of the demons through whose effigies human beings had tried to influence nature in magic rituals" (DE 3/5:27; translation modified). Indeed, "no difference is said to exist between the totemic animal, the dreams of the spirit-seer, and the absolute Idea" (DE 3/5:27). Ultimately "anything which does not conform to the standard of calculability and utility must be viewed with suspicion" (DE 3/5:28). In short, and strikingly, "enlightenment is totalitarian" (DE 3/5:28). Pushing the political metaphor, Horkheimer and Adorno claim that "enlightenment stands in the same relation to things as the dictator to human beings. He knows them to the extent that he can manipulate them" (DE 6/5:31). At the same time, since enlightenment is merely the removal of fear of the unknown, then humans only "believe themselves free of fear when there is no longer anything unknown" (DE 11/5:38). To achieve such a goal, and so far as anything potentially can be classified *as* something, truth is understood solely as classifying thought (DE 10/5:36). Fate, then, which enlightenment sought to combat in its battle with mythology, returns (DE 8–9/5:34–35). Horkheimer and Adorno emphasize that "abstraction, the instrument of enlightenment, stands in the same relationship to its objects as fate, whose concept it eradicates: as liquidation" (DE 9/5:36). Fate reappears in the form of science: where fate once explained everything as cosmically preordained, science performs the same procedure under lawful repetition through universal laws (DE 8/5:35). Furthermore, again invoking a political metaphor, "the distance of subject from object, the presupposition of abstraction, is founded on the distance from things which the ruler attains by means of the ruled" (DE 9/5:36). Through distance from the particular object to abstraction in the form of universality, enlightenment reverts to the very mythology it sought to overcome. Indeed, we are exactly where we started: everything is "reduced to a single common denominator"—"the subject" (DE 4/5:29). Not only that, Horkheimer and Adorno remind us that myth itself is already enlightenment, since myth likewise sought to classify and to "report, to name, to tell of origins . . . therefore to narrate, record, explain" (DE 5/5:30). Myth ultimately "becomes enlightenment" (DE 6/5:31). Mythology "set in motion the endless process of enlightenment," since "magic like science is concerned with ends" (DE 7/5:33). Ultimately, then, "just as myths already entail enlightenment, with every step enlightenment entangles itself more deeply in mythology" (DE 8/5:34).

For most readers this amounts to a relatively standard, albeit perhaps unusually forceful, account of instrumental rationality, with analogous arguments being found in Rousseau, Nietzsche, Weber, contemporary critics of a supposed enlightenment project,[29] critics of modern moral philosophy,[30]

---

29. For example, Alasdair MacIntyre, *After Virtue: A Study in Moral Theory* (Notre Dame, IN: University of Notre Dame Press, 1981).

30. For example, G. E. M. Anscombe, "Modern Moral Philosophy," *Philosophy* 33, no. 124 (1958): 1–19.

and many others. Of course, there are noticeable differences between all such critiques and *Dialectic of Enlightenment*, but the similarities enter exactly at the point where such critiques emphasize how theoretical reason undermines practical reason (and in this way *Dialectic of Enlightenment*'s intent to range over an array of domains ought not be overlooked). Nonetheless, even though the thesis that myth is already enlightenment gives the book a breadth (or, if one is unsympathetic, a lack of focus) that similar criticisms might lack,[31] the overall picture still is, purportedly, a thesis about instrumental rationality. Jürgen Habermas summarizes this common view when he claims that, according to Horkheimer and Adorno:

> Reason itself destroys the humanity it first made possible—this far reaching thesis, as we have seen, is grounded in the first excursus by the fact that *from the very start* the process of enlightenment is the result of a drive to self-preservation that mutilates reason, because it lays claim to it only in the form of a purposive-rational mastery of nature and instinct—precisely an instrumental reason . . . a rationality in the service of self-preservation gone wild.[32]

I think that for the most part this view has gained currency because *Dialectic of Enlightenment* is read in light of Horkheimer's later works,[33] where the instrumental rationalization of modern society is of central importance. There is no reason to opt for this hermeneutic strategy, however. In fact, it is more profitable to read *Dialectic of Enlightenment* in light of *Adorno's* later works, where the central theme is identity.[34]

Ultimately, while claims about instrumental rationality are crucial to *Dialectic of Enlightenment*, they are hardly the focus; indeed, the term "instrumental rationality" or a cognate never occurs in the text (admittedly, this point does not yet amount to much, since "autonomy" does not occur either). Instead, I suggest that for Horkheimer and Adorno instrumental

---

31. Cf. James Schmidt, "Genocide and the Limits of Enlightenment: Horkheimer and Adorno Revisited," in *Enlightenment and Genocide, Contradictions of Modernity*, ed. Bo Strath (Brussels: Peter Lang, 2000), 86.

32. Jürgen Habermas, *Philosophical Political Profiles*, trans. Frederick G. Lawrence (Cambridge, MA: MIT Press, 1983), 100. Cf. Habermas, *Philosophical Discourse of Modernity*, 111–12.

33. Especially Max Horkheimer, *Eclipse of Reason* (New York: Oxford University Press, 1947).

34. Cf. Hammer, *Adorno and the Political*, 43; Jameson, *Late Marxism*, 15–17.

rationality is merely symptomatic of a deeper problem centering on identity, both the identity of the subject (with herself) and the identity of the object (with itself and with the subject's appraisal of it). One way it ought to be clear how identity has been in the background is the identity of enlightenment with myth. That, however, is not the sense of identity I want to focus on. In order to stress the sense I have in mind, I must expound an additional argument running through *Dialectic of Enlightenment*.

The argument contains three distinct components, which will occupy me for the rest of the chapter. First, as I suggested earlier, it must be demonstrated how the dialectic of enlightenment potentially ranges over the gamut of human life—call this the "totality" claim. This claim needs to demonstrate only that the dialectic of enlightenment *can* apply to all areas of life. Second, it must be explained why the dialectic of enlightenment is necessary (and what sort of necessity it entails)—call this the "necessity" claim. This claim builds on the former claim and demonstrates that the dialectic of enlightenment *must* apply to all areas of life. Now, one might make the argument that, since mythology is already enlightenment and since enlightenment reverts to mythology, we are already always stuck in a circle that allegedly expands everywhere. This is not a strategy I pursue, since it fails to address the basic question here: *why* the trajectory of myth or enlightenment is to be totalizing (so, in this way, the totality claim and the necessity claim can be said to be related).[35] Why must rationality, whether in the form of myth *or* enlightenment, ultimately terminate in instrumental rationality? Finally, on the story thus far, while Horkheimer and Adorno have hinted (with political metaphors that are hardly accidental) at concrete social deformities like genocide, they have not provided an argument—even if we grant the tenability of their dialectic—for why *any* practical consequences follow from the dialectic—call this the "practical reason" question. Even if the dialectic of enlightenment applies to all areas of our lives, in that it is a claim about rationality (i.e., agency), it is not immediately obvious how this translates to any practical consequences.

---

35. Although I have learned a great deal from James Schmidt's work on *Dialectic of Enlightenment*, this is a central point of disagreement between us. Where he sees the claim "myth is already enlightenment" as the distinguishing feature of *Dialectic of Enlightenment* amid like-minded critiques (many of which he rightly believes to be "seeking to reactivate modes of thinking that had not been corrupted by enlightenment rationality"), I take *Dialectic of Enlightenment*'s distinctiveness to be in the way it shows how the dialectic is *necessary* (a point, admittedly, still to be developed). See Schmidt, "Language, Mythology, and Enlightenment," 827, and Schmidt, "Genocide and the Limits of Enlightenment," 87.

5. IMAGES AND SIGNS

Pace Habermas, who thinks that Horkheimer and Adorno simply presuppose or fail to address these issues,[36] I will show that they do have arguments for the three claims. Making good on this point, however, requires attention to several generally overlooked parts of *Dialectic of Enlightenment*. The first is the second section of the "Concept" essay, which opens with the cryptic statement that "the teachings of the priests were symbolic in the sense that in them sign and image coincide" (DE 12/5:39). Seemingly a non sequitur, this claim is crucial not only for our present concerns, but also for making sense of the essay as a whole.[37] Building on this statement, Horkheimer and Adorno tell a sort of primordial, quasi-historical story about the dawning of self-consciousness, which can here be understood simply as the most fundamental relation between subject and object. According to such a story, linguistic practices employ or are rooted in either "signs" or "images." The former calculate and categorize nature; the latter resemble it. On one hand, "as sign [*Zeichen*], language is to resign itself solely to calculation, and in order to know nature, must discard the claim to be akin to it" (DE 13/5:40; translation modified).[38] On the other hand, "as image" (*Bild*) language "is to resign itself to a likeness, and in order to be entirely nature, must discard the claim to know it" (DE 13/5:40; translation modified). Signs are classificatory, while images are mimetic.[39] At some prehistoric point the two coincided. This state of affairs, which Horkheimer and Adorno designate as "magical,"[40] is prior to both a mythological and

36. For Habermas's claim that Horkheimer and Adorno oversimplify modernity "so astoundingly," see Habermas, *Philosophical Discourse of Modernity*, 112.

37. Jay Bernstein has rightly noticed the importance of this section in J. M. Bernstein, "Negative Dialectic as Fate: Adorno and Hegel," in *The Cambridge Companion to Adorno*, ed. Tom Huhn (Cambridge: Cambridge University Press, 2004). Bernstein traces the importance of this section back to Hegel; I trace it back to Kant. Since Kant and Hegel are intimately related, both proposals might be right.

38. There is a lot more to be said here about Adorno's later work, in particular about his views of language. Indeed, mimesis is a key term for understanding this work. For more on Adorno's philosophy of language, see the essays by Michael K. Palamarek and Samir Gandesha in Donald A. Burke et al., eds., *Adorno and the Need in Thinking: Critical Essays* (Toronto: University of Toronto Press, 2007), 35–103.

39. Two lucid and concise overviews of mimesis in Adorno are Jarvis, *Adorno*, 175–79, and Hent de Vries, *Philosophy and the Turn to Religion* (Baltimore: Johns Hopkins University Press, 1999), 315–22.

40. Most interpreters overlook this tripartite rubric. An exception is Steven Vogel, *Against Nature: The Concept of Nature in Critical Theory* (Albany: State University of New York, 1996), 52–53.

an enlightening worldview and also is entirely unconsciously mimetic (DE 12–13/5:39–40). This is what I take to be the import of the claim that "neither the unity of nature nor the *unity of the subject* was presupposed by magical incantation. The rites of the shaman were directed at the wind, the rain, the snake outside or the demon inside the sick person, not at materials or specimens" (DE 6/5:31; emphasis added). Symbols, then, are the first properly mythological impulses, and in that symbolic practices are an instantiation of reason (albeit in a mimetic register), they are also *conscious*, imbued with the purpose of *doing* something *to* nature (DE 12/5:39).

Overall, it would be unfortunate to make too much of the historicity of such claims—at best they are facile; at worst they are simply wrong. Fortunately, Horkheimer and Adorno are not after a historical story. Their claims center on the idea that "the separation of sign and image is inevitable [*unabwendbar*]" (DE 13/5:40). That, and also the claim that "philosophy has perceived the abyss opened by this separation [*Trennung*] as the relationship between intuition [*Anschauung*] and concept [*Begriff*] and ever vainly [*vergebens*] tries to close it; indeed, philosophy is defined by this attempt" (DE 13/5:40; translation modified). Instead of being historical in nature, these claims are conceptual. Furthermore, the invocation of concepts and intuitions is meant to call to mind not only a Kantian distinction but, as I will argue shortly, specifically an entire Kantian framework. Famously, Kant distinguished between "intuitions," defined as immediate representations, and "concepts," which are used to make judgments about intuitions.[41] Hence Kant's famous slogan that "thoughts without content [i.e., without intuitions] are empty, intuitions without concepts are blind" (1C A51 = B75). If we represent the "magical" unity that Horkheimer and Adorno posit simply as a basic relation between subject and object, then this "magical" unity just describes a period prior to self-consciousness,[42] and it therefore matters little whether

41. There are many issues here, since Kant often employs another criterion (singularity) not only for intuitions, but also for how the status of judgment is itself variously understood. For an overview of the issues surrounding intuition, see Henry E. Allison, *Kant's Transcendental Idealism*, 2nd ed. (New Haven, CT: Yale University Press, 2004), 81–115, and Lorne Falkenstein, *Kant's Intuitionism: A Commentary on the Transcendental Aesthetic* (Toronto: University of Toronto Press, 2004), 72–145. The best, albeit contested, account of Kant on judgment is Béatrice Longuenesse, *Kant and the Capacity to Judge* (Princeton, NJ: Princeton University Press, 1998). Kant's own most lucid and useful discussion of intuitions and concepts occurs at sections 1–15 of the Jäsche logic in Immanuel Kant, *Lectures on Logic*, trans. J. Michael Young (Cambridge: Cambridge University Press, 2004), 589–97.

42. Formally speaking, during such a period there is no distinction between subject and object, since such a distinction requires self-consciousness. There is, however, a distinction between objects. This is what I take Horkheimer and Adorno to mean when they write: "The

we take this period to be historical, hyperbolic, or merely logical. I take Horkheimer and Adorno to argue for the latter: that we can posit a conceptual
space where self-consciousness did not yet exist. Once self-consciousness is
achieved, however, there must be a distinction between subject and object,
which in turn rests on a distinction between concept and intuition.

This last point, that self-consciousness, or the distinction between subject and object, fundamentally rests on a distinction between concept and
intuition, is one that cannot be rehearsed here (a truncated argument for it
can be found in DE 155–56/5:218–19), but it is precisely a central insight of
Kant's critical philosophy, especially as elaborated in the first *Critique*'s A
edition transcendental deduction. (One way to make this point compactly
is to refer to A90, where Kant explicitly notes that the transcendental deduction is necessary because the "stuff" of intuition might appear to us, but
might do so *without* being related to the concepts of the understanding—
and this is *the* problem of the A edition deduction.) What I do want to stress,
however, is Horkheimer and Adorno's invocation, at this point in their account, of this crucial Kantian dualism between intuition and concept. In
this context we should take very seriously the suggestion that not only
does philosophy "vainly" try to "close" this gap, but "philosophy is defined
by this attempt." This is a very strong philosophical claim, which invokes
not just Kant, but an entire tradition of post-Kantian philosophy, starting
with the German idealists and running to the present day. This is so much
so that one reductive, but nonetheless useful, way to see the trajectory of
much European and Anglo-American philosophy since Kant is as revolv-
ing around the issue of whether concepts and intuitions are to be seen as
merely distinguishable, but inseparable, or as fundamentally separable (and
of course distinguishable).[43] My goal here is not to engage these issues, but

---

spirit which practiced magic was not single or identical, it changed with cult masks which
represented the multiplicity of spirits. . . . [In] magic there is specific interchangeability [*Vertretbarkeit*]" (DE 6/5:31–32; translation modified). It is incorrect to gloss "*Vertretbarkeit*" as
"representation" here. Two additional points are worth mentioning. First, we should note the
stress on identity. The disenchantment story is here couched in terms of identity (as opposed to
instrumental rationality), the identity of the subject with herself, the identity of the subject's
estimation(s) of nature, and so forth. Second, the magical period already carries the seeds of its
demise. As Horkheimer and Adorno point out, "What is done to the spear, the hair, the name
of the enemy, is also to befall his person; the sacrificial animal is slain in place of the god. The
substitution which takes place in sacrifice marks a step toward discursive logic" (DE 6/5:31–32).
Self-consciousness is *over*determined.

43. Although he does not explicitly characterize this period in this way, I owe this phrasing
to Robert B. Pippin, "Concept and Intuition: On Distinguishability and Separability," *Hegel-
Studien* 40 (2005): 25–39.

only to emphasize that Horkheimer and Adorno take a very firm stand on the point, a stand that is wholly Kantian:[44] that closing the gap between these two is impossible.[45]

6. THE DISSOLUTION OF SUBJECTIVITY

Furthermore, it is not too much to say that this claim about the unavoidability of the separation between sign and image, and thereby about the inescapability of the separation between concept and intuition, grounds the claims of *Dialectic of Enlightenment*. Such a dichotomy performs two tasks. First, it anchors self-consciousness: the presence of subjectivity in the form of a subject and the presence of objectivity in the form of an object are the two poles required for self-consciousness. Second, once self-consciousness is achieved, this same duality structures the opposition between enlightenment and myth. The former, through categorization, classification, and so forth, proceeds by means of concepts, or signs, while the latter, through mimesis, proceeds by means of intuitions, or images. Together, mythological and enlightenment thinking both proceed self-consciously, in contradistinction to some magical period where mimesis was also the rule, but in a nonconscious or preconscious fashion. If we return to our earlier question about why rationality (whether in the form of myth *or* of enlightenment) must ultimately reduce to instrumental rationality, we can see that it need not. Indeed, instrumental rationality is only one manifestation of a much deeper problem—one that, as I stated before, concerns identity.

In conceiving of the two poles as myth and enlightenment or, just as accurately, nature and reason, or object and subject, we see that at one pole is pure objectivity, or pure nature, where the subject disappears entirely.

---

44. This statement must be qualified, since there is in the background a complex cluster of problems involving how to read the transcendental deduction. A lot hinges on Kant's famous claim that "the same function that gives unity to the different representations in a judgment also gives unity to the mere synthesis of different representations in an intuition" (1C A79 = B104). The question is how heterogeneous Kant himself takes the two to be (not whether the two are distinguishable, which they obviously are). For more on this point, see "Kant's Categories and the Capacity to Judge," in Béatrice Longuenesse, *Kant on the Human Standpoint* (Cambridge: Cambridge University Press, 2005), esp. 33. In short, whether Horkheimer and Adorno's stand is "wholly Kantian" is debatable insofar as Kant's own position is debatable.

45. Note that Horkheimer had already adopted something akin to this position as early as 1937. Even in "Traditional and Critical Theory" there is a stress on the point that the problems surrounding concepts/intuitions are crucial, that Kant never solved the schematism issue, and so forth. See Max Horkheimer, "Traditional and Critical Theory," in *Critical Theory: Selected Essays* (New York: Seabury, 1972), 204, 10.

This is the magical, preconscious period I just alluded to. At the other pole is pure subjectivity, or pure reason, where the objective realm disappears. In fact, paradoxically, at this pole self-consciousness is equally impossible, since without the presence of an objective realm, subjectivity fails to occur. Given this point, these poles ought to be understood heuristically. The claims here are *epistemological*: without some objective realm to oppose the subject, the subject will vanish—that is, everything is "reduced to a single common denominator," namely, "the subject" (DE 4/5:29). Horkheimer and Adorno stress this point in a plethora of places. Indeed, most of this argument has already been rehearsed, but it bears reviewing in this new context:

> Ruthless toward itself, enlightenment has eradicated the last remnant of its own self-awareness. (DE 2/5:26; translation modified)
>
> The identity of everything with everything is bought at the cost that nothing can at the same time be identical to itself. (DE 8/5:35)
>
> The self, entirely encompassed by civilization, is dissolved in an element composed of the very inhumanity which civilization has sought from the first to escape. (DE 24/5:53–54)
>
> What appears as the triumph of subjectivity, the subjection of all existing things to logical formalism, is bought with the obedient subordination of reason to what is immediately at hand. (DE 20/5:49)
>
> Enlightenment is more than enlightenment, it is nature made audible in its estrangement. (DE 31/5:63)

Again, it is not so much that reason devolves to instrumental rationality (although this too is a distinct modern deformity), but that in its attempt to master nature (or to overcome myth, whether instrumentally or otherwise), reason seeks and gains a greater and greater level of knowledge. As this knowledge ranges over more spheres of human life, it musters pretensions to speak to every facet of human life, and if this pretension is denied in a particular area, that area is decried as mythological, its status devalued, and, it is thereby all the same understood and identified as mythological. Horkheimer and Adorno's argument is that the more of the world that subjectivity seeks to identify and bring under its domain, the more it destroys *its own* conditions of possibility and thereby *itself*. Since all objectivity merely becomes the mirror of subjectivity, the distinction between the subjective and the objective disappears, and the pole of pure subjectivity looks entirely like the pole of pure objectivity; hence the return of fate, of myth, and of nature.[46] In this way we have the dialectic of enlightenment's claim to total-ity. To the extent that seemingly anything can be an object of knowledge (even if only to the extent that the *impossibility* of its being an object of knowledge is demonstrated), the dialectic of enlightenment can apply to everything.

7. THE DIALECTIC OF ENLIGHTENMENT AND KANT'S DIALECTIC OF REASON

Now, while we do have a sense of the potential scope of the dialectic, we still require an explanation for its necessity. After all, just because the dia-lectic can apply to any facet of human life, it hardly follows that it *must* apply to all facets. Once again, filling in certain Kantian details is fruitful. In advancing the overall trajectory of their thesis, Horkheimer and Adorno again invoke Kant, in a very technical way:

> The mastery of nature draws the circle in which the critique of pure rea-son holds thought spellbound. Kant combined the doctrine of thought's restlessly toilsome progress toward infinity with insistence on its insuf-ficiency and eternal limitation. The answer he issued is oracular: There is no being in the world that knowledge cannot penetrate, but what can be penetrated by knowledge is not being. Philosophical judgment, af-ter Kant, aims at the new yet recognizes nothing new, since it always merely repeats what reason has placed into objects beforehand. . . . Both subject and object are nullified. The abstract self, which alone confers the legal right to record and systematize, is confronted by nothing but abstract material, which has no other property than to be the substrate of that right. The equation of mind [*Geist*] and world is finally resolved,

46. I should note that such a view is in many ways apparent in Adorno's 1932 Kant Society lecture, "The Idea of Natural History." Although the lecture is a response to Heidegger, Adorno criticizes Heidegger on the same grounds: the ontological project to master history exactly loses any notion of the historical (see, e.g., Adorno's claims about the French Revolution, 114). Although deciding whether this is an accurate portrayal of Heidegger may be beyond the scope of this chapter (I happen to think it is not), what is important is that Adorno has already, in a deep sense, framed the stakes of such an inquiry: the necessity is to arrive at a means of making space for and giving primacy to the nonidentical (here, "transience"). And so a "positive proj-ect" is already suggested. The best analysis of Adorno's lecture is Robert Hullot-Kentor, "The Problem of Natural History in the Philosophy of Theodor W. Adorno" (PhD diss., University of Massachusetts, 1985). See also Hullot-Kentor, *Things Beyond Resemblance: Collected Essays on Theodor W. Adorno* (New York: Columbia University Press, 2006), 234–52. The lecture itself can be found in Hullot-Kentor, "The Idea of Natural History," *Telos* 60 (1984): 111–24.

but only in the sense that the two sides cancel out. (DE 19–20/5:48–49; translation modified)[47]

The reference to "restlessly toilsome progress toward infinity with insistence on its insufficiency and eternal limitation" invokes Kant's dialectic, which he elaborates in the concluding portion of the first *Critique* (and which, in fact, makes up more than half of that book). The dialectic of enlightenment, then, is to be understood as modeled after Kant's dialectic of reason,[48] to which I now turn.

In the preface to the first *Critique*, Kant claims that not only is reason in the continuous and unfortunate predicament of posing questions it cannot answer, but even worse, it is also in the unpleasant situation of repeatedly providing the wrong answers to such questions. To make sense of this

47. There is an ambiguous sentence here: "Auf das Neue zielt nach Kant das philosophische Urteil ab, und doch erkennt es nichts Neues, da es stets bloss wiederholt, was Vernunft schon immer in den Gegenstand gelegt." Generally, translators have rendered "nach Kant" as "philosophical judgment *according to* Kant." This is questionable in that Kant explicitly argued for only a *regulative* function to reason's concepts; but rendered this way, the sentence might suggest that reason has a *constitutive* role. I cannot see Adorno making this mistake, as both his writings and the writings of Hans Cornelius, the man who taught him Kant, make clear: Theodor W. Adorno, *Kant's "Critique of Pure Reason,"* ed. Rolf Tiedemann, trans. Rodney Livingstone (Cambridge: Polity Press, 2001), 38–39, 48–53; Hans Cornelius, *Kommentar zu Kants "Kritik der Reinen Vernunft"* (Erlangen, Germany: Verlag der Philosophischen Akademie, 1926), 26–29, 109–12. I have therefore rendered "nach Kant," as "after Kant," and thereby as a reference to post-Kantian philosophy (which makes the term oracular significantly more suggestive). I do not take a stand in this chapter on whether this characterization of post-Kantian philosophy is correct (I have doubts that it is), but I do think it is more in line with Adorno's (and Horkheimer's) general view of post-Kantian philosophy as "totalizing" and of Adorno's later view of Kant's transcendental idealism as in some measure commendable (centering, e.g., on Adorno's estimation of Kant's thing-in-itself as a sort of *aporetic* opposition to and within idealism).

48. Scholars have generally pointed to the allegedly Hegelian origins of the dialectic of enlightenment, finding it modeled on or borrowed from either the master/slave dialectic of Hegel's *Phenomenology of Spirit* or the religion/enlightenment dialectic of the same work. Cf. Bernstein, "Negative Dialectic as Fate," 22. Bernstein claims that *Dialectic of Enlightenment* was "explicitly conceived . . . to be a generalization and radicalization of 'The Enlightenment' chapter." I suspect Bernstein has in mind Adorno's letter to Löwenthal of June 3, 1945, where Adorno suggests that "the text, particularly the first chapter, describes the process of formalization and instrumentalization of reason as necessary and irresistible, in the sense in which Hegel dealt with enlightenment in the *Phenomenology*." Quoted from Wiggerhaus, *Frankfurt School,* 332. I think, however, that the letter allows for more speculation on this point, since in the next paragraph Adorno writes that all of philosophy (and notably Kant and Hegel) aims to produce objectivity from subjectivity. For additional claims that *Dialectic of Enlightenment* has an affinity to the master/slave dialectic, see Bernstein, *Adorno,* 95, and Willem van Reijen, *Adorno: An Introduction,* trans. Dieter Engelbrecht (Philadelphia: Pennbridge, 1992), 36–40. The Adorno letter can be found in the Houghton Library of Harvard University: bMS Ger 185(8) f.4#56. Thanks to Jennie Rathbun and Susan Halpert for procuring a copy for me.

claim, we need to understand the role Kant ascribes to human reason.[49] Reason (*Vernunft*) is one faculty of the mind, distinct from both sensibility (*Sinnlichkeit*) and the understanding (*Verstand*).[50] Sensibility, which is a passive faculty, provides us with the matter of intuitions, which occur in space and time, and the understanding makes judgments about these representations by employing concepts. For Kant, "The understanding is not capable of intuiting anything, and the senses are not capable of thinking anything. Only from their unification can cognition arise" (1C A51 = B75–76). The limits of experience are sharply delineated by the bounds of sensibility, that is, by the conditions of sensible intuition (that they occur in space and time). Or as Kant states it, "All objects of an experience possible for us, are nothing but appearances" (1C A490 = B518). Guided by the boundaries of sensibility, the only genuine knowledge available is either knowledge of the empirical world of objects or knowledge of the conditions of possibility of the same.

Reason, however, is not satisfied with such knowledge, for it strives to unify the various diverse claims of the understanding under principles—it aims to explain *why* appearances are the way they are. As Kant points out, "If the understanding may be a faculty of unity of appearances by means of rules, then reason is the faculty of the unity of the rules of understanding under principles" (1C A302 = B359). Reason is the "faculty of principles" (1C A299 = B356). Ultimately, its aims are "to find the unconditioned for the conditioned cognitions of the understanding" (1C A307 = B364). Reason aspires to grasp what, beyond the mere conditions of possibility, accounts for phenomena being the way they are. In this procedure of conceptualizing the unconditioned, reason creates various ideas: for example, God or the soul. These ideas in turn attempt to account, in absolute terms, for the knowledge provided by the understanding. Such a procedure, however, entangles reason in illusions. It ought to be obvious, even from my cursory discussion, that such ideas refer to objects beyond the bounds of sensibility. In positing them, reason fundamentally oversteps the bounds of experience by hypostatizing its requirement for unity. An eternal being, a first cause, or anything we do not have intuitional or transcendental experience of, cannot be known (it is neither part of possible experience nor, as Kant

---

49. In what follows, I consider, for example, the understanding and reason in their *transcendental* as opposed to merely formal uses. See 1C A299 = B356.

50. The best account of Kant on the faculties is still Gilles Deleuze, *Kant's Critical Philosophy: The Doctrine of the Faculties*, trans. Hugh Tomlinson and Barbara Habberjam (Minneapolis: University of Minnesota Press, 1983).

demonstrates, a condition of that experience). Reason, therefore, ultimately cannot ground such ideas. Furthermore, Kant shows that whatever concepts reason proposes as explanatory grounds, those concepts entangle reason in a dialectic that leaves one option as tenable as another. Reason can, for example, just as easily prove that the world has to be eternal as that it had to have been created in time (1C A426–34 = B454–62). Compounding this picture even further, Kant shows that this dialectical procedure is inherent to reason. Reason's drive toward unity accounts for its dialectical instability and is thereby the same drive that undermines the achievement of any secure foundation. It is this issue that leads him to distinguish between constitutive and regulative uses of reason. I will say more about this shortly.[51]

8. ADORNO ON KANT'S DIALECTIC

It is notoriously difficult to unpack Kant's claim that reason must seek such unity (that there is a "conative" urge to reason). One way to do so is to stress the link between this drive and Kant's conception of practical reason, especially the link between such a drive and Kant's notion of autonomy.[52] This is how Adorno understood the necessity of reason's drive for unity, that is, the necessity of the very project of the first *Critique* (I should quickly note that I do not plan to wade into the stormy waters of Kant interpretation; my goal is solely to make a case for the plausibility of Adorno's reading, and, even then, only as it helps us understand *Dialectic of Enlightenment*).[53] To understand how reason's drive toward unity and autonomy might be related, we can recall that in the preface to the first *Critique*, Kant wrote that

51. For this distinction, see Allison, *Kant's Transcendental Idealism*, 421ff. See also note 47 above.

52. See Onora O'Neill, "Vindicating Reason," in *The Cambridge Companion to Kant*, ed. Paul Guyer (Cambridge: Cambridge University Press, 1992); O'Neill, *Constructions of Reason: Explorations of Kant's Practical Philosophy* (Cambridge: Cambridge University Press, 1989); Richard L. Velkley, *Freedom and the End of Reason: On the Moral Foundation of Kant's Critical Philosophy* (Chicago: University of Chicago Press, 1989).

53. There are divergent opinions about how to account for reason's drive toward unity in Kant. Kant himself, in the first *Critique*, advances the claim that reason seeks this unity so that the understanding can function properly (1C A654 = B682), but this view is compatible with the strand that Adorno and others have tried to develop. For an overview on this point, see Michelle Grier, *Kant's Doctrine of Transcendental Illusion* (Cambridge: Cambridge University Press, 2001), 268–88. Alternatively, this drive can be explained by means of the third *Critique*; see Michelle Kosch, *Freedom and Reason in Kant, Schelling, and Kierkegaard* (Oxford: Oxford University Press, 2006), 39–43.

reason should take on . . . the most difficult of all its tasks, namely, that of self-knowledge, and to institute a court of justice, by which reason may secure its rightful claims while dismissing all its groundless pretensions, and this not by mere decrees but according to its own eternal and unchangeable laws; and this court is none other than the critique of pure reason itself. (1C Axii)

In discussing this claim in his lectures on the first *Critique* (1959), Adorno points out:

If you think your way through the implications of the metaphors of this passage, it will not escape you that the tribunal he is speaking of is a curious affair: it is a tribunal in which the judge, the prosecutor and the accused are actually one and the same person. However, I believe it would be a little facile to ridicule Kant for this because what we might call this paradoxical idea is actually the heart of the Kantian conception. What lies behind it—and in this respect we cannot really separate Kant's theoretical philosophy, that is, the critique of reason, from his practical philosophy, the *Critique of Practical Reason*—is Kant's remarkable conception which actually supplies the unifying factor. . . . [I]t is the idea that the freedom and sovereignty of spirit amounts to what he calls autonomy . . . and autonomy is the supreme concept in Kant's moral philosophy, and by implication also of Kant's theory of knowledge.[54]

Reconstructing the details of Adorno's reading presents a Kant interested foremost in autonomy, conceived as the ultimate species of self-knowledge. A "critique of pure reason" thereby just is the task of such "self-knowledge." Because a correspondence between how reason conceives the world to be and how it is cannot be presupposed, the only path left open to reason is to analyze its own functioning.[55] Owing to the unreliability of projecting itself outward in a presumed correspondence between its objects and reality, reason focuses inward, on its own functioning, and thereby

54. Adorno, *Kant's "Critique of Pure Reason,"* 54; emphasis added. Regarding the earlier discussion, such a reading is plausibly motivated by Kant's own ambitions, since Kant himself writes in the second *Critique* that "the concept of freedom . . . is the keystone of the whole architecture of the system of pure reason and *even of speculative reason*" (2C 5:3; emphasis added).

55. Cf. O'Neill, "Vindicating Reason," 282.

reveals a dialectical structure. In turn, because reason cannot point to a reality outside itself that ultimately justifies it, validates it, or serves as its foundation, the only option available is to pursue justification by means of some self-reflexive procedure, through, to, in, and for itself. If reason does not perform this procedure and, more important, in this fashion, then it will find itself subject to powers outside itself (and it matters little whether dogmatism appears here ecclesiastically, philosophically, or otherwise). Restating the whole position: according to Adorno, for Kant, if reason is not self-reflexive, then it is under the sway of nature.[56] Either autonomous reason or nature—it is all or nothing. This is what I take Adorno to imply when he claims that "autonomy is the supreme concept in Kant's moral philosophy, and by implication also of Kant's theory of knowledge."[57] Kant's claim in his popular essay "What Does It Mean to Orient Oneself in Thinking?" (1786) is apt here (especially since Kant himself took this essay as a clarification of his philosophical position in light of the *Pantheismusstreit*). There Kant points out that "if reason will not subject itself to the laws it gives itself, it has to bow under the yoke of laws given by an other; for without any law, nothing—not even nonsense—can play its game for long" (8:145; translation modified). Reason, then, must both subject itself to itself and give itself the law by which it subjects itself.[58] Equally suggestive in this context is a footnote in the same essay, where Kant writes that "reason does not feel; it has insight into its lack, and through the *drive for knowledge* [*Erkenntnistrieb*] it produces [*wirkt*] the feeling of a need [*Bedürfnis*]" (8:140; translation modified).[59] A perceived lack of unity drives reason both to need and to seek such unification. In light of these passages, I take it that linking autonomy and reason in Kant's thought is not entirely implausible.

Adorno's understanding of Kant's position, then, is this: Because we think and act, we must have a means of guiding these endeavors. Skepticism is not viable at this practical level of reason (although there is more to be said here; see section 10 below). Indeed, because we think and act, reason must set the ends that guide these actions. To function in this way,

56. Such a reading stresses Kant's proximity to Rousseau. Cf. Velkley, *Freedom and the End of Reason*. Few scholars have connected Rousseau and Horkheimer/Adorno, perhaps because the two hardly ever mention him. An exception is Hans Robert Jauss, "Der literarische Prozess des Modernismus von Rousseau bis Adorno," in *Adorno-Konferenz*, ed. Ludwig von Friedeburg and Jürgen Habermas (Frankfurt am Main: Suhrkamp, 1983).

57. Adorno, *Kant's "Critique of Pure Reason,"* 54.

58. One can speak here of a "Kantian paradox"; see note 9 of the introduction.

59. For more on the "conative character" of reason, see Pauline Kleingeld, "The Conative Character of Reason in Kant's Philosophy," *Journal of the History of Philosophy* 36, no. 1 (1998): 85.

reason must set *some* end—reason must be oriented somewhere. We can ask, however, about the origins of such ends. How might we justify them? As already suggested, to count as autonomous, such ends cannot be imposed externally, whether in the form of religion, as mere submission to the forces of nature, or as any other form of heteronomy. Such external aims would make reason instrumental, serving a merely technical purpose. In this way Kant's position vis-à-vis autonomy can be understood, to take a term from Wilfrid Sellars, as an argument about the "space of reasons": nothing can count as a reason for a subject unless she takes it as a reason for herself.[60] Sellars elaborates this view in the realm of knowledge as follows: "In characterizing an episode or a state as that of *knowing*, we are not giving an empirical description of that episode or state; we are placing it in the logical space of reasons, of justifying and being able to justify what one says."[61] Putting aside temporarily the issues surrounding the success of such self-grounding,[62] according to Kant, through an introspective and self-reflexive examination of itself, reason must restrict the employment of its own self-generated ideas to regulative, as opposed to constitutive, roles.[63] Such ideas thereby can *guide* inquiry into various areas of life, but they cannot be taken to *constitute* that reality (1C A642–68 = B670–96). In this way I stand at the center of my world; thus Kant's Copernican revolution.[64]

9. THE NECESSITY OF THE DIALECTIC OF ENLIGHTENMENT

Returning to Horkheimer and Adorno's dialectic, we can begin to understand its necessity when we realize that the dialectic of enlightenment is formally analogous to Kant's dialectic. In the preface to *Dialectic of Enlightenment*, Horkheimer and Adorno write: "We have no doubt—*and herein lies our petitio principii*—that freedom in society is inseparable [*unabtrennbar*] from enlightenment thinking" (DE xvi/5:18; emphasis added). It is striking

---

60. See Wilfrid Sellars, *Empiricism and the Philosophy of Mind* (Cambridge, MA: Harvard University Press, 1997).

61. Ibid., 76.

62. In a sense this entire book is about the issue, so it is implicit to the development of my argument as a whole. For another take on the issue of self-grounding, see Robert B. Pippin, *Modernism as a Philosophical Problem: On the Dissatisfaction of European High Culture*, 2nd ed. (Oxford: Blackwell, 1999).

63. See note 51 above.

64. This paves the way for seeing transcendental illusion as a "social problem." See Timo Jütten, "Adorno on Kant, Freedom and Determinism," *European Journal of Philosophy* 20, no. 4 (2010): 548–74.

that the question they beg just is the Kantian notion of autonomy. Their
dialectic is structured by this assumption. As modern agents, we undertake
to be autonomous. Our fears of the unknown are dissolved to the extent
that we can cognize any potential unknown, and knowing the conditions
of the possibility of cognition itself, we can be said to know significantly
enough about anything that might ever be an object of experience for us
(i.e., the transcendental deduction is taken to succeed; self-consciousness is
taken to be tied to the constitution of objectivity). In so doing, we extricate
ourselves from nature, from anything truly opposed—beyond—reason (in
one sense nothing we can know is beyond, and in another, what cannot be
known is nothing for us, it will not even appear; see especially 1C A120).[65]
The more we undertake this procedure, however, the more our subjectivity
is involved in a dialectic radically similar to Kant's, where a correspondence
is posited between reality and notions that originate through autonomous
reason. The more reason knows and identifies nature, the more it destroys
(via identification, repetition, and totalization) the presence of objectivity,
and ultimately the more it reverts to nature. (This can be seen as a rough
summary of sections 4–6 above.)[66] Whereas Kant's dialectic is restricted in
scope to the constructed ideas of reason, Horkheimer and Adorno extend
the scope of this dialectic to all human reasoning and cognition. As we
strive for autonomous agency, and considering that only self-reflexively
can we ground such autonomy, we repeat this dialectical procedure at *every* level of human activity. As Horkheimer and Adorno point out, "philosophical judgment . . . aims at the new yet recognizes nothing new, since
it always merely repeats what reason has placed into objects beforehand"
(DE 19–20/5:48–49). The continual references to Kant, then, are neither accidental nor metaphorical; Kant's notion of autonomy exactly drives the
dialectic of enlightenment (and here we might highlight even the opening
references to Bacon in *Dialectic of Enlightenment*, which are exactly a nod
to Kant's own dedication to Bacon in the B edition of the first *Critique*).

From here it is a small step to the necessity claim. *If* one understands
oneself as an autonomous agent (Horkheimer and Adorno's *petitio principii*),
then no external justification, no justification apart from one's own reason,
can serve to ground that autonomy. Because we are "*condemned* to choice

65. For Kant, however, there is practical reason, which allows us to introduce (practically)
certain objects beyond the bounds of sense. I pursue this point in significantly more detail in the
next chapter. See also the conclusion to this chapter.

66. Cf. Hammer, *Adorno and the Political*, 47. In particular, Hammer is exactly right in
stressing that "repetition, totality, and identity" are "*themselves . . . the subjective principles of
the mythical imagination.*"

and action,"[67] we must give reasons for our actions and choices, we must justify our claims, and only we, no one else, can do so. Ultimately we might say, with a nod to Kant, that we cannot but act under the idea of freedom. To be a particular self is just perpetually to be faced with *some* choice or claim (to be *me* is to have a view from *somewhere*). Another way to put all this is to highlight how Kant's dialectic (and thereby the dialectic of enlightenment to the extent they are formally analogous) rests on Kant's broader moves in the transcendental deduction (especially the B edition). Because the synthetic unity of apperception is the supreme principle of the understanding, all consciousness is apperceptive (B138). That is, *I* am taking things a particular way rather than merely finding them a particular way (for, importantly, I might take things to be wrong). Experience does not come prefabricated, falling upon me passively. Instead, I constitute my world in that I employ the categories in judgment—I take it that things are *this* way and not another, and so I also take myself *to have* taken it that things are this way. (I realize that the amount of ink spilled over B138 is almost indescribable—my aim here, however, is not to vindicate Kant but merely to suggest how a certain reading of Kant helps us understand *Dialectic of Enlightenment*.)[68] As Adorno puts the point in describing Kant's position on this point, apperception "is not just something in me, but is always and at the same time present in the experiences concerned, because the experiences, the appearances, are in truth always only *mine*, they are mediated through me."[69] In Kant we see this explicitly when he argues in the B edition transcendental deduction that the categories (and thereby always my employment of them by way of my synthetic activity) apply to "*whatever* objects may come before our senses" (1C B159; emphasis added). Horkheimer and Adorno's

---

67. Christine M. Korsgaard, *Self-Constitution: Agency, Identity, and Integrity* (Oxford: Oxford University Press, 2009), 1. Horkheimer and Adorno, then, with their *petitio principii*, also presuppose a constitutive standpoint. In addition to Korsgaard's, there are many forms of constitutivism; see, for example, Peter Railton, "On the Hypothetical and Non-hypothetical in Reasoning about Belief and Action," in *Ethics and Practical Reason*, ed. Garrett Cullity and Berys Gaut (Oxford: Oxford University Press, 1997), 53–79; J. David Velleman, *The Possibility of Practical Reason* (Oxford: Oxford University Press, 2000). For Horkheimer and Adorno, the point is that if we are to call ourselves agents, then when we act, we have to give some reason—they are not presupposing any broader commitment to, for example, such facts' being justified by the drive for self-knowledge or the ability of such facts to imply broader moral commitments (indeed, Adorno explicitly rejects deriving morality from the mere fact of agency at ND 264/6:241).

68. A powerful account of the radical significance of Kant's picture relevant to my context here is Robert Brandom, *Making It Explicit: Reasoning, Representing, and Discursive Commitment* (Cambridge, MA: Harvard University Press, 1998), 3–64.

69. Adorno, *Kant's "Critique of Pure Reason,"* 140.

radical suggestion is that with the synthetic unity of apperception, I am already entangled in the dialectic of enlightenment—it penetrates to the very core of my experience, much as a sequence of DNA rests at the core of any living organism. Since I am the one taking things a particular way, then the pole of objectivity is already always compromised, contaminated by the pole of subjectivity, and from here, for Horkheimer and Adorno, it is a small dialectical step to the complete dissolution of subjectivity (see section 6 above). Furthermore, since this concerns the very makeup of who we are—what it means to be an agent and even to have a world, indeed to take a first-person perspective at all[70]—the problem that emerges is global, indicting a variety of practices and orientations (whether theoretical or practical). (This incidentally is also why the argument cannot center *solely* on B138 and the synthetic unity of apperception. The elements of "myth," in other words those objects that cannot be objects of experience—for example, God or other ideas—*also* fall under the sway of the dialectic of enlightenment; see section 6 above and the claim to totality.)[71] Ultimately, our way of being agents, that is, Kantian autonomy, "already contains the germ of the regression which is taking place everywhere today" (DE xvi/5:18). The omnipresence of identity thinking, the dissolution of subjectivity, the rise of instrumental rationality, the disenchantment of the world, and so forth, are grounded in our very standing as autonomous agents. In this way we have the claim to necessity. This necessity, I ought to add, is obviously conditional—following only so far as I assume the stance of an autonomous agent.[72] It might be possible to develop views of agency that do not trade on concepts of autonomy or any sort of "condemnation to action."

70. There is a lot more to be said here about the difference between first- and third-person perspectives in this context. See Richard Moran, *Authority and Estrangement: An Essay on Self-Knowledge* (Princeton, NJ: Princeton University Press, 2001).

71. Thanks to Gordon Finlayson for getting me to think about this point.

72. There is a question here about the nature of our being "condemned" to action, that is, about constitutivism. Especially I have in mind the sort of objections raised in David Enoch, "Agency, Shmagency: Why Normativity Won't Come from What Is Constitutive of Action," *Philosophical Review* 115, no. 2 (2006): 169–98. The Kantian assumption is that any determination of oneself must be rule-bound—the only question is *how* the rule originates (autonomously or heteronomously). Enoch argues that this truth about ourselves cannot be justified along normative lines and can be understood only as a brute fact, which does not get us what we need (normativity). I will have more to say about this, but for now I just want to highlight how so far Horkheimer and Adorno's argument is merely about the *assumption* of Kantian autonomy. Indeed, they themselves condemn Kant's fact of reason as merely a "psychological fact" (DE 160/5:114). In other words, Adorno's mature position will not rely on constitutivism.

10. THE DIALECTIC OF ENLIGHTENMENT
AND PRACTICAL REASON

As potentially worrisome as all this might sound, it also might seem largely divorced from actual events, at both ends of the account (that is, whether on the "genetic" side about the origins of human reason or on the "practical" side of the process of human reasoning). Worries at the former end will manifest in worries about the absence of material factors in the account: it seems that the misery of early human lives and the concomitant desire to alleviate this misery ought to play some explanatory role in our account (see PMP 4). Worries at the latter end will arise from a concern with practical reason, specifically how the dialectic of enlightenment leads to *any* practical consequences. One way to underscore this last point is by imagining a utopia of radically different material conditions (so as not to get embroiled in controversies about conceptions of utopia, one might say this logical space is to be occupied by the best of all possible utopian pictures). If such material conditions were to appear tomorrow, what would be at stake in having our utopian world populated by agents under the sway of the dialectic of enlightenment? That is, would there be something objectionable about having a world free of material suffering (poverty, homelessness, hunger, and so forth) that was also a world of agents entirely formed and guided by the dialectic of enlightenment as a principle of reason? In this sense, to riff on one of Richard Rorty's ideas ("take care of freedom, and truth will take care of itself"),[73] we might say: Why not take care of material suffering, and autonomy will take of itself—or it will not? . . . But in any case, no matter. I take such concerns to allege that my account might be seen as a sort of problematic reductive idealism.[74]

All such worries require that we better understand the nature of Horkheimer and Adorno's account. They explicitly tell us that it is not meant to comprehensively explain the ills of modernity; indeed, it is "merely" meant to ask after the "self-destruction of enlightenment" (DE xvi/5:18; cf. section 3 above). Seeing Kant's dialectic of reason as the formal model, I have glossed this as an argument about how the concept of autonomy

---

73. Richard Rorty and Eduardo Mendieta, *Take Care of Freedom and Truth Will Take Care of Itself: Interviews with Richard Rorty* (Stanford, CA: Stanford University Press, 2006).

74. For a crisp statement of Adorno's distaste for such, see Theodor W. Adorno, *Beethoven: The Philosophy of Music*, trans. Edmund Jephcott (Stanford, CA: Stanford University Press, 1993), 80.

breaks down under its conceptual weight. This is not to deny, however, that any such agency would be affected by material conditions; indeed, there are certain practices, social configurations, and economic policies that might make particular forms of agency more likely (i.e., make autonomy and the dialectic of enlightenment more likely). Nonetheless, the "problem" of the dialectic of enlightenment is not reducible to worries about these conditions. Putting things this way invariably suggests a variety of questions about modern material conditions, questions far beyond the scope of my account here, especially about distinctly modern phenomena like commodity fetishism, monopoly capitalism, state socialism, fascism, and so forth (on this point, see also chapter 3, sections 4 and 7). Not only that, broader questions emerge about the effect of economic conditions on subjectivity.[75] Such questions are important, and I do not mean that Horkheimer and Adorno were not concerned with them;[76] but, while related, I take them fundamentally to be questions crucial to a different project than the one pursued here (cf. HF 187). As I mentioned in the introduction, my aim in this book is to tease out Adorno's thinking about freedom and autonomy. Since this project depends on understanding Horkheimer and Adorno's critique of Kantian autonomy, I have focused on (what I take to be) the "problem" of the dialectic of enlightenment: that it dissolves agency.

Making that point more plausible, however, requires clarifying exactly *how* (or perhaps whether) Horkheimer and Adorno's account *is* historical (and this is just a further permutation of the idealism worry). If the account is allegedly about agency and modernity, then it seems deeply anachronistic. On one hand, the dialectic of enlightenment seems aimed at a historical concept of modernity—it explicitly presupposes (and attacks) the notion of autonomy. On the other hand, they at the same time trace the dialectic's origins to the most basic attempt at enlightenment thinking. A rather peculiar historical account is then emerging. If the assumption necessary to get the account going is a thoroughly modern one and yet the account is meant to comment on at least some facet of premodern practices, then we have a bewildering sleight of hand. In response, I would stress that while

75. For a penetrating discussion of this issue, see Elizabeth Anderson, *Value in Ethics and Economics* (Cambridge, MA: Harvard University Press, 1995), 147–68.

76. See especially Theodor W. Adorno, "Sociology and Psychology 1," *New Left Review* 46 (1967): 67–80; Adorno, "Sociology and Psychology 2," *New Left Review* 47 (1967): 79–99; and Adorno, *Can One Live After Auschwitz? A Philosophical Reader*, ed. Rolf Tiedemann (Stanford, CA: Stanford University Press, 2003), 93–126. Highly useful is Deborah Cook, *The Culture Industry Revisited: Theodor W. Adorno on Mass Culture* (Lanham, MD: Rowman and Littlefield, 1996).

Horkheimer and Adorno acknowledge that autonomy, taken as a basic impulse, stretches all the way back to the dawning of self-consciousness (see section 5), they also take autonomy to reach its conceptual culmination (say, its full development as an original impulse) in modernity, achieved especially in Kant's conception of the issues. All this is neither to deny nor to minimize the complex historical circumstances that must also have taken place for such a conceptualization to appear and take hold.[77] One might say that self-consciousness makes the dialectic of enlightenment a possibility, while the problematizing of the relation between self-consciousness and autonomy drives the dialectic to its completion (glossed here as the idea that a vindication of the claims of self-consciousness requires an understanding of autonomy).[78] Because Kant links autonomy and self-consciousness (see the conclusion of section 9 above), it is no surprise that he is the central focus for Horkheimer and Adorno.[79] But all of this only reinforces the distinct level at which discussion is being pitched.

This point becomes more apparent if we return to the utopian thought experiment mentioned above. The problem with any material utopia circumscribed by the dialectic of enlightenment is that it lacks a proper space for subjects. Although the argument of this entire book roughly is meant to vindicate the following claim, I take Adorno still to defend the importance of subjectivity (albeit of a certain sort). In this way I take it that any utopia would involve a variety of concepts that can be understood only as being "subject-referring."[80] I have in mind here concepts like shame or envy or, in a more utopian tenor, dignity, respect, integrity, and so forth. Such concepts simply cannot be understood without reference to a subject. Our interpretation of them is constitutive of our experiencing them: in conceiving of something as shameful, we undergo a distinct sort of experience, not achievable by means other than self-interpretation. More generally, we can say that "certain modes of experience are not possible without certain

77. Cf. Pippin, *Modernism as a Philosophical Problem*, xv–xviii.

78. This is one way, I think, to understand Adorno's fascination with Alfred Sohn-Rethel's work. For that encounter, see Stefan Müller-Doohm, *Adorno: A Biography* (Cambridge: Polity Press, 2005), 220–22. Thanks to Max Pensky for turning me on to this encounter. Exploring this in more detail is a worthwhile topic but outside my present inquiry.

79. One of the clearest accounts of how these are linked is John McDowell, "Self-Determining Subjectivity and External Constraint," in *Having the World in View: Essays on Kant, Hegel, and Sellars* (Cambridge, MA: Harvard University Press, 2009), 90–107.

80. Charles Taylor, "Self-Interpreting Animals," in *Human Agency and Language* (Cambridge: Cambridge University Press, 1985), 54. I pursue this point in more detail in chapter 3.

self-descriptions."[81] I do not want my claims here to hinge on an alleged picture of utopia, nor do I want to argue about which concepts would or would not be present in a utopia. Instead, I am raising the more general point that subjects seem necessary for any conception of utopia (and all without suggesting that "subject" or "subjectivity" is somehow understood here undialectically or naively—a point I pursue in more detail in chapter 3). Insofar as *any* notion of utopia involves the notion of a world of subjects, it depends crucially on elements of self-interpretation for its actualization (i.e., it is not enough merely to be a satisfied pig; Socrates too must have his satisfaction). Subjectivity is, at the very least, just as important as material conditions. And all this is just to claim, not surprisingly, that the dissolution of subjectivity engendered by the dialectic of enlightenment is a serious problem for subjects. My aim, then (and I take myself to be following a strand of Adorno's thinking), is to limit my analysis here to the conceptual issues surrounding this problem, that is, the issues surrounding Kantian autonomy and freedom more broadly (and again without dismissing or minimizing the importance of material conditions to any overall account of modernity, *or* to an understanding of Adorno's thought as a whole).

Stressing the importance of subjectivity in this way, however, just raises again the "problem" with the dialectic of enlightenment. After all, why not just say so much the worse for subjectivity. Here I want to suggest that our story can only be historical. There is no suprahistorical reason we ought to be subjects. For Horkheimer and Adorno, subjectivity is an achievement, one that requires a distinct form of life. One side of this point is that we just now do embody the sort of life to which subjectivity is central. This is exactly why agency seems "inescapable" to a strand of contemporary thinking.[82] The flip side of this point, however, and in contradistinction to such thinking, is that we may yet become a form of life that does say so much the worse for subjectivity. A thought of Stanley Cavell's is apt here. He asks whether we might imagine our civilization's being replaced by another:

> In particular, is it being replaced by one in which nothing that happens any longer strikes us as the objectification of subjectivity as the act of an answerable agent, as the expression and satisfaction of human freedom, of human intention and desire? What has a beginning can have an

81. Charles Taylor, "What Is Human Agency?" in *Human Agency and Language* (Cambridge: Cambridge University Press, 1985), 37.

82. See Luca Ferrero, "Constitutivism and the Inescapability of Agency," *Oxford Studies in Metaethics* 4 (2009): 303–33. See also note 72 above.

end. If this future (civilization?) were effected its members would not be dissatisfied. They would have lost the concept of satisfaction. Then nothing would (any longer) give them the idea that living being, human things, could feel. So they would not (any longer) be human. They would not, for example, be frightened upon meeting others—except in the sense, or under circumstances, in which they would be frightened upon encountering bears or storms, circumstances under which bears would be frightened. And of course particular forms of laughter and amazement would also no longer be possible, ones which depend upon clear breaks between, say, machines and creatures. (CR 468)

What is striking about Cavell's account is the way it recreates the end-point of the dialectic of enlightenment. Cavell's next few lines are especially poignant. He points out how this new picture of agency would "betoken the success of the picture of science, of knowledge, *as subjugation*—not now as that by which the human being subjugates the world, and overcomes superstition and magic, but now as that by which the human being is subjugated. *So science falls back, or forward, into magic*" (CR 468; emphasis added). The analogy to the dialectic of enlightenment cannot be overlooked: Cavell's picture is just a return to the magical period that Horkheimer and Adorno describe, the period before self-consciousness (see section 5 above). Furthermore, it may be that the dialectic of enlightenment is just the next step in the process of modernization—perhaps to be truly modern is to no longer be a subject. Furthermore, none of this imagery, no matter how worrisome, is *in itself* an argument against a form of life defined by subjectivity.

This is no strike against my inquiry here. It is rather an admission not only about its nature (analytic as opposed to predictive), but also about its orientation (thoroughly historical—in this way analogous to the Hegelian suggestion that the owl of Minerva takes flight only at dusk). Indeed, it is difficult to imagine what an argument "against" such a form of life might look like in this context. (At this level of discussion, how might one provide an argument against a historical possibility?) The point is that the possibility of an 'agency' permeated by a dissolved subjectivity would be actualized historically, in concrete forms of life, not in philosophical arguments. In this way material concerns resurface in our discussion: through evolution or (say, chemical) revolution, it may occur that agency ceases to involve subjectivity. A utopia of lobotomies is a historical possibility. And such a utopia might occur *even if* we were to resolve the philosophical issues emerging around the dialectic of enlightenment. This is what I take to be the power of Cavell's hypothetical example.

In this sense, as far as questions of practical reason go, I do not take the dialectic of enlightenment to entail *any* distinct practical projects. Here, for the sake of analysis, I am opposing a strand found in Adorno's thought. He often goes in for a strong claim, for example, that genocide is an extension of modern reason—of the dialectic of enlightenment. This sentiment is expressed in *Minima Moralia*: "Accordingly the destructive tendencies of the masses that explode in both varieties of totalitarian state are not so much death-wishes as manifestations of what they have *already* become. They murder so that whatever to them seems living, shall resemble themselves" (MM 231/4:262; emphasis added). One finds an analogous argument in *Negative Dialectics*: "Genocide [*Völkermord*] is the absolute integration. It is on its way wherever men are leveled off—"'polished off,'" as the German military called it—until one exterminates them literally, as deviations from the concept of their total nullity. Auschwitz confirmed the philosopheme of pure identity as death" (ND 362/6:355).[83]

The claim is that the dissolution of subjectivity that follows with the dialectic of enlightenment leads to genocide (among other totalitarian projects). While such an interpretation might not be unwarranted (and it is certainly common enough),[84] it does require far more empirical work than we currently have available.[85] More important, however, it is a different argument than the one being developed here, which is an argument also found in Adorno's corpus and that, unlike the stronger claim, has thus far received inadequate attention.

This argument suggests that the relation between the dialectic of enlightenment and practical reason is this: Practical reason, in that it serves as the capacity for generating practical reasons, under the dialectic of enlightenment and with subjectivity, is *dissolved*. The dialectic of enlightenment deals with the possibility of reason *as such*, as opposed to this or that reason. In this way it is a piercing critique, more ambitious than even

83. Adorno's position here is hardly fixed—an opposite view is found in the German of *Minima Moralia* 4:286–87 (for whatever reason, these pages are not translated in the English edition).

84. For hesitations about such interpretations, see Shuster, "Philosophy and Genocide," 228–35.

85. Studies that might be taken to be pitched in this tenor include Donald Bloxham, *Genocide, the World Wars and the Unweaving of Europe* (Middlesex, UK: Mitchell Vallentine, 2008); Bloxham, *The Final Solution: A Genocide* (Oxford: Oxford University Press, 2009); Mark Levene, *Genocide in the Age of the Nation State*, 4 vols. (London: I. B. Tauris, 2005); Michael Mann, *The Dark Side of Democracy: Explaining Ethnic Cleansing* (Cambridge: Cambridge University Press, 2005); and A. Dirk Moses, *Empire, Colony, Genocide: Conquest, Occupation, and Subaltern Resistance in World History* (London: Berghahn Books, 2008).

strands of contemporary moral theory that illustrate how certain concepts might break down with the employment of certain modes of subjectivity. Horkheimer and Adorno's position is not merely that some subjective capacity (e.g., reflection) *can* undermine practical reason,[86] but rather that a certain sort of subjectivity (enlightenment thinking—Kantian autonomy) *does* undermine practical reason (and everything else subjective besides). Reflection destroys reflection, destroys itself. And this is *all* the practical reason claim can amount to in this context. One way to stress the importance of the problem I take to arise here, then, is to focus on how, *independent* of material conditions, the dialectic of enlightenment is a conceptual problem that must be resolved, or subjectivity ceded. In putting things this way I do not mean there is no relation between material conditions and subjectivity, only that they can be divorced heuristically and worked through independently.[87] Any achievement of free conditions *will* involve a material component, but it will *also* require a solution to the problem of the dialectic of enlightenment. Similarly, stressing an earlier point, resolving the issues surrounding the dialectic of enlightenment is no guarantee that a world free of subjectivity will not arise. (We might, in the end, all turn out to be organisms instead of agents). If the problem of the dialectic of enlightenment *can* be solved, then my sole claim will be that such a world will not arise *because* of the dialectic of enlightenment (it might, however, arise through actions initiated through such agency or entirely by chance).[88]

11. CONCLUSION

All this raises the question of how we ought to understand our commitment to autonomy. Could we not be subjects without the notion of Kantian autonomy (or indeed any notion of autonomy)? Why not simply give up that concept and conceive of agency differently? Certainly there are many options on the menu, from various naturalisms to materialisms to determinisms—some more coherent than others, but all potentially options. My gambit, following Adorno, is *not* to move to such questions, but instead to ask how (initially, whether) we can conceptualize a notion of autonomy that does not succumb to the dialectic of enlightenment. This is

86. See, for example, chapter 9 of Bernard Williams, *Ethics and the Limits of Philosophy* (London: Routledge, 1993).

87. See note 75 above.

88. I take Hannah Arendt to have explored the first option with the "thoughtlessness" of agents like Adolf Eichmann in Hannah Arendt, *Eichmann in Jerusalem* (New York: Viking Press, 1963).

the issue I take much of Adorno's later work to be concerned with, and it is
the problem for which Horkheimer and Adorno had no solution during the
writing of *Dialectic of Enlightenment*—that is, why no positive account of
enlightenment ever materialized in that work.

Before turning to Adorno's later work, however, I want to consider a
possible Kantian rejoinder. In fact, this rejoinder is essential to understanding Adorno's later project. The significance of Kant's project in this context
comes out most clearly if we consider how we also might bind ourselves
to a variety of objects outside ourselves (from God to the Party or beyond).
That is, we might limit our autonomy without entirely abdicating it (servitude as opposed to complete dissolution). With such "servitude" we anchor
our subjectivity to an object we take to be distinct from that subjectivity (which we thereby see as objective), and to this extent such an object
checks the dissolution of subjectivity that the dialectic of enlightenment
engenders. We need not minimize how much, in a dogmatic register, this
is a contradictory stance, performatively confused, "taking" something to
be the case (any such claim is still a normative claim) while at the same
time claiming to be responding to an outside object.[89] Insofar as we might
say that the "trail of the human serpent is . . . over everything,"[90] such
a solution is no real (rational) solution to the dialectic of enlightenment.
(One might speak here of both the temerity and the fragility of faith.) This
solution, does, however, allow us to situate Kant's alternative. In the case
of what I am calling servitude, we set up a variety of objects for ourselves
(*take* them to be authoritative), and to do so we limit our autonomy. We
might nonetheless retain some commitment to autonomy (and thus still be
subject to the dialectic of enlightenment) but do so only in a few areas of our
lives, compartmentalizing ourselves in such a way as to entirely abdicate
autonomy in others (a position quite easy and common in late capitalism).[91]
This would then lead to only a partial dissolution of selfhood. Understood
in this way, and by virtue of its basis in contingent epistemic orientations
(as much as its contradictory normative stance), such a "solution" is at
best a stopgap. (This is meant neither to deride nor to underplay the practical possibility of religious life; it is only one way of arriving at it. Furthermore, there is certainly no practical impossibility in living a contradiction,

89. It is useful here to distinguish between "grounding" and "receiving" the object. See
Charles Taylor, *A Secular Age* (Cambridge, MA: Harvard University Press, 2007), 8–9.

90. William James, "What Pragmatism Means," in *Essays in Pragmatism*, ed. Alburey
Castell (New York: Free Press, 1948), 150.

91. Here one might think again of Arendt or of Adorno's own studies on "authoritarian
personalities."

perhaps even indefinitely.) The question I want to raise at this juncture is this: What if reason itself not only could, but perpetually *must* project objects of this sort, objects that constantly anchor our subjectivity through their presence "outside" us? Indeed, what if such projection was *itself required* for a full conceptual elaboration and understanding of autonomy? Could these objects then save reason from the dialectic of enlightenment— from itself? Might there be a *nondogmatic* way of adopting such a stance?

In fact, this is Kant's suggestion: that autonomous reason must project certain objects outside itself. Viewed in this way, Kantian morality responds to the critique sketched thus far. By invoking the highest good, God, and an immortal soul as the necessary objects of (practical) reason, Kant indexes autonomy to these objects. In doing so he is also able to ward off the dialectic of enlightenment, since not only is autonomy possible *only by virtue of* a commitment to these objects, but thereby our commitment to them in no way limits our autonomy—rather, it actualizes it. Ultimately, the dialectic of enlightenment is avoided to the extent that I *must* carve out a space outside my subjectivity, outside myself. Furthermore, it is important to note that this Kantian interjection is hardly contrived; it is exactly how Adorno conceived of the relation between Kant's project and the dialectic of enlightenment. In the concluding pages of *Negative Dialectics*, Adorno writes that "Kant's rescue of the intelligible sphere . . . is . . . an attempted intervention in the dialectics of enlightenment, at the point where this dialectics terminates in the abolition of reason" (ND 385/6:378). Kantian morality is taken exactly as an alleged response to the dialectic of enlightenment. For this reason, before proceeding to Adorno's own development of the concept of autonomy, I turn to Kant's linking of morality and autonomy in order to evaluate its status as a rejoinder to the issues raised here.

CHAPTER TWO

Beyond the Bounds of Sense:
Kant and the Highest Good

1. INTRODUCTION

In *On the History of Religion and Philosophy in Germany* (1834), Heinrich Heine mocks Kant by fabricating a scene where Kant's servant, Lampe, stands with umbrella in hand, dismayed before the storm Kant has unleashed. Heine imagines that seeing this,

> Kant takes pity and shows that he is not merely a great philosopher but also a good person. He thinks, and half with goodwill and half with irony, he speaks: "Old Lampe has to have a God, otherwise the poor man cannot be happy—people, however, should be happy in this world—that is what practical reason says—well, what do I know?—maybe we can let practical reason vouch for the existence of God." As a result of this argument, Kant distinguishes between theoretical and practical reason and with the latter, as with a magic wand, he again animates the corpse of deism which had been killed by theoretical reason.[1]

While Kant's philosophy is not as simple as Heine's mockery has it, Heine captures a common sentiment: that Kant's rational theology arises *in spite of* the critical philosophy, that is, that Kant's rational theology is a vestige of the very dogmatism he set out to overthrow. My discussion centers on this suspicion. It is only if Kant's rational theology arises as a consequence of his conception of autonomy that rational theology can serve as a response to the dialectic of enlightenment. Having the objects of practical

---

1. Heinrich Heine, *On the History of Religion and Philosophy in Germany and Other Writings*, ed. Terry Pinkard (Cambridge: Cambridge University Press, 2007), 87.

reason be necessitated by the notion of autonomy guarantees a limited sphere in which the dissolution of subjectivity is averted. If, on the other hand, the projections of practical reason are just an afterword to Kant's critical philosophy, then the potential intervention into the dialectic of enlightenment is entirely feeble and no different from any other dogmatic claim (see the conclusion to chapter 1). The locus for these issues is Kant's notion of the highest good, where his claims are as radical as they are controversial: allegedly, in order to be autonomous agents, we must affirm the notion of a highest good, and this notion requires the additional notions of God and immortality of the soul. There can be no autonomous action without belief in the highest good, for autonomy implies rational theology.

Understanding the necessity of rational theology to Kant's project of autonomous self-determination thereby hinges on grasping the role the highest good plays in his critical philosophy. Since the notion undergoes radical change from the first *Critique* to the third, it is worth examining its evolution in detail. (Indeed, my argument will be that the notion becomes plausible only with its presentation in the third *Critique*.) Ultimately, in assessing the accuracy of Heine's sentiment and the nature of his position, Kant's practical commitments must be clarified along with explaining how they arise. It is only then that we can assess their potential suitability as a response to the issues of the previous chapter. In this chapter, then, I will present Kant's position, saving for chapter 3 an assessment of its success as a rejoinder to Horkheimer and Adorno.

2. MORALITY AND THE HIGHEST GOOD

The clearest way into all these issues is through Kant's insistence that morality requires *both* the categorical imperative and a belief in the highest good. Commentators have traditionally been puzzled by this insistence, often failing to see any connection between two claims: The first is Kant's well-known claim in the *Groundwork* that "the good will is not good because of what it effects or accomplishes or because of its competence to achieve some intended end; it is good only because of its willing (i.e., it is good in itself)" (G 4:394). The second is Kant's claim in the second *Critique* that "since the furthering of the highest good . . . is an *a priori necessary* object of our will and is inseparably related to the moral law, the impossibility of the highest good must prove the falsity of the moral law" (2C 5:114; emphasis added). The tension between these claims is captured by Lewis White Beck's famous dismissal of the duty to promote the highest good: "And it is easy to see why this command of reason is not fully expounded: it does not exist. Or at least it does not exist as a separate command, independent of the categorical imperative, which is developed without this concept."[2]

Beck's criticism can be broken down into two issues, one a subset of the other. The first concerns the nature of the relation between the highest good and the moral law (expressed as worries about how the highest good is a duty and about how the relation between the highest good and the rest of Kant's critical philosophy ought to be understood).[3] The second issue is the problem of motivation. The categorical imperative demands that one not act morally because of the motivational pull of the highest good, yet this motivational element constantly threatens to explain motivation. Schopenhauer evinces this sentiment when he writes, "Now the supreme happiness in the highest good should not really be the motive for virtue; yet it is there like a secret article, the presence of which makes all the rest a mere sham contract. It is not really the reward of virtue, but yet is a voluntary gift for which virtue, after work has been done, stealthily holds its hands open."[4]

Although my discussion will focus largely on the first issue (the relation between the highest good and the moral law in Kant's philosophy), I will have a few things to say about the latter issue (and I can note that Kant himself was certainly aware of them as distinct; see LE 66/27:274). In evaluating Kant's notion of the highest good, I begin with the alleged duty to promote the highest good (for this reason my discussion largely avoids any critical discussion of the postulates themselves; my goal is to understand the reasons *for* the postulates). Ultimately it will come out that not only is the highest good necessary for Kantian morality, but that without the highest good, Kantian autonomy is impossible.[5] To make this plausible, however, requires carefully working through the notion of the highest good in Kant's

2. Lewis White Beck, *A Commentary on Kant's "Critique of Practical Reason"* (Chicago: University of Chicago Press, 1960), 244.

3. A quick way to bypass this issue altogether is to show that Kant addresses the highest good for nonphilosophical reasons. Frederick Beiser suggests this (although he does not endorse it) when he writes that "some answer to the problem of the highest good was *de rigeur* in eighteenth-century Germany; no respectable philosopher, least of all one of Kant's stature, could afford to ignore it." See Beiser, "Moral Faith and the Highest Good," in *The Cambridge Companion to Kant and Modern Philosophy*, ed. Paul Guyer (Cambridge: Cambridge University Press, 2006), 594.

4. Arthur Schopenhauer, *The World as Will and Representation*, 2 vols. (New York: Dover, 1958), 1:524.

5. Unsurprisingly, given how closely morality and autonomy are linked, see the "reciprocity thesis" in Henry E. Allison, *Kant's Theory of Freedom* (Cambridge: Cambridge University Press, 1990), 201–14.

critical writings,[6] especially understanding how the notion self-destructs in each critique except the last, where it finally achieves conceptual stability and thereby gains plausibility.

3. THE HIGHEST GOOD IN THE *CRITIQUE OF PURE REASON*

Before we can understand the role of the highest good in Kant's practical philosophy, we must clarify what he means by the highest good. In contemporary discussions, it is common to see two strands of the highest good, one "secular" and one "theological."[7] Such a distinction obfuscates the matter, however, not only because it is foreign to Kant, but because he explicitly points out that even *without* religion, the concept of the highest good arises for reason (see 19:188–89 R6876). I do not mean Kant did not have varying conceptions of the highest good, only that these conceptions must be contextualized within broader shifts in his corpus. (In this way we cannot underestimate the significance of the fact that Kant's philosophical output spanned roughly five decades.)

In the first *Critique*, Kant's notion of the highest good requires both perfect morality and general happiness. Kant describes it as a "self-rewarding morality" (1C A809 = B837). According to such a view, the highest good requires only human effort and rests "merely" on "the condition that everyone do what he should; that is, that all actions of rational beings occur as if they arose from a highest will that comprehends all private choice in or under itself" (1C A810 = B838). If this were to happen, general happiness would follow, since "the system of morality is therefore inseparably combined with the system of happiness" (1C A809 = B837). In his lectures of 1784, Kant explains it like this: "For God wills the happiness of all men, and this by human agency, and if only all men together were unanimously willing to promote their happiness, we might make a paradise in Novaya

6. I do not discuss Kant's precritical views of the highest good. See Richard L. Velkley, *Freedom and the End of Reason: On the Moral Foundation of Kant's Critical Philosophy* (Chicago: University of Chicago Press, 1989), 89–136.

7. This reading was popularized by Yirmiyahu Yovel, *Kant and the Philosophy of History* (Princeton, NJ: Princeton University Press, 1980). Its seeds can be found in John R. Silber, "Kant's Conception of the Highest Good as Immanent and Transcendent," *Philosophical Review* 68 (1959): 469–92. More recently it is in Andrews Reath, "Two Conceptions of the Highest Good in Kant," *Journal of the History of Philosophy* 26, no. 4 (1988) 593–619. Cf. the analogous distinction between "ectypal world" and a world of "happiness according to worth" in Thomas Auxter, "The Unimportance of Kant's Highest Good," *Journal of the History of Philosophy* 17, no. 2 (1979): 121–34.

Zemlya. God *sets us on a stage where we can make one another happy; it rests entirely upon us*. If men are wretched, it is their own fault" (LE 78, 27:285–86). What is crucial is that the highest good could be achieved *if* everyone were to act morally. As Kant writes: "God does not wish a single one of us to fare ill. He has determined us all to unite in helping one another" (LE 79, 27:286).[8] If everyone were to act morally, then everyone would also be happy, because general happiness is more than just the "satisfaction of all of our inclinations" (1C A806 = B834).

But what is general happiness? Furthermore, why is it not just the satisfaction of inclinations? Responding to such potential questions, Kant points out the difficulties involved with the satisfaction of inclinations. Not only is it not obvious how particular inclinations are best satisfied, but it is equally puzzling what our inclinations actually are—what we really want (cf. G 4:418). In light of this uncertainty, it is impossible to achieve general happiness based just on the satisfaction of everyone's inclinations. A general happiness achieved through the moral action of all allegedly is possible. Kant makes this clear in a *Reflexion* from the late 1770s:

> *Only* a universally valid will can provide the ground for the assurance of happiness; *hence we either cannot hope to be happy at all, or we must bring our actions into concordance with the universally valid will*. For in that case alone we are capable of happiness in accordance with the idea, i.e., the representation of the whole, and since this capability is a consequence of our free will, worthy of it. The extent of our happiness depends on the whole, and our will must be substituted for the *originario*. (19:216–17 R6971; emphasis added)

In considering a moral world, we thereby abstract "from inclinations and natural means of satisfying them, and consider . . . only the freedom of a rational being in general and the necessary conditions under which alone it is in agreement with the distribution of happiness in accordance with principles" (1C A806 = B834). Given that the satisfaction of contingent, empirical desires proves to be unstable or even impossible, we can ask how the world would look if it were arranged according to rational (moral) principles. Kant's answer is unequivocal: it is a world where we abstract from

---

8. There are deep questions here about the broader connection between morality and religion. While this is outside my scope, see Beiser, "Moral Faith and the Highest Good," and Allen W. Wood, *Kant's Moral Religion* (Ithaca, NY: Cornell University Press, 1970). See also note 54 in this chapter.

hindrances (both to morality and happiness) and instead envision a world structured entirely according to rational principles, which in turn entails a requisite amount of happiness for the agents involved. (Without this, such a vision would have no motivational pull—more on this shortly.) Only in light of such a holistic vision can general happiness be instantiated.

Of course, Kant realizes that not everyone acts morally. In light of this he asks, What ought I to do? Furthermore, given that I *have* acted morally, what can I hope for? Such questions reflect the dual elements of our discussion: morality and happiness. Since not everyone acts morally, achieving general happiness through morality appears as impossible as achieving it through the satisfaction of inclinations. Nonetheless, "the obligation from the moral law remains valid for each particular use of freedom even if others do not conduct themselves in accord with this law" (1C A810 = B838). Kant's suggestion is thereby that only if I can hope for more than the present world can I then be motivated to do what is moral. The moral world can be hoped for only if it is imagined as "grounded on a highest reason, which commands in accordance with moral laws" and is "at the same time the cause of nature" (1C A810 = B838). In short, although a moral world arising from the world as it now stands cannot be imagined (since not everyone does as he should),[9] such a moral world can, with the addition of a ground in reason, be imagined in the future (cf. R5445 and R5446). Because such a world is ultimately structured by reason, it also offers the guarantee of general happiness—for agents would have no motivation to act morally unless doing so made them worthy of happiness. Furthermore, conceptualizing a moral world requires not only postulating immortality as the means by which a share in the eventual moral world is guaranteed, but also believing in God as the means by which such a world is secured, both practically and theoretically. God guarantees the parity between happiness and morality and the possibility of the latter.

Practically, then, the importance of God comes out most forcefully with the issue of motivation. For Kant, the question What should I do? is just as important as the question What may I hope? If God and immortality are not postulated as a means of securing the eventual existence of the moral world (and, if we so warrant it, our place in it), then not only are moral laws "empty figments of the brain" (*leere Hirngespinste*), but morality itself, while admirable, offers no incentive for "resolve and realization"

9. Kant is not thereby committed to the idea that the moral world *cannot* be instantiated in the natural world. For an opposing view, see Reath, "Two Conceptions of the Highest Good in Kant," 608n19.

(1C A811 = B839; A813 = B841). The postulates are introduced to guarantee the binding force of morality.[10] Kant puts the point as follows: "Thus without a God and a world that is now not visible to us but is hoped for, the majestic ideas of morality are, to be sure, objects of approbation and admiration, but not incentives for resolve and realization" (1C A813 = B841). God and immortality are two ideas of reason required to make morality and the moral world a practical possibility, and thereby serve as a spur for moral action (cf. 1C A808 = B836).

God, however, also occupies a related role in the Canon, serving as the *theoretical* nexus for morality. The standpoint of the highest good requires us to speak of a "purposive unity" and of seeing actions "as if they arose from a highest will." Examples of this way of seeing the issue are numerous in the Canon:

> The idea of a moral world thus has objective reality, not as if it pertained to an object of an intelligible intuition (for we cannot even think of such a thing), but as pertaining to the sensible world, although as an object of pure reason in its practical use and a corpus mysticum of the rational beings in it, *insofar as their free choice under moral laws has thoroughgoing systematic unity in itself.* (1C A808 = B836; emphasis added)
>
> But this system of self-rewarding morality is only an idea, the realization of which rests on the condition that everyone do what he should, i.e., *that all actions of rational beings occur as if they arose from a highest will that comprehends all private choice in or under itself.* (1C A808 = B836; emphasis added)
>
> I call the idea of such an intelligence, in which the morally most perfect will, combined with the highest blessedness, is the cause of all happiness in the world, insofar as it stands in exact relation with morality, the ideal of the highest good. *Thus only in the ideal of the highest original good* can pure reason find the ground of the practically necessary connection of both elements. . . . *Now since we must necessarily represent ourselves through reason as belonging to such a world.* (1C A 810 = B838; emphasis added)

This last point, that we must necessarily represent ourselves as belonging to such a world, is the most significant. The ideal of the highest good is exactly required for the existence of moral reason; it is what guarantees that

10. Cf. Eckart Förster, *Kant's Final Synthesis* (Cambridge, MA: Harvard University Press, 2000), 120–21.

morality is more than just an "empty figment of the brain." Only through God can the moral world gain the requisite unity, a unity that requires viewing its contents (the aggregate sum of all moral actions) as having arisen "from a highest will." Such a procedure has something in common with Leibniz's "ultimate reason for things" in God,[11] albeit in a practical, transcendental register.[12] It is not surprising then to find that Kant mentions Leibniz in the Canon:

> Leibniz called the world, insofar as in it one attends only to rational beings and their interconnection in accordance with moral laws under the rule of the highest good, the realm of grace. . . . Thus to regard ourselves as in the realm of grace, where *every* happiness awaits us *as long as we do not ourselves* limit our share of it through the unworthiness to be happy, is a practically necessary idea of reason. (1C 680–81 A812 = B40; emphasis added)

Exactly this view of morality is on display when Kant conceives of the necessity of moral theism: "The end here is inevitably fixed [*unumgänglich festgestellt*], and according to all my insight, there is possible only one condition under which this end connects with all ends, and thereby has practical validity, namely, that there is a God" (1C A828 = B856; translation modified). Again, *Reflexionen* from the 1770s give a more robust picture of this view:

> Moral laws are those which contain the conditions through which free actions are concordant [*einstimig*] with the universally valid end, thus the private will with the original and supreme will. . . . The will is thus considered in accordance with the unity of the ground, namely insofar as all wills lie in a single will: that which is the cause of nature and every other. (18:184 R5446)
>
> In the intelligible world the substratum is intelligence, the action and cause is freedom, the community is happiness from freedom [*Glückseligkeit aus Freiheit*], the primordial being is an intelligence through

11. See "Principles of Nature and Grace, Based on Reason," in G. W. Leibniz, *Philosophical Essays* (Indianapolis, IN: Hackett, 1989), 206–13.

12. Cf. Kant's remark in the debate with Eberhard that the first *Critique* can be seen as a "genuine apology" for Leibniz, in Immanuel Kant, *Gesammelte Schriften*, ed. Preussischen Akademie der Wissenschaften, 29 vols. (Berlin: Walter de Gruyter, 1912), 8:250. For an overview of the debate, see Henry E. Allison, *The Kant-Eberhard Controversy* (Baltimore: Johns Hopkins University Press, 1973), 1–21.

idea [*eine Intelligentz durch Idee*], the form is morality, the nexus is a nexus of ends. This intelligible world already lies at the basis of the sensible world and is the truly self-sufficient. (18:83 R5086)

Kant describes this dual necessity of God, as theoretical nexus and practical guarantor of morality, as an efficient cause:

> It is necessary that our entire course of life be subordinated to moral maxims; but it would at the same time be impossible for this to happen if reason did not link with the moral law, which is a mere idea, an efficient cause [*wirkende Ursache*] which determines [*bestimmt*] for such same conduct in accord with this law as an outcome [*Ausgang*] precisely corresponding to our highest ends, whether in this or in another life. (1C A812 = B840; translation modified)

The clearest analogy to such a necessity for God in the Canon is the transcendental ideal of the Dialectic. There Kant introduces the idea of a thoroughgoing determination (*durchgängige Bestimmung*), which is a synthetic a priori principle having as its presupposition a "transcendental substratum that contains as it were the entire storehouse of material from which all possible predicates of things can be taken" (1C A575 = B603).[13] This substratum is "nothing other than the idea of an all of reality [*omnitudo realitatis*]" (1C A575 = B603). Single and individual, such a transcendental idea is thereby a transcendental ideal (1C A568 = B696, A576 = B604). Determination is conceived of as parasitic on such an "all of reality," as a sort of storehouse of predicates; determination only through limitation.[14] What is essential for an *omnitudo realitatis* is that it be an idea of reason, not that it have actual existence. God and the highest good perform an analogous function in the Canon, addressed to practical instead of theoretical reason. I take Kant to broach this analogy explicitly in a *Reflexion* from the late 1770s:

> Moral laws do not spring from reason, but rather contain the conditions through which alone it is possible for free actions to be determined and cognized in accordance with the rules of reason. This happens, however, when we make the universally valid end the basis of actions. Thereby do particular ends agree with those which one can regard as if through them

13. For a discussion, see Henry E. Allison, *Kant's Transcendental Idealism*, 2nd ed. (New Haven, CT: Yale University Press, 2004), 397–405.

14. Cf. ibid., 400.

all things were possible. The morally good demands complete unity of the ground of the action before reason, consequently that it be derived from the *idea archetypa*, which is the end of the entire world. (18:184 R5445)

With this *Reflexion*, we can see that, while already in possession of the categorical imperative,[15] Kant also viewed morality as a sphere of ends unified through an ultimate end.[16] Germane to our broader discussion, we can see here, for better or for worse, that Kant already envisions reason as projecting an ultimate end (the highest good), thereby deriving particular moral ends from this projection.

In summary, God both guarantees happiness *practically* through the promise of parity between morality and happiness, and also establishes the *theoretical* unity necessary to conceptualize a moral world (and I note here that this theoretical function will importantly reappear in the second *Critique*). Without God, immortality, and the highest good, morality would be impossible. Together they guarantee not only the very standpoint of morality (a moral image of the world), but also the requisite motivation for moral action.[17] Only through the spur of an eventual reward of happiness is Kant able to neutralize the threat posed by the obvious immorality of the present world. Prudence and morality are two sides of the same coin. Without the highest good, there is no reason to choose morality over happiness where the two conflict. With the highest good, however, moral action gains its proper motivation. Or so it seems.

4. THE GARVE REVIEW

Although the *Groundwork of the Metaphysics of Morals* (1785) makes no mention of the highest good, it is nonetheless crucial for understanding the evolution of the notion in Kant's critical works. The starting point for

15. See Dieter Henrich, "The Concept of Moral Insight," in *The Unity of Reason*, ed. Richard L. Velkley (Cambridge, MA: Harvard University Press, 1994), 72; Josef Schmucker, *Die Ursprünge der Ethik Kants in seinem vorkritischen Schriften und Reflektionen* (Meisenheim am Glan, Germany: Anton Hain, 1961), 253–59.

16. Cf. Dieter Henrich, "The Moral Image of the World," in *Aesthetic Judgment and the Moral Image of the World* (Palo Alto, CA: Stanford University Press, 1994), 20–22. Henrich discusses this notion extensively, as well as Kant's reasons for abandoning it.

17. Cf. Paul Guyer, "Moral Faith and the Highest Good," in *The Cambridge Companion to Kant and Modern Philosophy*, ed. Paul Guyer (Cambridge: Cambridge University Press, 2006), 614–15; Steven G. Smith, "Worthiness to Be Happy and Kant's Concept of the Highest Good," *Kant Studien* 75 (1984): 175.

understanding the *Groundwork* must be Christian Garve's review of the first *Critique*, which profoundly influenced the writing of the *Groundwork*.[18] In 1782 an anonymous review of the first *Critique* appeared in the *Göttinger Anzeigen von Gelehrten Sachen*. Kant seems to have been so displeased by the review that he issued a challenge to it in the appendix to the *Prolegomena* (1783), demanding that the reviewer reveal himself so a proper debate about the merits of the review and the *Critique* could occur (4:378–79). Roughly a year later, on August 21, 1783, Kant received a letter from Garve stating that although "you demand that the reviewer of your book in the Göttingen journal identify himself. I cannot in any way recognize that review, in the form that it was published, as my own" (10:328). Garve then describes his own displeasure at how his review was mangled by J. G. H. Feder, enclosing with his letter the full copy of his own, longer review.[19] It is this version of the review that ought to be examined in attempts to understand the *Groundwork*.[20] There, after describing Kant's agnosticism about skeptical reason, Garve writes that, for Kant, "moral concepts, which are necessarily and *a priori* true, come to the help of these speculative [ones]. They show us that a certain type of acting is right [*Art zu handeln als Recht*], and also present it to us as a claim to happiness."[21] In describing the moral world, Garve also mockingly writes, "How wisely and happily is the nature of men arranged!"[22] He then points out that it is unlikely someone could practically value God and immortality when, theoretically, knowledge of them is conclusively shown to be impossible in the Dialectic. As Garve puts it: "That one can dwell and live in the kingdom of Grace after the kingdom of nature has disappeared before our eyes, will, I believe find its way into the minds and hearts of very few people."[23]

More fundamentally, however, Garve shows that Kant's account in the first *Critique* suffers from a vicious circularity.[24] God and immortality are

18. On this point see Förster, *Kant's Final Synthesis*, 117–47. Also relevant is Klaus Reich, "Kant and Greek Ethics (II)," *Mind* 48 (1939): 446–63.

19. This review appeared in its entirety in 1783 in *Allgemeine Deutsche Bibliothek*. Kant was also displeased with this longer review, claiming he was treated like an idiot—see the letter from Hamann to Herder of December 8, 1783, in Johann Georg Hamann, *Briefwechsel* (Wiesbaden, Germany: Insel, 1994), 5:107.

20. Found in Immanuel Kant, *Prolegomena zu einer jeden künftigen Metaphysik, die als Wissenschaft wird auftreten könne*, ed. Rudolf Malter (Stuttgart: Reclam, 1989), 219–46.

21. Ibid., 237.

22. Ibid.

23. Ibid., 238.

24. Cf. Förster, *Kant's Final Synthesis*, 124–26; Terry F. Godlove Jr., "Moral Actions, Moral Lives: Kant on Intending the Highest Good," *Southern Journal of Philosophy* 25, no. 1 (1987): 51.

introduced to secure the viability of the moral standpoint, but since they are also to serve as *incentives* to morality, they ultimately rest on our desire for happiness (in the form of the happiness promised by the *worthiness* to be happy, inherent in the highest good). But this leaves morality as fundamentally derivative, since it too rests on the desire for happiness. In short, Kant—at this point—has no argument for why we should follow the dictates of morality beyond the dictates of prudence. Indeed, it may be that the entire moral standpoint is a mere "empty figment of our brain," since what *really* counts is our happiness; morality is just the handmaiden of happiness. Since God and immortality are introduced to anchor the moral standpoint, it is difficult to see how they could also serve as an incentive for that very standpoint. Put another way, there is no way the moral law retains its binding force, as Kant claims (1C A810 = B838), since this binding force is guaranteed by the postulates and yet the binding force is what precipitates the postulates in the first place.[25] Many issues arise for Kant here. Kant's proposed solution to the bigger issue of motivation (i.e., his "deduction" of freedom in the *Groundwork* and his shift in the second *Critique*) is beyond my scope here.[26] Instead, I want to move directly to the second *Critique* to see how Kant refashions the notion of the highest good in light of his realizing this circularity.

25. Cf. Thomas Wizenmann's response to Kant in the *Deutsches Museum* of February 1787, titled "An den Herrn Professor Kant von dem Verfasser der *Resultate*," in Karl Gottlob Hausius, *Materialien zur Geschichte der critischen Philosophie* (Leipzig: Breitkopf, 1793), 2:127. For more on Wizenmann see Lewis White Beck, *Early German Philosophy: Kant and His Predecessors* (Cambridge, MA: Harvard University Press, 1969), 372–74.

26. In fact, even the relation between the *Groundwork* and the second *Critique* is a point of contention. Generally it is agreed that the deduction in the final pages of the *Groundwork* is a failure. The estimation of this failure ranges from merely "ambiguous" to one of the "most spectacular train wrecks" in philosophy (for the former see Allison, *Kant's Theory of Freedom*, 214–30; for the latter see Paul Guyer, "Naturalistic and Transcendental Moments in Kant's Moral Philosophy," *Inquiry* 50, no. 5 (2007): 445). An exception that reads the argument as successful is Onora O'Neill, "Reason and Autonomy in *Grundlegung* III," in *Constructions of Reason: Explorations of Kant's Practical Philosophy* (Cambridge: Cambridge University Press, 1989), 51–66. Analogously, there is debate over the position Kant takes in the second *Critique*, that is, over the nature of the "fact of reason." Is it another attempted deduction or an illustration of how that task is abandoned? For claims to the former see Paul W. Franks, *All or Nothing: Systematicity, Transcendental Arguments, and Skepticism in German Idealism* (Cambridge, MA: Harvard University Press, 2005), 260–301. Although she takes a different tack than Franks does, cf. Carol W. Voeller, *The Metaphysics of the Moral Law: Kant's Deduction of Freedom* (New York: Garland, 2001). For the latter position see Karl Ameriks, "Kant's Deduction of Freedom and Morality," in *Interpreting Kant's Critiques* (Oxford: Oxford University Press, 2003), 161–93.

5. THE HIGHEST GOOD IN THE
CRITIQUE OF PRACTICAL REASON

With the *Groundwork*, Kant realizes that nothing can serve as an incentive for moral action except the moral law. What has puzzled interpreters, however, is that Kant continues to maintain in the second *Critique* that the highest good is a necessary duty (2C 5:114) and that if the highest good is impossible, then the moral law is false (2C 5:114). If all that is not enough, Kant also employs a notion of happiness quite distinct from the one in the first *Critique*. I turn to these points below.

In the *Critique of Practical Reason* (1788), the highest good appears in the Dialectic,[27] where Kant points out that no less than with theoretical reason, practical reason also seeks the unconditioned.[28] Kant writes:

> Pure practical reason . . . likewise seeks the unconditioned for the practically conditioned (which rests on inclinations and natural needs); and this unconditioned is not only sought as the determining ground of the will but, even when this is given (in the moral law), is also sought as the unconditioned totality of the object of the pure practical reason, under the name of the *highest good*. (2C 5:108)

Kant adds that "though the highest good may be the entire object of a pure practical reason, i.e. of a pure will, it is still not to be taken as the *determining ground* of the pure will" (2C 5:109). Furthermore, Kant also insists that the concept of the highest good involves proportionality between virtue and happiness. He introduces the point as follows:

> The concept of the "highest" contains an ambiguity which, if not attended to, can occasion unnecessary disputes. The "highest" can mean the "supreme" (*supremum*) or the "perfect" (*consummatum*). The former is the unconditional condition, i.e., the condition which is subordinate to no other (*originarium*); the latter is that whole which is no part of a yet larger whole of the same kind (*perfectissimum*). That virtue (as the worthiness to be happy) is the supreme condition of whatever appears

---

27. That there is a dialectic in the second *Critique* (in the realm of practical reason) is a significant departure from the first *Critique*. Cf. Reinhard Brandt, "Analytic/Dialectic," in *Reading Kant: New Perspectives on Transcendental Arguments and Critical Philosophy*, ed. Eva Schaper and Wilhelm Vossenkuhl (Oxford: Blackwell, 1989), in particular 185–91.

28. On the notion of reason having "needs," see chapter 1, section 7.

to us to be desirable and thus of all our pursuit of happiness and, consequently, that it is the supreme good have been proved in the Analytic.
But these truths do not imply that virtue is the entire and perfect good
as the object of the faculty of desire of rational finite beings. For this,
happiness is also required. (2C 5:110)

This proportionality requirement, with the question of the necessity of
the highest good as an object of pure practical reason in the first place, leads
many commentators to throw up their hands (if they are not already using
them to tear their hair out). Lewis White Beck summarizes the frustration:

> For suppose I do all in my power—which is all any moral decree can de-
> mand of me—to promote the highest good, what am I to do? Simply act
> for respect for the law, which I already knew. I can do absolutely noth-
> ing else toward apportioning happiness in accordance with desert—that
> is the task of a moral governor of the universe, not of a laborer in the
> vineyard. It is not my task; my task is to realize the one condition of the
> summum bonum which is within my power.[29]

Beck's point is a familiar one: If the categorical imperative is unconditional, then why the added duty to promote the highest good? Furthermore,
why is parity between happiness and virtue necessary to the highest good,
let alone a necessity for me to further? As Beck says, perhaps we should just
let the "eschatological chips fall where they may."[30] Any requirement for
parity, however, raises an even more basic question about the relation between happiness and virtue. Here, in contrast to the first *Critique*, Kant rejects a conception of happiness operating on the model of general happiness.
Instead, happiness is now conceived as the satisfaction of inclinations.[31]

---

29. Beck, *Commentary on Kant's Critique of Practical Reason*, 244–45.

30. Ibid., 275.

31. Cf. Förster, *Kant's Final Synthesis*, 118–22. See also Pauline Kleingeld, "What Do the
Virtuous Hope For? Re-reading Kant's Doctrine of the Highest Good," in *Proceedings of the
Eighth International Kant Congress* (Milwaukee, WI: Marquette University Press, 1995), 94;
Smith, "Worthiness to Be Happy and Kant's Concept of the Highest Good," 174. For an opposing
viewpoint, see Paul Guyer, "Beauty, Systematicity, and the Highest Good," *Inquiry* 46 (2003):
206–8. For a rebuttal of Guyer, see Eckart Förster, "Reply to Friedman and Guyer," *Inquiry* 46
(2003): 234. For an (unsuccessful) attempt to rescue Guyer's position, see Sean ☐ ⁻nberg, "From
Canon to Dialectic to Antinomy: Giving Inclinations Their Due," *Inquiry* 48, n☐ (2005): 232–
48. For more on Kant's various conceptions of happiness, see Klaus Düsing, "Das ⁻blem des
höchsten Gutes in Kants praktischer Philosophie," *Kant Studien* 62 (1971) 5–42. ☐ Victoria S.
Wike, *Kant on Happiness in Ethics* (Albany: State University of New York Press, 1994), 1–27.

With the second *Critique*, it is impossible that virtue inherently leads to happiness or vice versa (2C 5:110–13). This is so much so that one early reviewer of the book characterized Kant as "tougher than Zeno" when it came to virtue, but with regard to happiness, as "more lax than Epicurus."[32] One way to understand the problem of the second *Critique*, then, is, again, as the task of making happiness and virtue compatible, but this time in light of a notion of happiness distinct from the first *Critique*.

Fundamental to that task is understanding *why* happiness is necessary for the highest good. Why is virtue alone insufficient? In the first *Critique*, happiness and virtue were intimately related. In the second they are divorced. Kant offers hints throughout the second *Critique* about the necessity of happiness to the highest good, but he never offers an explicit argument. This suggests that the point was too obvious to elaborate, or that Kant himself was uncertain about the necessity. Opting for the first option, it can be shown that the point *is* entirely obvious. The highest good is introduced as the highest object of practical reason—it is thereby meant to unify all the other objects of practical reason; these objects are to be arranged with the highest good at the top (in the same way that, say, ranks are arranged in a military structure). It is *trivially true* that such objects include not only the objects of *moral* reasoning, but also the objects of the other side of practical reason, namely, *prudential* reasoning. Through the highest good, these objects will all be unified and ordered with goodness (virtue) at the top, restricting the claims of nonmoral reasoning via the moral law. Since practical reason entails the unified perspective of a single agent, prudential claims are not voided or abandoned.[33] They cannot be, on pain of schizophrenia. Kant illustrates how the moral law *restricts* (but does not destroy) selfishness (*Eigenliebe*): "Pure practical reason *merely checks* selfishness, for selfishness, as natural and active in us even prior to the moral law, is *restricted* [*einschränkt*] by the moral law to agreement with the law; when this is done, selfishness is called rational self-love" (2C 76, 5:73; emphasis added). In other words, if happiness is "the satisfaction of all of our inclina-

32. See Herman Andreas Pistorius's review (1794) in Hausius, *Materialien zur Geschichte der critischen Philosophie*, 172. For more on Pistorius, see Frederick Beiser, *The Fate of Reason: German Philosophy from Kant to Fichte* (Cambridge, MA: Harvard University Press, 2006), 188–92. See also note 45 below.

33. My understanding of the necessity of prudential claims to the highest good is indebted to Stephen Engstrom, "The Concept of the Highest Good in Kant's Moral Theory," *Philosophy and Phenomenological Research* 52, no. 4 (1992): 756–67. Engstrom presents a formal argument for parity using beneficence. For a discussion of this latter concept, see Bruce Aune, *Kant's Theory of Morals* (Princeton, NJ: Princeton University Press, 1979), 181–88.

tions" (1C A806 = B834; cf. 2C 5:124), and insofar as practical reason is also in charge of the satisfaction of these inclinations, then it just is the case that the highest good involves unifying all aspects of practical reason, including prudential reasoning.

In the second *Critique*, Kant makes such an argument explicit in several places, but he does so in a cryptic manner, with allusion to the judgment of an "impartial" (*unparteiischen*) reason.[34] In defining the highest good, he writes that, in addition to virtue, "happiness is also required, and indeed not merely in the partial eyes of a person who makes himself his end but even in the judgment of an impartial reason, which impartially regards persons in the world as ends-in-themselves" (2C 5:110). The reason these pronouncements seem mysterious is that Kant often accompanies them with talk of "an omnipotent rational being," as he does in this case, continuing: "For to be in need of happiness and also worthy of it and yet not to partake of it could not be in accordance with the complete volition of a rational being, *who also would be all powerful*, assuming the latter only for the sake of the thought experiment [*wenn wir uns auch nur ein solches zum Versuche denken, gar nicht zusammen bestehen*]" (2C 5:110; translation modified and emphasis added; cf. 2C 5:124). Given that we are unifying *human* happiness and virtue, it is peculiar to talk of omnipotence. But such phrasing is not as mysterious as it might appear. In fact, it is merely a restatement of the moral image of the world perspective from the first *Critique*; that is, it is what the world would look like if ordered with virtue in mind, but this time from the perspective of a *humanly* rational will that also employs prudential reasoning. The invocation of omnipotence is not a reference to God but is assumed solely "for the sake of the thought experiment" (i.e., to lend plausibility to the possibility of such ordering). Additionally, just as in the first *Critique*, such a perspective is built on inquiring what our world would be like if it were ordered according to such highest reason, that is, the highest good. Cases of individual action do not require this perspective; rather, it naturally arises when one tries to order the entirety of goods present to one. Kant is explicit about this point when he writes in a relatively late *Reflexion* (later than 1790): "If we look merely to actions, we do not require this belief [in the highest good]. If, however, we wish to extend ourselves through our actions to the possession of the end that is thereby possible, we must assume that this end is thoroughly possible" (16:515 R2793). In this sense, Kant's procedure here is akin to the one in the first *Critique*,

---

34. There is more to be said about this notion, especially in broader contexts. See Hannah Arendt, *Lectures on Kant's Political Philosophy* (Chicago: University of Chicago Press, 1982).

the difference being that where in the first *Critique* the unifying nexus for the highest good was God, here it is the standpoint of morality as the project of autonomous moral action (as conditioned by empirical nature) that garners such unity. This standpoint serves as the grounding for morality—*I am the nexus*. Proportionality, then, is inherent in the highest good insofar as reason unifies all the items it reasons about, whether moral or prudential. In this way it ought to be obvious that the parity requirement cannot be grounded outside reason,[35] it cannot be proposed to reason but can arise only *from* reason.[36] Anything else would be heteronomy.[37] Since the highest good is the organizing principle of practical reason, then, happiness just is part of the highest good.

Nonetheless, even if happiness must be part of the highest good, why seek the highest good? This question suggests that Beck's worry admits of two strands, for one of which we have an answer: the highest good must involve happiness (i.e., parity is a requirement of the highest good). The second worry, however, is about the necessity of the highest good in the first place—How is the highest good an a priori object of pure practical reason? Unless it can be shown that pure practical reason *must* unify the various goods that fall under its domain, it does not matter whether the highest good must contain elements from prudential reasoning, since we cannot explain how the highest good arises as an object for practical reason in the first place. Another way to put this point, then, is to say that the perspective of pure practical reason as involving the highest good must be shown to be inescapable, in much the same way that Kant, in the first *Critique*, had shown that apperception was inescapable (see the brief discussion in section 9 of chapter 1). Furthermore, in showing that the highest good is a necessary a priori object of practical reason, we will also have shown that

---

35. In this context see John Rawls, *Lectures on the History of Moral Philosophy*, ed. Barbara Herman (Cambridge, MA: Harvard University Press, 2000), 314–17. Rawls disagrees, taking proportionality to arise from a divine will. Nonetheless, as I will argue, Rawls is right when he suggests that the necessity of the highest good arises only with an alliance of the agent's will with the will of God.

36. This undercuts arguments that suggest Kant cannot achieve the parity requirement because of the inscrutability of motives. Such arguments attack Kant too late, at the level of realization. What is at stake, however, is reasoning. For example, see R. Z. Friedman, "The Importance and Function of Kant's Highest Good," *Journal of the History of Philosophy* 22, no. 3 (1984): 107; Jeffrie Murphy, "The Highest Good as Content for Kant's Ethical Formalism," *Kant Studien* 56 (1965): 102–10.

37. Similarly, the postulates arise not *because* of desert, but because of reason's *need* to achieve unity. Cf. Engstrom, "Concept of the Highest Good in Kant's Moral Theory," 778–79.

the highest good involves happiness, since prudential reasoning just is a part of practical reason.

One way to broach this point is to refer to the earlier *Reflexion*. Why can we not "look merely to actions" (to the form of the categorical imperative), but instead ought also to form the notion of the highest good? As I have stressed above, even if the highest good can be understood as expressing the unity of practical reason, an additional argument is required for the necessity of this unity. In the second *Critique*, Kant has an argument for the necessity of such unity, but it suffers from the same defect as the argument of the first *Critique*—circularity. This circularity is apparent when we sketch how the postulates arise in the second *Critique*. According to Kant, the antinomy of practical reason arises because the connection between virtue and happiness is synthetic (it requires a third term to guarantee the connection). Because the highest good both requires such a connection (between happiness and virtue) and requires "complete fitness of intentions to the moral law," the postulate of immortality is adduced in order to guarantee progress toward this goal (2C 5:122). Immortality solves the "first problem" of the highest good: how to achieve the requisite amount of virtue (2C 5:124). Immortality allows for the possibility of the highest good as the ordering principle of an agent's practical standpoint (given enough time, the form of my practical reasoning can come to have virtue as its pinnacle). God accordingly enters the picture to guarantee that happiness is also achieved when the concept of the highest good does come to organize an agent's practical reasoning standpoint. What is problematic, however, is how Kant frames this point:

> The supreme cause [*oberste Ursache*], however, must contain the ground of the agreement [*grund der Übereinstimmung*] of nature not merely with a law of the will of rational beings [*einem Gesetze des Willens der vernünftigen Wesen*], but with the idea of this law so far as they place [*setzen*] it as the supreme ground of determination of the will [*obersten Bestimmungsgrunde des Willens*]. Thus it contains the ground of the agreement of nature not merely with actions moral in their form [*mit den Sitten der Form*] but also with their morality as the motives [*Bewegungsgrunde*] to such actions, i.e., with their moral comportment of mind [*Gesinnung*]. (2C 5:125; translation modified)

What might Kant mean with his distinction between "actions moral in their form" and "morality as the motives to such actions?" One way to understand this distinction is as an uncontroversial claim: God is introduced to guarantee parity between virtue and happiness, but such a parity is due only to *truly* virtuous actions, as opposed to actions that appear virtuous from an external perspective ("actions moral in their form"). This is hardly satisfactory, however, since actions "moral in their form" already are "truly" virtuous. It is impossible that an action that is moral in *its form* could only "appear" to be virtuous. Put another way, from an external perspective, helping you in a time of need because of moral motives and because of immoral ones *may* be indistinguishable (e.g., because I hate to see you suffer or in order to gain your confidence so I can abuse it later). Actions moral in their form, however, inherently carry an "internal" perspective—they conform to the categorical imperative. Moral actions could never contain ulterior or nonmoral motives as their justificatory grounds exactly because they would *not* be "moral in their form," since such form just is the categorical imperative. What else might Kant have in mind, then?

I think this passage becomes clear if we read it in light of something else Kant writes about God in the second *Critique*:

> Through the concept of the highest good as the object and final end of pure practical reason, the moral law leads to religion. Religion is the recognition of all duties as divine commands, not as sanctions, i.e., arbitrary and contingent ordinances of a foreign will, but as essential laws of any free will as such. *Even as such, they must be regarded as commands of the Supreme Being* because we can hope for the highest good . . . *only from* a morally perfect (holy and beneficent) and omnipotent will; and, therefore, *we can hope to attain it only through harmony with his will.* (2C 5:129; emphasis added)

Kant adds that "here again everything remains disinterested and based only on duty, without being based on fear or hope as incentives, which, if they became principles, would destroy the entire moral worth of the actions" (2C 5:129). This rings hollow, however, because Kant's position here is fundamentally analogous to the first *Critique*. Both views trade on an idea summarized by an early *Reflexion* (ca. 1772–78) where, attempting to prove the existence of God, Kant claims, "We have the concept of God necessarily as the supreme ground [*obersten Grundes*] of things by means of freedom . . . to determine the final ends and hopes of rational beings [*die letzte Zwecke und Hoffnungen Vernünftiger Wesen zu bestimmen*]" (17:603 R4589). Here, in the second *Critique*, the same view is deployed, albeit in a different context. Although Kant is not trying to *prove* the existence of God here, he is presuming that God is the reason *by which* practical reason achieves its unity. The unity of an agent's practical reason (where the highest good orders all of practical reason from top to bottom) cannot be achieved unless the agent has aligned her will with the will of God. To hearken explicitly to the first *Critique*, this position is exactly the same as the one where Kant invokes God as a moral nexus by means of which morality is made possible, and through which we align our motivations with those of God (cf. section 3 above). That this is not an adequate answer ought to be obvious. The central question can just be repeated in a different register: Why does an agent *need* to align her will with the will of God? Nonetheless, explicitly elaborating this failure in the terms of Kant's account of rational agency is fruitful here, since this contextualizes the way he revises the notion of the highest good in the third *Critique*. What follows, then, are some basic points about his conception of rational agency.

The backbone of Kant's account is what he terms a maxim, which is "a subjective principle of volition" (G 4:400). Likewise, for Kant, the will cannot be determined to act by an incentive (*Triebfeder*) unless an agent has incorporated that incentive into her maxim (R 6:24).[38] An action thereby can be attributed to an agent only where there is a maxim "underwriting" it. Actions without maxims are not attributable to free agency (this is not to say that every action must have a *conscious* maxim—only that a maxim can ultimately be provided for any action). Maxims, in turn, are general enough that several actions may fall under them.[39] Heuristically, we might think of maxims as filters. They not only filter particular intentions, they color the ways these intentions manifest themselves. For example, if I have adopted as my maxim the idea that I should make my students feel welcome in class, I may not only design and deliver my lectures in a particular way, but likewise perform those designs and deliverances in a particular manner (e.g., gently correcting mistakes as opposed to rolling my eyes at them). There is, then, a sort of hierarchy that unfolds with every particular maxim. I may design the class in a particular way, deliver it in a particular way, even use a particular type font when printing the syllabus, dress a certain way on the day of the lecture, and so forth. Yet all these actions would fall under one maxim.[40] In turn, this maxim may fall under another maxim,

38. Aptly dubbed the "incorporation thesis" in Allison, *Kant's Theory of Freedom*, 39–40.

39. They are, in this regard, instructively compared to concepts in ibid., 91.

40. This hierarchical interpretation of maxims is illustrated in O'Neill, *Constructions of Reason*, 83–89. A question about the scope of maxims emerges here. We may take maxims to be akin to a "life rule" (*Lebensregel*) and thereby rare, or we may take them to be more common. For the former, see Otfried Höffe, *Ethik und Politik: Grundmodelle und Probleme der praktischen Philosophie* (Frankfurt am Main: Suhrkamp, 1979), 90–92. More recently, see Manfred

one that centers on acting in such a way as to develop my talents (which
in this case, happens to refer to teaching, but in another situation may refer to Olympic weight lifting or to playing chess, which themselves would
carry nested maxims, actions, and so forth). Likewise, this maxim may fall
under another maxim that centers on helping those around me, which in
turn may fall under another maxim that centers on valuing humanity, and
so forth. This nested procedure is crucial to understanding human action,
since two people performing the same action (e.g., a deadlift at the gym)
may be doing it for two radically different reasons (contrast the vanity of
a bodybuilder with the physical conditioning of a firefighter). These basic
points about maxims are important because in the second *Critique* and in
Religion within the Boundaries of Mere Reason (1793), Kant begins to speak
of a highest or supreme maxim, a "supreme ground for the determination of
choice" and a "first ground of the adoption of our maxims" (2C 5:22; R 47,
6:21). According to Kant, there are only two options for a highest maxim:
either the principle of self-love or the moral law. The prioritizing of one or
the other is what Kant terms *Gesinnung*,[41] or one's "fundamental comportment of mind."[42]

In the second *Critique*, Kant thinks the highest good cannot be a supreme end for a will unless that will has aligned itself with the will of God.
He writes explicitly: "The moral law commands us to make the highest
possible good in a world the final object of all our conduct [*letzten Ge-
genstande alles Verhaltens*]. This I cannot hope to effect *except* through
the agreement of my will with that of a holy and beneficent Author of the
world" (2C 5:129; emphasis added). The analogy to the moral image of the
world in the first *Critique*, then, is readily apparent here. A supreme maxim
can be achieved only through an alliance between our will and the will of
God. Through such comportment, all the agent's maxims are arranged in
light of the final end presented by the divine will. In this way it is allegedly explained how the highest good is arrived at as an a priori object. Since
I must believe in God, I also must believe in a supreme maxim, that is,
the highest good. But this account is just as circular as the one in the first

---

Kuehn, *Kant: A Biography* (Cambridge: Cambridge Univesity Press, 2001), 144–47. For the latter, see Barbara Herman, *The Practice of Moral Judgment* (Cambridge, MA: Harvard University
Press, 1993), 217–24. My argument here requires only that maxims be nested in nature.

41. There are many issues here. See Allison, *Kant's Theory of Freedom*, 136–45, and G.
Felicitas Munzel, *Kant's Conception of Moral Character* (Chicago: University of Chicago Press,
1999).

42. In choosing this translation instead of the more general "character," I follow Kuehn,
Kant, 368–69, and Munzel, *Kant's Conception of Moral Character*, xv–xviii, 65–70.

Critique. If the highest good is what causes the notion of God to arise in the first place, it cannot also be that God is what causes the notion of the highest good to arise as an a priori object of reason. If God enters in order to guarantee parity between happiness and virtue, it cannot be that God also guarantees that this parity should be an object of our will. It still remains, then, to be established why practical reason must seek such unity.[43]

6. THE HIGHEST GOOD IN THE *CRITIQUE OF JUDGMENT*

Here is one way to understand the problem that has emerged: First, there is a plurality of goods that need to be conditioned and ordered with the highest good at their pinnacle. Second, there is also a plurality of maxims that need to be nested and ordered with the supreme ground as their locus. Right now, "the highest good" and "the supreme ground" appear to designate two separate justificatory grounds. What needs to be shown is that these are two sides of the same object. We can make headway here if we remember how Kant stresses in the second *Critique* that the good is viable only as "an effect possible through freedom" (2C 5:57).[44] Nothing is good before being determined as good by the will.[45] Put this way, on pain of heteronomy and schizophrenia, "highest good" and "supreme ground" *must* be two sides of the same thing. The *Critique of Judgment* (1790) exactly shows how this is so. Before elaborating this point, we can summarize the problem the second *Critique* presents as the fact that while the agent autonomously imposes the highest good as an *end*, in aligning her will with the will of God, she *heteronomously* imposes the *Gesinnung* necessary to that end. And this is a problem on top of the still unanswered question of why reason *needs* to unify its ends in the form of the highest good. With the third *Critique*, Kant

43. For this reason, in an otherwise excellent account, I think the case for the hope of "participating in the highest good" being the mark of freedom is overstated in Paul Ricouer, "Freedom in the Light of Hope," in *The Conflict of Interpretations: Essays in Hermeneutics* (Evanston, IL: Northwestern University Press, 1974), 420.

44. This does not require that only actions are moral goods. See Wood, *Kant's Moral Religion*, 62–68.

45. This element of the second *Critique* originates from Pistorius's review of the *Groundwork* (cf. 2C 5:8). See Rüdiger Bittner and Konrad Cramer, eds., *Materialien zu Kants "Kritik der praktischen Vernunft"* (Frankfurt am Main: Suhrkamp, 1975), 144–61. See also note 32 above. Pistorius argues that Kant makes a cardinal mistake in not first establishing the nature of good. Much of the second *Critique* is concerned with illustrating precisely why Pistorius is incorrect. On how Kant prioritizes the "right over the good," see Charles Larmore, *The Morals of Modernity* (Cambridge: Cambridge University Press, 1996), 19–41. Cf. John R. Silber, "The Copernican Revolution in Ethics: The Good Re-examined," *Kant-Studien* 51 (1951): 185; and Silber, "The Importance of the Highest Good in Kant's Ethics," *Ethics* 73 (1963): 179–97.

solves both problems by showing how humanity must be seen as the final end of creation.

Unpacking Kant's argument there requires first understanding the notion of a natural end that surfaces in the concluding sections of the third *Critique*. Kant stresses that when the faculty of judgment forces us to view organisms as natural ends (3C §§64–66), we are also led to view the whole of nature teleologically, since living organisms and their environments admit of teleological explanation (3C §67). A question arises about whether there is a final end to all of creation. Because we can always ask *why* any particular thing, living or otherwise, exists, we are drawn to the possibility of teleology.[46] Does the object in question exist as a means for something else, or is it a final end? Kant points out that "if we go through the whole of nature, we do not find in it, as nature, any being that can claim the privilege of being the final end [*Endzweck*] of creation; and one can even prove *a priori* that whatever could be an ultimate end [*letzter Zweck*] for nature could never . . . be, as a natural thing, a final end" (3C 5:426). We might initially be tempted to see humanity as an ultimate end, say, because the rest of the world seems to exist to support its existence, or because humans appear to be the only beings on earth who form a concept of ends for themselves. All such views are ultimately unjustifiable, because, as Kant points out, following Carl Linnaeus (Carl von Linné), we might just as easily decide the opposite: humans are the best means for keeping other systems (say, vegetative, animal, or otherwise) in check—we exist exactly *for them*. While this point reflects skepticism toward the matter, Kant deploys a far stronger objection when he suggests that it can be shown a priori that no natural end could *ever* be a final or ultimate end.

Kant begins by proposing that humanity might be hypothesized as being the ultimate end of creation. If this were so, then the end would be such that it is "either the kind of the end that can be satisfied by the beneficence of nature itself, or it is the aptitude and skill for all sorts of ends for which . . . we can use nature. . . . The first end of nature would be . . . happiness, the second the culture of the human being" (3C 5:429–30). In short, if humanity is the final end of creation, then our ultimate end is instantiated either through happiness or through human culture. Kant dismisses the option of happiness by means of two arguments. The first is a familiar one: our own idea of happiness is so fickle and amorphous that even were it the end, we

---

46. There is a lot more to be said about teleology in this context. See James Kreines, "The Inexplicability of Kant's *Naturzweck*: Kant on Teleology, Explanation and Biology," *Archiv für Geschichte der Philosophie* 87, no. 3 (2005): 270–311.

could never satisfy it because we could never even properly delineate what it consists in (3C 5:430; cf. G 4:395–96; 2C 5:25–27). The second argument, however, is novel and relevant to our larger discussion. Kant points out that we need only to look around us at the magnitude of natural and human suffering to see that it is impossible that nature is designed with our happiness in mind. Kant makes this point forcefully in the note to section 84: "It is easy to decide what sort of value life has for us if it assessed merely by what one enjoys (the natural end of the sum of all inclinations, happiness). *Less than zero*: for who would start life anew under the same conditions" (3C 5:434; emphasis added).

Human culture proves equally incapable of serving as the final end of creation. Here Kant defines culture as the "production of the aptitude of a rational being for any ends in general (and thus those of his freedom)" (3C 5:431). This is congruent with his account in an earlier essay, "Idea for a Universal History from a Cosmopolitan Point of View" (1784).[47] There he suggested that culture might be conceived of as progressively developing the capacities of humanity through an "unsocial sociability" (*ungesellige Geselligkeit*).[48] On such a view, human calamity ultimately makes human prosperity possible. In the third *Critique*, however, Kant is clear that no matter how great the achievements of culture, no such achievement can ever be a final end, because all the achievements of culture are conditioned. With all cultural ends, we can always ask for the reason behind them. Ultimately, why must humanity exist from the standpoint of culture?

The existence of humanity can be absolutely justified only from a moral point of view. Seeing this requires a few steps. First, Kant writes, "Now of the human being . . . as a moral being, it cannot be further asked why (*quem in finem*) it exists" (3C 5:435). Considered this way, the human being is "the only natural being in which we can nevertheless cognize on the basis of its own constitution, a *supersensible faculty* (freedom) and even the law of the causality together with the object that it can set for itself as the highest end (the highest good in the world)" (3C 5:435; emphasis added). Only from this perspective can a human being be conceived of as a final end. As Kant

---

47. Immanuel Kant, *On History*, ed. Lewis White Beck, trans. Lewis White Beck, Robert E. Anchor, and Emil L. Fackenheim (New York: Bobbs-Merrill, 1963), 11–26.

48. My use of "might be conceived of" should not be overlooked. The "Idea" in the title of the 1784 essay implies that it is not meant to be a constitutive interpretation of history. Cf. Reinhard Brandt, "Zum 'Streit der Facultäten,'" in Reinhard Brandt and Werner Stark, eds., *Neue Autographen und Dokumenten zu Kants Leben, Schriften und Vorlesungen, Kant Forschungen* (Hamburg: Felix Meiner, 1987), 1:31–78, 42–43. For an opposite view see Yovel, *Kant and the Philosophy of History*, 155–56.

puts it, "a good will is that alone by means of which . . . existence can have an absolute value and in relation to which the existence of the world can have a final end" (3C 5:443). Any such conceptualization, however, exactly requires seeing the human being as more than a mere *natural* specimen.[49] Although implicit in the *Groundwork*, this claim is available more immediately through several innovations in Kant's critical philosophy. With the third *Critique*'s concept of reflective judgment in mind,[50] Kant claims that the entirety of nature can be conceived of as a purposive whole. One might then always ask after the purpose of the whole. In the realm of nature, there are no ultimate purposes. In the realm of morality, however, the moral person creates her own purpose: freedom. Kant stresses this alternative when he contrasts two ways of conceiving of rational beings: "If . . . there were also rational beings, but ones whose reason was able to place the value of the existence of things only in the relation of nature to themselves (to their well-being), and were not able to themselves to create such an original value (in freedom), then there would be . . . no (absolute) final end" (3C 5:449). The absolute freedom of the moral law, then, provides a possibility for conceiving of the moral person as a final end. In conceiving of myself as a moral creature, I view myself autonomously—I see myself as absolute and unconditioned. As Kant puts it, the "final end can be nothing other than the human being under moral laws" (3C 5:445).

Given that the *whole* of nature is to be conceived purposively, we must thereby see ourselves as part of a greater purposive whole. It is only now that the second formulation of the categorical imperative (G 4:429) is properly grounded: the kingdom of ends is underwritten as a proposal of practical reason by the formal purposiveness of nature. I am one human among others. What might the *entirety of creation* look like when conditioned by freedom? What would humanity look like if it consisted of moral creatures? This, then, is exactly the perspective of the second *Critique*, where we imagine the world ordered according to an omnipotent moral observer (5:110), but it now arises *autonomously*. Furthermore, the innovation here beyond the *Groundwork* is that the moral person is viewed as the final end of creation exactly because nature as a whole is taken as purposive.

49. This is a reversal of Kant's position from the late 1770s, where he claims in a *Reflexion* that the human being can always be placed within a yet higher systematic whole, so this discovery "strikes down every pretension of the human being to a special provision . . . and so squelches him in his own eyes that he does not ascribe to himself enough importance to be an end of creation [*Zweck der Schöpfung*]" (18:476 R6165).

50. On the development and importance of this notion, see Förster, *Kant's Final Synthesis*, 5–11.

With the principle of reflective judgment, a perspective that takes stock of the moral person as embedded within the whole of nature is necessitated by reason. It is not enough just to set ends, because even if set morally, such ends might be embedded in an entirely natural framework, one that is amoral (not to say possibly immoral). If human beings are not the final end of creation, then even *moral* human beings might turn out to be merely natural ends to or for something else. This leads Kant to distinguish between "technically practical" and "morally practical" bases for action (3C 5:172). He points out that it might be left "indeterminate with regard to the practical whether the concept that gives the rule to the causality of the will is a concept of nature or a concept of freedom" (3C 5:172). Without organizing our ends according to a highest ground (a supreme *Gesinnung*),[51] which must be the highest good seen as the final end of creation, we ultimately leave matters akin to the realm of culture, and thereby nature. Kant's point is that, without such a conception of the highest good, moral ends might still turn out to be *technically* practical, and thus we must posit the highest good as the final end of creation.

Ultimately, in response to Beck, Kant can now say: Even if I were to act virtuously in every moral situation I was confronted with, if I *had not* actively willed the highest good as the supreme ground of my action and seen humanity as the final end of creation, then my individual ends—even if they are moral—might nonetheless be ends in the service of nonmoral or amoral ends. If, on the other hand, I will them in the context of seeing myself as the final end of creation, then I will them as embedded in the context of the highest good, and thereby of autonomy.[52] As Kant puts the point, a good will in the context of the highest good guarantees that a person is more than a "link in nature" (*Naturglied*) (3C 5:443). It is in this tenor that we ought to read Kant's notorious footnote in "On the Common Saying." There he writes that "not every end is moral, but this [the final end] must be an unselfish one; and the need for a final end assigned by pure reason

51. Several commentators have noted the link between a supreme *Gesinnung* and the highest good. Cf. Matthew Caswell, "Kant's Conception of the Highest Good, the *Gesinnung*, and the Theory of Radical Evil," *Kant Studien* 97 (2006): 184–209; Kleingeld, "What Do the Virtuous Hope For?" 95; Sharon Anderson-Gold, "The Good Disposition and the Highest Good," in *Akten des Siebenten Internationalen Kant-Kongresses*, ed. Gerhard Funke (Berlin: Bouvier, 1991), 2:2.229–37; Anderson-Gold, *Unnecessary Evil: History and Moral Progress in the Philosophy of Immanuel Kant* (New York: State University of New York Press, 2001), 33–53.

52. This can be seen as one way Kant is thoroughly "modern." On this point see Bernard Williams, *Shame and Necessity* (Berkeley: University of California Press, 2008), 166. Williams opposed Kant to a common tradition in antiquity and modernity that refuses such a purposive assessment.

and comprehending the whole of all ends under one principle . . . is a need of an unselfish will *extending itself beyond observance of the formal law to production of an object.*"[53] Without willing this final end, the absolute worth of life would be nothing, since a human could not yield any reason for why she should exist in the whole of creation (3C 5:442). Ultimately, again, a good will is "that alone by means of which . . . *existence* can have an absolute value and in relation to which the *existence of the world can have a final end*" (3C 5:443; emphasis added).

Connecting to the earlier question about the necessity for practical reason to unify its objects, reason *must* unify its goods exactly in light of this expanded perspective. The highest good *just is* viewing humanity as the final end of creation, seeing the entirety of existence as ordered by human autonomy. By viewing the whole, any such view inherently involves all the objects of practical reason. In seeing humanity as the final end of creation, I see myself as one end within that kingdom of ends, and in turn I see all my maxims as ordered within a broader matrix of ends, with the final end of creation (the highest good) at its summit. Furthermore, reason *must* seek this unity through willing the moral law in the form of the highest good *as the final end of creation* or else its ends, *even moral ones*, might be in the service of natural, and thereby amoral, ends. With the highest good in the third *Critique*, *autonomy* is now at stake. Kant's suggestion here is not that moral ends not willed in the context of the highest good are thereby cultural ends, but rather that such ends are *formally akin* to cultural ends. This is what I take Kant to mean when he writes that "in the absence of a final end, which only pure reason can provide *a priori* (since *all* ends in the world are empirically conditioned, and *can contain nothing except what is good for this or that as a contingent aim, and nothing that is absolutely good*)" (3C 5:441; emphasis added). Without the highest good, even moral actions might be "links in nature," links in an *a*moral chain. Freedom therefore finally *is* truly the capstone of the Kantian architectonic. In this way the concept of autonomy guarantees that the "highest good" and "supreme ground" are the same. In conceiving of ourselves as moral—autonomous—we must will the highest good as the final end of creation. And only such an expanded perspective can truly underwrite autonomy.

---

53. "On the common saying: this may be true in theory but it does not apply in practice," in Immanuel Kant, *Practical Philosophy*, ed. and trans. Mary J. Gregor (Cambridge: Cambridge University Press, 1996), 282; emphasis added.

7. CONCLUSION

Because we can conceive of the highest good as the final end of creation only if there was a moral author of the world (3C §§87–90), here belief in God arises truly autonomously for the first time. Faith is not necessary for morality; rather, faith "is necessary for perseverance in the moral life."[54] In conclusion, and in preparation for a rapprochement between Adorno and Kant, I want to highlight how far Kant is committed to a supersensible context for all his mature claims. In the third *Critique* Kant asserts repeatedly (and not just in the context of a final end) that *we cannot but* refer to this supersensible realm (3C 5:412, 5:435). It is not possible that the final end could be an end "that nature would be sufficient to produce in accordance with its idea," because *everything* in nature is conditioned (3C 5:435). Several points emerge here. First, in opposition to many interpreters, for Kant it is not enough simply to speak of a commitment to normativity; it must be a *particular sort* of normativity, since setting norms could itself be compatible with the ends of nature. It is ambiguous, then, to say that nothing in Kant's account "requires any ontological claims, or requires that we be radically different sorts of creatures than the mundane rational animals we suppose ourselves to be."[55] Part of Kant's point is that as mundane rational animals we must view ourselves as underpinned by a supersensible substratum. In a *Reflexion* from the late 1790s Kant puts the point this way: "For we must also set before ourselves such ends which we cognize a priori (not empirically), because they concern the supersensible, and these concepts must precede *a priori* all disclosure [*Offenbarung*] of the supersensible and lie at its ground" (19:315 R7316). In the third *Critique* he puts it simply as that "we could not even make comprehensible the kind of purposiveness related to the moral law and its object . . . without an author and ruler of the world who is at the same time a moral legislator" (3C 5:455). For Kant, then, neither culture, nor a civil constitutional state, nor even perpetual peace through a cosmopolitan order is sufficient for autonomous reason. A

---

54. John E. Hare, *The Moral Gap: Kantian Ethics, Human Limits, and God's Assistance* (Oxford: Oxford University Press, 1996), 94. See also the importance of Kant's "reasoned hope" in Onora O'Neill, "Kant on Reason and Religion," in *The Tanner Lectures on Human Values*, ed. Grethe B. Peterson (Salt Lake City: University of Utah Press, 1996), 18:267–308; Ricouer, "Freedom in the Light of Hope."

55. Christine M. Korsgaard, *Creating the Kingdom of Ends* (Cambridge: Cambridge University Press, 1996), 183. Cf. Henry van der Linden, *Kantian Ethics and Socialism* (Indianapolis, IN: Hackett, 1988), 140.

metaphysical picture is required: it is not enough simply to set ends; those ends must be set in a particular way. Returning to Kant's earlier claim that "the impossibility of the highest good must prove the falsity of the moral law also" (2C 5:114), we can now see that without the highest good willed as the final end of creation, any particular moral ends are amoral. In such a case, moral reasons would be embedded in an amoral realm. The formal purposiveness of nature necessitates a perspective that expands the scope of morality to cosmic proportions. Willing the highest good is part of morality. Finally making good on claims in the first and second *Critiques*, belief in God is now a requirement of autonomy.

Kant's critical philosophy, as it culminates in the third *Critique*, then, does offer a plausible rejoinder to Horkheimer and Adorno. This rejoinder, however, occurs in a distinct transcendental register, one that requires the highest good and the supersensible commitments that go with it. Furthermore, this gives us a powerful and plausible reading of Kant, one that is, I hope, motivated from the "inside out" and able to stand on its own. It is a vision that presents a distinct sort of moral and supersensible purposiveness and that alleges a full vindication for autonomy. In the next chapter I turn to Adorno's later work, showing that he finds such supersensible commitments deeply problematic, illustrating not only an implausible view of agency but also a morally flawed one, and thereby structures his later philosophy in opposition to such commitments. Another way to understand the emerging issue, at least implicitly, is to see it as *not* centering on morality or a morality system.[56] Instead, the questions are about *autonomy*. On one hand, for Adorno autonomy is untenable *because* it is framed as involving the dialectic of enlightenment. On the other hand, for Kant autonomy is untenable *unless* it involves the commitments sketched in this chapter. In broad strokes, a question worth asking is whether a notion of autonomy might be found that succumbs neither to the Charybdis of the dialectic of enlightenment nor to the Scylla of the highest good. And that remains to be seen.

---

56. In distinction to Bernard Williams and many other critics of Kantian morality, Adorno's point will be that Kant's failure occurs as much at the level of his conception of autonomy as at that of his conception of morality. For more on the "morality system" see Williams, *Ethics and the Limits of Philosophy* (London: Routledge, 1993), 174–96.

CHAPTER THREE

Adorno's Negative Dialectic as a Form of Life: Expression, Suffering, and Freedom

I. INTRODUCTION

I take Adorno's late work to be concerned with providing a middle ground between two positions. The first is the dialectic of enlightenment, with its threat being the dissolution of agency (see especially sections 6 and 10 of chapter 1). The second position is Kant's rational theology, but its exact threat will emerge only at the conclusion of this chapter because Adorno's critique of Kant's rational theology hinges, at least in part, on the presentation of Adorno's own position. For this reason I take up Adorno's worries about Kant's rational theology only after I have presented Adorno's own position on freedom. That position centers on developing an alternative understanding of freedom that retains elements of the idea of autonomous self-determination while rejecting the idea of autonomy as a causal power for self-determination.[1]

The nexus for all these issues is Adorno's new categorical imperative, which I will unpack so we can understand both the picture of action that underpins it and the conception of morality and freedom it presupposes. (For Adorno as for Kant, morality and action are interconnected.) Since a certain conception of action underpins Adorno's theory of freedom, I start with the theory of action. Doing so, in turn, requires understanding Adorno's broader philosophical commitments, especially with respect to agency. Only through all these connected discussions does a picture emerge

---

1. Adorno does not thereby entirely reject the notion of autonomy. Cf. Iain Macdonald, "Cold, Cold, Warm: Autonomy, Intimacy and Maturity in Adorno," *Philosophy and Social Criticism* 37, no. 6 (2011): 669–89; Brian O'Connor, "Adorno and the Rediscovery of Autonomy," in *Nostalgia for a Redeemed Future: Critical Theory*, ed. Stefano Giacchetti Ludovisi (Rome: John Cabot University Press, 2009).

of Adorno's conception of freedom. This conception can then be compared with Kant's, especially with an eye to the impasse of the previous chapter. In this way, I will first present Adorno's views about agency and action and only then move to Adorno's moral thought. A preliminary consideration of Adorno's new categorical imperative can show why this approach is warranted.

Adorno's new categorical imperative is found in the concluding section of *Negative Dialectics*, "Meditations on Metaphysics," where he writes, "Hitler has forced [*aufgezwungen*] a new categorical imperative upon humans in the condition of their unfreedom: to arrange their thoughts and actions so that Auschwitz will not repeat itself, so that nothing similar will occur" (ND 365/6:358; translation modified; cf. M 116). Adorno continues:

> This imperative is as rebellious toward its justifications as the given one of Kant's. To deal with it discursively would be an outrage [*Frevel*]: for it causes us to feel, bodily, the moment of the moral addendum [*Hinzutretenden am Sittlichen*]. Bodily, because it is now the abhorrence, become practical, of the unbearable physical agony to which individuals are exposed, even as individuality, as a form of mental reflection, is about to vanish. It is only in the unvarnished materialistic [*materialistichen*] motive that that morality [*Moral*] lives on. (ND 365/6:358; translation modified)

The new imperative raises various questions. The most basic is what it means to have something "forced" on us (and forced, crucially, by Hitler). Above all, this suggests a deeply historical quality to the new categorical imperative; it is born from and somehow justified by concrete historical circumstances. In this way, contra Kant's imperative, "it is not grounded in an *a priori* way, but is based on the historical experience of suffering; and it is also not the ultimate ground or something unconditioned, but dependent on the objective existence of suffering and the reality causing it."[2] Such a historical dimension raises questions about the necessity of the imperative, centering on how suffering comes to register for an agent (a point I will return to). A related point arises with the suggestion of a *forced* imperative.

---

2. Fabian Freyenhagen, "No Easy Way Out: Adorno's Negativism and the Problem of Normativity," in *Nostalgia for a Redeemed Future: Critical Theory*, ed. Stefano Giacchetti Ludovisi (Rome: John Cabot University Press, 2009), 49. Cf. Rahel Jaeggi, " 'No Individual Can Resist': *Minima Moralia* as Critique of Forms of Life," *Constellations* 12, no. 1 (2005): 76–77; Manuel Knoll, *Theodor W. Adorno, Ethik als erste Philosophie* (Munich: Wilhelm Fink, 2002), 33–44.

Such phrasing might suggest a Humean picture, where in light of the Nazi genocide, we have (or ought to have) certain passions, and because of such passions, with reason serving as an intermediary, we undertake particular actions. Such a suggestion raises tensions with a notion of autonomy as self-determination. And the site of such tensions is the mechanism(s) for action; so this is where I begin my analysis.

2. TOWARD AN UNDERSTANDING OF THE MORAL ADDENDUM

Adorno is not a Humean, and he does not reject the idea of self-determination. Thus it is essential to understand his moral psychology and conception of agency. The notion that unifies these issues is what Adorno terms the "moral addendum" (which, as will emerge, is a species of "addendum" generally—thus my beginning with action more broadly). To see how we get there, I focus on Adorno's 1963 lectures on moral philosophy. There, the concept of the moral addendum is introduced with a specific example: Adorno discusses meeting a German army officer involved in an attempt to assassinate Hitler.[3] Asked about his motivation, the lieutenant explains that he simply could no longer take living in his situation. Adorno responds this way:

> I believe that this act of resistance—the fact that things may be so intolerable that you feel compelled to make the attempt to change them, regardless of the consequences for yourself, and in circumstances in which you may also predict the possible consequences for other people—is the precise point at which the irrationality, or better, the irrational aspect of moral action is to be sought, the point at which it may be located. (PMP 9)

He continues:

> At the same time, you can see that this irrationality is only one aspect, because on the level of theory the officer concerned knew perfectly well how evil, how horrifying this Third Reich was, and it was because of his critical and theoretical insight into the lies and the crimes that he had to deal with that he was brought to the point of action. *If he had not had*

3. Although he is not named there, Adorno refers to Fabian von Schlabrendorff (1907–80). See LND 240.

this insight . . . he would quite certainly never have been moved to that
act of resistance. (PMP 8; emphasis added)

From this Adorno concludes that "the task of moral philosophy is *above*
all else the production of consciousness" (PMP 9; emphasis added).

This example suggests what Adorno refers to as "the addendum" (*das*
Hinzutretende).[4] This notion involves two additional components. The first
is Adorno's idea that "the subject's decisions do not roll off in a causal chain;
what occurs is a jolt [*Ruck*]" (ND 226–27/6:226). The second is the claim
that any such jolt or impulse or addendum is "intramental and somatic at
the same time, driv[ing] beyond the conscious sphere to which it belongs
just the same" (ND 228–29/6:228; translation modified). By developing and
understanding these thoughts, we can begin to understand the "addendum"
as well as its significance to Adorno's broader concerns in relation to action,
freedom, and ultimately morality.

Chiefly, Adorno opposes a view of agency found in transcendental philosophy of various stripes, but especially in Kant. For Adorno, Kant's chief
mistake is in imagining our freedom to be a sort of causality. Adorno makes
this point in various ways throughout the "Freedom" section of *Negative*
Dialectics. Some of Adorno's arguments on this point are not particularly
good,[5] and I ignore them, so this discussion is not meant to be exhaustive.
Instead, I focus on what I take to be the strongest case, best exemplified by
the following: "In the name of spontaneity, of that which in the subject is
not objectifiable at any price, the will is defined as nothing other than the
subject—and yet, solid and identical like reason, it is objectified into a hypothetical but factual power [*Vermögen*] amidst the factual-empirical world,
and thus made commensurable with that world" (ND 235/6:233–34). I take
Adorno here to reject what Kant describes in the *Groundwork* as a "will."

---

4. The most comprehensive discussion of this notion in Adorno is Eckart Goebel, "Das
Hinzutretende: Ein Kommentar zu Seiten 226–230 der '*Negativen Dialektik*,'" in *Frankfurter*
Adorno Blatter, ed. Theodor W. Adorno Archiv (Munich, 1992). Other discussions include J. M.
Bernstein, *Adorno: Disenchantment and Ethics* (Cambridge: Cambridge University Press, 2001),
386–88; Espen Hammer, *Adorno and the Political* (London: Routledge, 2006), 118–19; Christoph
Menke, "Virtue and Reflection: The 'Antinomies of Moral Philosophy,'" *Constellations* 12, no. 1
(2005): 38–40.

5. See the discussion of how Adorno conflates the senses of necessity at play in "practical
necessity" and "natural-scientific necessity" (two necessities Kant takes pains to distinguish),
in Robert B. Pippin, "Negative Ethics: Adorno on the Falseness of Bourgeois Life," in *The*
Persistence of Subjectivity (Cambridge: Cambridge University Press, 2005), 114ff. But as I will
suggest, there are strands in Adorno's thinking that Pippin neglects and that do not trade on this
mistake.

There Kant claims that the "will is a kind of causality of living beings so far as they are rational, freedom would be that property of this causality by which it can be effective independent of foreign causes determining it, *just as* natural necessity is the property of the causality of all irrational beings by which they are determined to activity by the influence of foreign causes" (G 4:446). Adorno rejects any such agent causation.[6] Furthermore, for Adorno the mistake of such a view is *as much* in speculating about the existence of such causation as in *conceiving* of our agency as involving it (so Kant's recourse to transcendental idealism would be of no help with this issue, since the latter point is conceptual, as opposed to metaphysical).[7] Adorno ultimately takes such a view to imply a mistaken view of both our agency and the freedom involved in such agency (ND 235/6:233–34).

We can see this if we see the force of this objection as underwritten by the claim that the subject is inseparable from concrete historical situations (already implicit with the new categorical imperative). In this way Adorno's target is the general notion of voluntarism, since it crucially, and mistakenly, presupposes the ability to do otherwise, suggesting a view of the self as somehow separable from its concrete situation. Understood as agent causation, autonomy is illusory (cf. ND 219/6:218; 221/6:220–21). Part of Adorno's story will be (and it will take some work to get there) that freedom consists not in the ability to do otherwise, but in the necessity of doing what one's embodied and socially and historically situated being in the world demands.[8] An equally important part, however, will be an acknowledgment that *the* problem with contemporary society is that situated existence is from the start deformed, scarred, wrong, and so forth (PMP 99).[9]

6. For a discussion of this notion, see Robert Kane, *The Significance of Free Will* (Oxford: Oxford University Press, 1996), 120–23. For an argument *against* lumping Kant into this camp, see Henry E. Allison, *Kant's Theory of Freedom* (Cambridge: Cambridge University Press, 1990), 49–53.

7. For such a defense, see Eric Watkins, *Kant and the Metaphysics of Causality* (Cambridge: Cambridge University Press, 2005), 18ff.

8. In this Adorno's theory of action is very similar to the sorts of expressivist notions of freedom proposed in Hegel scholarship from Charles Taylor onward. Most recently, see especially Terry Pinkard, *Hegel's Naturalism: Mind, Nature, and the Final Ends of Life* (Oxford: Oxford University Press, 2012); Robert B. Pippin, *Hegel's Practical Philosophy: Rational Agency as Ethical Life* (Cambridge: Cambridge University Press, 2008). Cf. Charles Taylor, "Hegel's Philosophy of Mind," in *Human Agency and Language: Philosophical Papers* (Cambridge: Cambridge University Press, 1985), 1:77–97. There are important differences, however, and I will have more to say about this.

9. This is Adorno's "negativism." Cf. James Gordon Finlayson, "Adorno on the Ethical and the Ineffable," *European Journal of Philosophy* 10, no. 1 (2002): 2–4; Fabian Freyenhagen, "Moral Philosophy," in *Adorno: Key Concepts*, ed. Deborah Cook (Stocksfield, UK: Acumen,

Therefore one's situated being cannot be *all* there is to agency (this is what it means to be an agent "after Auschwitz").

Although Adorno does not draw the distinctions that follow, I am proposing them as a heuristic in order to build his theory one layer at a time. The bottom layer might be seen as Adorno's nonvoluntaristic theory of action. We can elaborate this originally without reference to his moral thought, and I will develop this first. At another level, however, Adorno is radicalizing this theory of action explicitly in a moral pitch, arguing that the modern world seems to be such that the actions agents express are from the beginning malformed, damaged, and immoral (more on this shortly). Crudely put, at this point I would like to distinguish the sequence in which Adorno's worries about "damaged life" occur. "Damaged" in this context generally refers to the suffering associated with actions, not to their form (conceived as voluntaristic or nonvoluntaristic). Put another way, and again crudely, it is important to understand that Adorno thinks there would be inherent problems with a voluntaristic picture of action even if the world were *not* damaged (and similarly, a nonvoluntaristic picture of action does nothing to guarantee that the world will not turn out to be damaged). On Adorno's behalf, to the extent that it relies a fundamentally flawed view of action, I take it that a voluntaristic conception of action *guarantees* we will not be able to respond to the dialectic of enlightenment, while a nonvoluntaristic picture at least offers us the hope of doing so (but this point still needs to be argued in full).

With all that said, in his lectures Adorno introduces the argument against voluntarism by claiming that the "subject is not what it is explicitly called . . . the sphere of 'absolute origins'" (HF 221; cf. ND 223/6:222). In *Minima Moralia* (1951) Adorno flatly writes, "Not only is the self entwined in society; it owes society its existence in the most literal sense. All its content comes from society, or at any rate from its relation to the object" (MM 154/4:173). Ultimately, "detached from the object, autonomy is fictitious" (ND 223/6:222). Formally, in line with the discussion of chapter 1, "object" here designates the other to the "subject" in the self-consciousness pair. For Adorno, any such object is "filled in" or actualized along two interpenetrating axes: social and somatic. Much more needs to be said about such a proposal, but its basic contours ought to be plausible from the discussion in chapter 1. As we saw, the dialectic of enlightenment relies on the idea that, detached from an object, "the subject is a fiction, or else such a

---

2008), 100–104; Freyenhagen, "No Easy Way Out"; Freyenhagen, "Adorno's Ethics without the Ineffable," *Telos* 2011, no. 155 (2011): 127–49.

thin and abstract principle that it can be of no assistance in telling us about the actual behavior of human beings" (HF 222; cf. ND 223/6:222). This is so much so that "even that which is immediate, nearest, most assured to the subject, its own personality, requires mediation" (ND 276/6:272).

Going forward, a recurring strategy Adorno employs is to stress the ways philosophy of action has overlooked this point, most obvious even at the level of its construction of examples. For Adorno, because of the simple fact that choice is always *about something* and *by someone*, the formal quality of choice is insufficient for philosophical analysis. In fact, even terms like "something" and "someone" are misleading, since they really mean *you* or *this* (in the sense of already being demonstratively saturated). Adorno's bold claim is that the variety of thought experiments prevalent in philosophy of action really boil down to variations of the example of Buridan's ass, where a donkey is presented with two equal, equidistant bundles of hay.[10] Making light of the example, Adorno first states that "such identical bundles of hay that are supposed to provide us with a test of free will may perhaps exist for asses" (HF 222; cf. ND 224/6:222). He then continues, "but even there this won't happen often, for what farmer would take the trouble to provide his ass with two identical bundles of hay equidistant from the animal, unless he has already been corrupted by philosophy?" For Adorno the logical error lies "in failing to recognize that such a thought experiment would only be compelling in empirical conditions in which real people exist, while, on the other hand, as soon as you introduce a degree of reality into the experiment, you inevitably introduce elements that would deprive the example of its cogency" (HF 222). Indicting an entire tradition of philosophy is perhaps no joking matter, and certainly such rhetorical moves require significant elaboration before this line of thought might become plausible. Furthermore, why should we not tease out and analyze *formal* qualities that *all* particular choices might share? Adorno is sensitive to such worries. To state his view in full now, so as to lend it at least some plausibility in the face of this indictment of a certain tradition on action, Adorno's position is that actions are best understood as *drawn out of us*, that is, as environmentally situated.[11] And this is the sole formal account we can provide—everything

10. Likely mistakenly attributed to John Buridan, since it is not found in his corpus. Cf. Kane, *Significance of Free Will*, 109.

11. The view has points in common with the "situational environmentalist" view of Abraham S. Roth, "Reasons Explanations of Actions: Causal, Singular, and Situational," *Philosophical and Phenomenological Research* 59, no. 4 (1999): 839–74. Roth builds on Donald Davidson, "Actions, Reasons, and Causes," in *Essays on Actions and Events* (Oxford: Clarendon Press, 2001), 3–21; and Fred Dretske, *Explaining Behavior: Reasons in a World of Causes* (Cambridge,

else will have to be analyzed at the level of particular empirical details
(including not only a concrete embodied situation, but also its historical,
perhaps even genealogical, descent). For this reason, Adorno takes voluntaristic examples of "doing otherwise" as failing to recognize this point. All
this requires significantly more detail. Fortunately, in his reading of *Hamlet*, Adorno gives us a rich analysis to draw on.[12]

In Adorno's reading, Hamlet finds himself in the predicament of not being able to do what he has "decided" to do: take revenge. Most significant
in Adorno's eyes is that "at the end, in the final scene, events, and here this
means the most horrific killings, suddenly crowd in on us in a way reminis-
cent of puppets on a string" (HF 233). Indeed,

> up to now Hamlet, whose thoughts have prevented him from carrying
> out the deed that follows from his thoughts, and who has not succeeded
> in breaking the spell of thinking and escaping from his *monologue inté-
> rieur* . . . has suddenly, and I would add, irrationally [*widervernünftiger*],
> in a matter that leads directly to his own death, gone on a killing spree
> and has stabbed everyone who crosses his path. (HF 233)

According to Adorno, this aspect of the play is best understood through
the notion of the addendum. Hamlet, who—rightly or wrongly—feels the
obligation to obtain revenge, "can only succeed in carrying out his intention with the aid of a sudden, violent impulse that in the play stems from
the fact that he himself has been wounded" (HF 234). Adorno elaborates:

> The addendum, that is to say, the element in his taking action that goes
> beyond rationality, can be studied here as in a test tube. And it is prob-
> ably only the convention, a convention implanted in us for centuries,
> that compels us to measure this factor, without which there could be no
> action, against the yardstick of rationality. This explains why we tend
> to think that these final events are somehow puppet-like or ridiculous,

---

MA: MIT Press, 1991). Roth rightly shows how Dretske's view allows the environment to play
only a structuring role as opposed to triggering action, but Roth's view nonetheless ends up
insufficiently distinct from Davidson's causal view. Adorno's model will be similar but will be
underwritten by an idea of agency that does not rely on any causal model of the will or on the
sort of representationalism Dretske still maintains.

12. There are worries here about using literature for philosophical aims, but they are not fatal. Cf. Alice Crary, *Beyond Moral Judgment* (Cambridge, MA: Harvard University Press, 2007),
127–63; John Gibson, *Fiction and the Weave of Life* (Oxford: Oxford University Press, 2008); and
Candace Vogler, "The Moral of the Story," *Critical Inquiry*, no. 34 (2007): 5–35.

since we fail to notice that what is happening is that this additional spontaneous factor, or what we might even call this irrational [*irratio-nale*] element, forces its way to the surface. (HF 234; cf. ND 229/6:228)

Many questions emerge here. Foremost among them is *what* the addendum supplies or adds to a discussion of action. Equally important, however, are a variety of worries about the suitability of this example. Is this even a case of action attributable to an agent, or are we dealing here with an unconscious action more akin to a nervous twitch or reflex? Adorno is adamant that he is not endorsing some irrational theory of the will (HF 234). But this is hardly obvious, and at the very least Hamlet's actions, if not irrational, certainly do not appear self-determined. What is at stake here is how far and by what means we can ascribe Hamlet's actions to Hamlet. Call this desideratum the self-ascription requirement; it suggests that actions are the sorts of performances about which we can ask, Why? In other words, they are intentional under some description (I §5).[13]

Adorno's strategy for keeping the possibility of self-ascription available consists in suggesting that we conceive the relation between "inner" intentions and "outer" actions in a way distinct from a variety of philosophy of action. In his lecture courses, Adorno frames the point this way: "This moment, which I have called the addendum or the irrational, survives as if it were the indestructible phase in which the separation between inner and outer *had not yet been consolidated*" (HF 234; emphasis added; cf. ND 228/6:227–28). Adorno glosses this situation as a moment "integral to the constitution of what we call will and freedom," best understood through the idea that "this impulse is both somatic *and* mental at the same time" (HF 235; emphasis added; cf. ND 228–29/6:228). In light of this claim, and before moving to the nitty-gritty mechanics of Adorno's philosophy of action, I want to elaborate Adorno's broader commitments about the relation between the "somatic" and the "mental" (and normativity more broadly). With such an elaboration in place, we can then move back to a proper discussion of action.

3. NATURAL AND NORMATIVE: SOME VARIATIONS

My guiding assumption is that understanding the relation between the "somatic" and the "mental" requires mapping out a more overarching concern

---

13. Cf. Davidson, "Actions, Reasons, and Causes."

about the relation between the natural and the normative. In *Minima Moralia*, Adorno frames the relation this way: "Nothing less is asked of the thinker today than that he should be at every moment both within things and outside them—Münchhausen pulling himself out of the bog by his pig-tail becomes the pattern of knowledge which wishes to be more than either verification or speculation" (MM 74/4:82). What I take from this quotation for the broader discussion is that we cannot conceptualize our freedom merely as verification or speculation (cf. BPS 240/3:190–91); so, respectively, no bald naturalism and no uncritical idealism.

Adorno claims the philosopher must be able to countenance *both* perspectives. In a 1962 lecture, "Progress," he proposes an analogous synthesis when he claims that "spirit is not what it enthrones itself as, the other, transcendent in its purity, but rather *is also* a piece of natural history" (CM 156; emphasis added).[14] For Adorno, it is crucial to avoid three options for conceptualizing freedom:

Metaphysical: where freedom consists in some appeal to any sort of metaphysical substratum (or "causality") for our freedom (agent causation again).

Normative: where freedom consists in something like a "fact of reason," where that fact is taken *just as* the fact that we must reason, that we are so comported to the world, and in being such a fact requires no further explanation or underpinning.

Natural: where freedom can be elaborated somehow in terms of strictly natural, nonnormative facts about ourselves.

In Adorno's terminology, the first two succumb to "speculation," and the latter defers to "verification." For Adorno, freedom is speculative when elaborated merely psychologically (as an appeal to a *fact* of reason) or metaphysically (as an appeal to a fact of *reason*), while freedom is bald nature if it refuses to acknowledge our ability to take a normative stance toward ourselves. Opposed to such options, Adorno goes in for a much more ambitious

---

14. In that I stress certain Hegelian elements in Adorno, my reading of Adorno is indebted in many ways to Pippin's reading of Hegel. See Robert B. Pippin, "Naturalness and Mindedness: Hegel's Compatibilism," *European Journal of Philosophy* 7, no. 2 (1999): 194–212. Particularly relevant in this context is the analogy Pippin draws to Sellars (203–4), which applies just as well to Adorno (and in this context, see especially Adorno's own rejection of the "myth of the given" in H3S 53–89). For more on Sellars and his relation to the post-Kantian tradition, see Terry Pinkard, "Sellars the Post Kantian?" in *The Self-Correcting Enterprise: Essays on Wilfrid Sellars*, ed. Michael P. Wolf and Mark Norris Lance (New York: Editions Rodopi, 2007).

claim when he suggests that "we are no longer simply a piece of nature from the moment we recognize that we are a piece of nature" (PMP 103). He continues by pointing out that the denial of such a view "succumbs to the delusion that all is natural conditioning" (PMP 103). To the extent that we can take a reflective and normative stance toward ourselves, and that such reflection potentially comes to be tied to and embedded within historical and social practices,[15] we cannot understand ourselves simply in nonnormative terms. Adorno continues: "Any being that stands outside nature and might be described as a human subject can be said to possess consciousness of self, the capacity for self-reflection in which the self observes: I myself am part of nature—*and straight thereby* is the human subject liberated from the blind pursuit of natural ends" (PMP 104; translation modified and emphasis added).[16] On such a view, even the distinction between "inner" (intentions) and "outer" (actions), as opposed to representing fixed facts, might come to be seen as a fluid (perhaps even unstable) distinction drawn by agents.[17] All this will require more support, but that is the general picture I propose.

Turning back to the addendum, we can see that this understanding of the relation between the natural and the normative is key for elaborating Adorno's conception of freedom and action. Earlier, two issues had arisen. First, we needed to show how the addendum could satisfy the self-ascription requirement. Second, we had to show how the addendum could be both somatic and mental. Both of these worries arose with claims by Adorno like the following: "The impulse, intramental and somatic in one, drives beyond the conscious sphere to which it belongs just the same. With that impulse freedom extends to the realm of experience; this animates the concept of freedom as a state that would no more be blind nature than it would be oppressed nature" (ND 228–29/6:228). With such talk of freedom "extending" into the realm of experience, I take it that the addendum is not something irrational (incapable of being rationalized; without endorsing his view, we might nod to Davidson and say that the addendum *can rationalize* an action).[18] When Adorno points out that we "may" term the addendum

15. See Robert Brandom, "Freedom and Constraint by Norms," *American Philosophical Quarterly* 16, no. 3 (1979): 192.

16. It is crucial *not* to render the German *"und gerade dadurch"* as "by virtue of that fact," since that implies that some fact about ourselves underpins our freedom.

17. There would here be a significant overlap with a certain reading of Hegel and Wittgenstein. For such a reading, see Terry Pinkard, "Innen, Aussen und Lebensformen: Hegel und Wittgenstein," in *Hegels Erbe* (Frankfurt am Main: Suhrkamp, 2004), 254–92.

18. Davidson, "Actions, Reasons, and Causes," 3–4.

the "irrational element," he ought to be taken to mean that only within
a particular chain of rational reflection does it occur as an irrational jolt
(HF 234). Such a jolt, or break, in the chain of reflection appears irrational
from the perspective of that chain. As a jolt, it seems to come from no-
where. Such a jolt, however, can serve as a reason, and this means that, *after*
the act/jolt in question, it is acknowledged as *my* act because *I* can give
reasons for it, reasons that are genuinely mine.

   Hamlet illustrates the point nicely. Hamlet's actions at the conclusion
of the play do not occur blindly, for "no reason." Instead, certain reasons
seem foreign to Hamlet's current state of mind. Because of his particular
context, some reasons might be so foreign as to be consciously inaccessible (but nonetheless they are still *his*, in that if they were presented, by,
say, a psychiatrist during a session, Hamlet would accede to them). Thus
Adorno suggests that Hamlet's actions only "*seem* to be unconnected with
the complex, elaborate and rational reflections that have preoccupied him
throughout the drama" (HF 234; emphasis added). Instead, he points out
that for Hamlet to carry out his plan of revenge, his environment requires
alteration: "The situation is that Hamlet has, rightly or wrongly, felt himself to be under an obligation to obtain revenge. . . . Once he has felt this obligation, he can only succeed in carrying out his intention with the aid of a
sudden, violent impulse that in the play stems from the fact that he himself
has been wounded" (HF 234). Two points about agency can be teased out of
Adorno's analysis of *Hamlet*. First, our agency, the possibility of attribut-
ing actions to ourselves, is not dependent on seeing an anterior, somehow
"internal" desire or want as causing that action. Rather, as will emerge
more clearly, the assigning or determining of such intentions is itself intimately related to ongoing activity.[19] In turn, the thought that underpins
this idea is the claim that actions occur along a complex web of mediation
in the form of various institutions and historical valences, and this web is
as much somatic as mental (with a slight difference of inflection, and in a
way I will elaborate, it would not be inappropriate to call this web a "form
of life"). (Again, none of this is meant to deny Adorno's suspicions, worries,
and misgivings about the seemingly damaged, deformed, and wrong nature

   19. On this point I have benefited greatly from G. E. M. Anscombe, *Intention* (Cambridge,
MA: Harvard University Press, 2000); Robert Brandom, "Action, Norms, and Practical Reasoning," *Noûs* 32, no. S12 (1998): 127–39; and Michael Thompson, *Life and Action: Elementary
Structures of Practice and Practical Thought* (Cambridge, MA: Harvard University Press, 2008),
85–149.

of our modern form of life. But I will take up that worry only after we have this alternative view of action on the table.)

Both of these thoughts require significant elaboration. Once again, we must take a step back and start with even broader claims, this time about our embodied nature. Adorno again harks back to Buridan's ass when discussing the "jolt" that Hamlet undergoes. In this case, however, Adorno stresses a certain merit to the example, especially when taken to illustrate something like the jolt,

> when we consider that even the ass, stupid though it may be, still has to exert itself, to make a gesture of some sort, to do something or other that *goes beyond the thought-processes or non-thought-processes* of its pathetic brain. That is to say, it experiences some kind of impulse, I would almost say a physical impulse, a somatic impulse that goes beyond the pure intellectualization of what is supposed . . . alone to constitute the will. (HF 228; emphasis added)

Foremost in Adorno's mind is the simple idea that being a subject requires a body. In part this is just the claim that a subject requires embodiment.[20] As Adorno puts it in "On Subject and Object," we can conceive of objectivity "without a subject, but not likewise subjectivity without an object" (CM 249; translation modified; cf. ND 183/6:184). More forcefully, however, this hints at Adorno's broader conceptualization of subjectivity: that to be a subject *just is* to be embodied, to be already always in and part of the world, a world as much natural as normative. Consciousness is embodied.

To underwrite this claim we can double back to the relation between the somatic (say, needs, wants, desires, and so forth) and the mental (say, consciousness and self-consciousness). Speaking of the allegedly clearest example of the nonsomatic—thinking—Adorno stresses, "If I am to reflect, I have to *wish* to do so; in order to reflect, I have to *want* to reflect. Otherwise, in the absence of this element of will, even the simplest act of thought is inconceivable" (HF 259; emphasis added). For Adorno, then, it is not that when one feels or thinks, one adds a distinct state "on top" of consciousness. Such feelings or thoughts, rather, are already tied together—the somatic and the mental are inseparable, and both involve our being immersed in a world of concerns. On such a view, when particular facts about a situation are

---

20. Although far afield of my concerns and discussion, see also Lisa Yun Lee, *Dialectics of the Body: Corporeality in the Philosophy of Theodor Adorno* (London: Routledge, 2004).

taken to be a "salient fact about the situation," then that individual "is in a psychological state that is essentially practical"; that is, desires are not thereby added "on top of" cognitive states.[21] Thinking is an activity tied to being in the world, a practice. "Will," in turn, is no more a type of causality added "on top" of embodied existence than embodied existence is added on top of a disembodied will. Embodied existence is rather the experience of a mutually saturated exchange between two distinguishable, but inseparable aspects of our experience. The somatic and the mental are just two aspects of something called "experience."

With respect to action, and once again putting the whole proposal forward at once: Adorno's claim will be that the addendum or impulse must be understood as the idea that the world solicits and draws out of us certain actions (we may say it offers us certain "affordances" for action).[22] And in that the addendum is mental *and* somatic, such actions are always mine because the world itself is already always normatively constituted and saturated. Only because we are in the world in a particular way—our *experience* is a certain sort of experience—are we capable of acting in a particular way. Actions are impossible without the distinct experiential frame in which they occur. Adorno summarizes this position with the idea that "consciousness, rational insight, is not simply the same as a free act. *We cannot flatly equate it with the will*" (ND 227/6:224; emphasis added).

My suggestion (forming the first of several comparisons to Stanley Cavell) is that the best way to understand the ground for such a proposal is to see it as underpinned and elaborated by a conception of Wittgenstein's notion of a "form of life" (*Lebensform*),[23] if that notion is understood along the lines of Stanley Cavell's interpretation.[24] In *The Claim of Reason*, Cavell at one point asks how the gap between mind and world might be closed. He

21. John McDowell, "Virtue and Reason," in *Mind, Value, and Reality* (Cambridge, MA: Harvard University Press, 1998), 70.

22. See James J. Gibson, *The Ecological Approach to Visual Perception* (Boston: Houghton Mifflin, 1986), 127–38. And these affordances need not be read as "nonconceptual"—a point argued in section 4 below and in Marianne Janack, *What We Mean by Experience* (Palo Alto, CA: Stanford University Press, 2012), 154–58.

23. For a view that broaches a similar comparison (but thereby reads Wittgenstein in a very different way from Cavell, seeing the two thinkers in tension), see Albrecht Wellmer, "Ludwig Wittgenstein: On the Difficulties of Receiving His Philosophy and Its Relation to the Philosophy of Adorno," in *Endgames: The Irreconcilable Nature of Modernity, Essays and Lectures* (Cambridge, MA: MIT Press, 1988), 239–51. See also Rolf Wiggerhaus, *Adorno und Wittgenstein: Zwei Spielarten modernen Philosophierens* (Göttingen: Wallstein, 2000).

24. This comparison is not entirely unwarranted in that both are best understood as post-Kantian thinkers. On this point, concerning Cavell, see Paul W. Franks, "The Discovery of the Other: Cavell, Fichte, and Skepticism," *Common Knowledge* 5, no. 2 (1996): 72–78.

answers, "In Wittgenstein's view the gap between mind and the world is closed, or the distortion between them straightened, in the appreciation and acceptance of particular human forms of life" (CR 109). Subsequently he distinguishes between vertical and horizontal senses of the notion form of life (UA 40–45). These two senses correspond to an ethnological (horizontal) and a biological (vertical) sense. In the former sense, the differences might be "between promising and fully intending, or between coronations and inaugurations," while in the latter the differences are between "poking at your food, perhaps with a fork, and pawing at it, or pecking at it" (UA 41, 42). Cavell refers to these two senses as constituting a "mutual absorption of the natural and the social," which he sees as a consequence of what can be called "the human form of life" (UA 44).[25] He writes: "In being asked to accept this [form of life], or suffer it, as given for ourselves, we are not asked to accept, let us say, private property, but separateness; not a particular fact of power but the fact that I am a man, therefore of *this* (range or scale of) capacity for work, for pleasure, for endurance, for appeal, for command, for understanding, for wish, for will, for teaching, for suffering. The precise range or scale is not knowable *a priori*" (UA 44). (One way we might understand the relation between Adorno's broader worries about modernity and Cavell's picture of forms of life is in light of Cavell's subsequent emphasis that the range or scale of forms of life can be artificially fixed; it is this, then, that the dialectic of enlightenment may be taken to confirm.) In this way we can understand how actions can be seen to occur along a complex web of mediation in the form of various institutions and historical valences. (However, it will soon emerge that this cannot be the *only* story we tell about actions—being able to act contrary to prevailing norms is essential to Adorno's moral theory.) The horizontal sense of forms of life corresponds to our shared history, while the vertical corresponds to how certain facts of our nature come to be navigated in light of the former.

4. THE ADDENDUM

With the invocation of forms of life, we can profitably turn to Adorno's discussion of the addendum, which I will use as a springboard to say some general things about his philosophy of action. In this way I do not take Adorno to be committed to the implausible idea that "addendum actions" explain all action. Instead, examples of addendum actions are a powerful way for us

25. Relevant here is Brian O'Connor, "The Concept of Mediation in Hegel and Adorno," *Bulletin of the Hegel Society of Great Britain* 39/40 (1999): 84–96.

to tease out a broader theory of action. Ultimately, the freedom that underwrites addendum actions "may be said to be something like a reconciliation of spirit, the union of reason and nature as it survives in this impulse"
(HF 237). In this way, for Adorno freedom is not some special causality added
to our natural existence as human animals, nor is it just a complex amal-
gamation of reflex responses. Freedom is instead an activity that involves
already always *being in the world*,[26] which should be understood as a complex procedure that precludes any bald natural immediacy as much as any
mediation that completely dissolves the natural in favor of the conceptual.
On this suggestion, the very act of consciousness and self-consciousness
reveals how the natural and the normative are intermixed. Consciousness is
not merely conceptual activity; it is just as much a somatic activity, albeit
one where even our bodily uptake of the world is already saturated with
(but, as I will argue, not entirely defined by) our norms, conventions, and
spiritual life.

Looking now at the "jolt" that Hamlet experiences, one can claim,
based on the earlier discussion, that it is irrational given Hamlet's path of
reflection from *one view* of this particular situation (say, the perspective of
a typical bourgeois from the period). It is not, however, thereby rendered
irrational from Hamlet's perspective, for viewed from another perspective
that Hamlet *equally* embodies (say, the perspective of unwavering revenge),
his actions are rational in that they form a plausible means-end relation. In
light of any broader discussion of agency, Adorno's suggestion is not that we
instantiate certain mental states that then cause us to act, but rather that
at every moment we are environmentally formed and situated—embodied,
and already always *in* action. Actions are best explained by other actions,
not by wants, desires, or other propositional states (more on this shortly),[27]

---

26. I do not mean this as a point of commonality between Adorno and Heidegger. Adorno
is still committed to a dialectical (what I have called mutually saturated) version of the subject/
object divide, whereas Heidegger's notion elides it. There are nonetheless many points of
connection between Adorno and Heidegger. See Lambert Zuidervaart, "Truth and Authentication: Heidegger and Adorno in Reverse," in *Adorno and Heidegger*, ed. Iain Macdonald and
Krzysztof Ziarek (Stanford, CA: Stanford University Press, 2008); Fred R. Dallmayr, *Life-World,
Modernity and Critique: Paths between Heidegger and the Frankfurt School* (Cambridge: Polity
Press, 1991); Alexander García Düttmann, *The Memory of Thought: An Essay on Heidegger
and Adorno*, trans. Nicholas Walker (London: Continuum, 1991); Hermann Mörchen, *Macht
und Herrschaft im Denken von Adorno und Heidegger* (Stuttgart: Klett Cotta, 1980); Mörchen,
Adorno und Heidegger: Untersuchung einer philosophischen Kommunikationsverweigerung
(Stuttgart: Klett Cotta, 1981).

27. On this point and many others I am indebted to G. E. M. Anscombe and Michael
Thompson.

and reflection on this model is an element of action that might interrupt or qualify prior action. So I might begin to think about something because I am doing something else (or even because I am doing the very thing I am thinking about). In an example germane to Adorno's concerns, I might be trying furiously to surmise how to desert from the army or kill my commanding officer even as I carry out his orders to kill this civilian. Alternatively, but just as realistically, I might be thinking about a more efficient way to kill the next civilian as I am killing this one.[28]

Actions are ultimately drawn out of agents based on the interactive equilibrium between their surroundings and their individual embodied constitution (which here includes our reflective capacities).[29] We come to have certain ends because we exist in the world in a certain way. In this way the entirety of one's embodied being is implicated in any action. So while Hamlet may not at present be planning revenge and his present actions seem to happen *to* him, they are *not* externally imposed (as with a twitch or some pathology). Hamlet's actions, rather, arise from his commitments, which could not be actualized before this moment. Certain affordances were not "lit up" and therefore were "missing" from the world (and I do not take this phrasing as pushing us back to voluntarism). Adorno suggests such a picture when he writes that, for Hamlet, "two epochs stand on a knife's edge" (HF 234). Hamlet has undertaken both a commitment to the bourgeois view of the world and, in Adorno's words, a more "archaic" commitment to revenge. In Adorno's eyes, "revenge . . . is . . . an archaic phenomenon that is not really compatible with a rational, bourgeois order of things" (HF 235). So revenge is archaic, but it is *not* irrational. On the contrary, revenge is a sort of rationality—it presupposes an entire institution of rational human commitments and backgrounds, with their own practices and histories.[30] The issue that arises for Hamlet is that a commitment to revenge is fundamentally incompatible with contemporary commitments also undertaken by Hamlet. Hamlet has earlier *become* the sort of individual who would carry out revenge (demonstrated, I suggest, when he remorselessly kills Polonius). Only at the end of the play, however, does revenge become

28. Compare "reaching for a cookbook" while "making an omelet" in Thompson, *Life and Action*, 113.

29. An analogy arises here with perception. Cf. Brandom, "Action, Norms, and Practical Reasoning," 137. See also the last two chapters of Wayne Martin, *Theories of Jud   nent: Psychology, Logic, Phenomenology* (Cambridge: Cambridge University Press, 2006).

30. For example, the Hebrew Bible has laws aimed at revenge, including the   ablishment of cities of refuge. See A. Grame Auld, "Cities of Refuge in Israelite Tradition," *Jou nal for the Study of the Old Testament* 4, no. 10 (1979): 26–40.

"rationally necessary" for him. When Adorno claims that "two epochs stand on a knife's edge," he means that Hamlet is so constituted that it is rationally necessary that he carry out revenge (so, speaking of a "second nature" is appropriate here). At the same time, given his bourgeois commitments, it is *also* rationally necessary that he not do so (HF 234). Hamlet's embodied equilibrium is thereby contradictory, perhaps even unstable. At the conclusion of the play, however, things change, and revenge becomes the action that is drawn out of him by his practical standing in the world. Speculating, we might theorize that, in light of the interpenetration of the mental and the somatic, when Hamlet undergoes a particular sort of physical stimulus, certain affordances—routes of normative salience—light up for him, and certain actions thereby become necessitated by his (new) practical engagement and standing within the world. I say "routes" here because there generally are multiple routes for accomplishing any desired action. Often one route shines brightest, is most salient, but this need not always be so. In consequence, there might be multiple routes, and our choosing *this* route over that route is largely a matter of whim or chance (although this does not mean that such a route is *entirely* random or that *any* route will do just fine). In undertaking an action, an agent might be seen as committing herself to a *range* of actions, not only as "basic" and "complex" acts, but also as the idea that "any intentional action (proper) figures in a space of reasons as a region, not as a point."[31] Coming back to Hamlet, his wound literally alters the way he exists in the world, perhaps moving practical constitutive commitments like avoiding violence or danger to a position of irrelevancy[32] and allowing other commitments to gain a greater constitutive role. Such an alteration, however, is not a foreign imposition upon Hamlet insofar as it merely involves reprioritizing or shifting commitments that were already part of who he was (e.g., the commitment to revenge). Owing to other commitments, however, such commitments may not have encroached on his experience in the way they do *after* the wound. Such a shift produces a different being in the world (and it is possible that such shifts can occur in less violent ways—e.g., conversation or reflection). Furthermore, an added

31. See Thompson, *Life and Action*, 112. For the former distinction, see Arthur Danto, *Analytical Philosophy of Action* (Cambridge: Cambridge University Press, 1973). I have also benefited from Hector-Neri Castañeda, "Conditional Intentions, Intentional Action and Aristotelian Practical Syllogisms," *Erkenntnis* 18, no. 2 (1982): 239–60.

32. It may be useful to speak here of a "self-network," as in Kane, *Significance of Free Will*, 139.

dimension to this view is that a person's present state of embodiment might affect his capacities for action.[33]

Another way to frame the theory of action undergirding Adorno's thinking is to look at how far our descriptions in cases of action make a difference for our theory and understanding of action. It is plausible, for example, that Hamlet's actions might be justified by other actions, as in "I'm organizing this play because I'm carrying out revenge" (cf. I §23–26).[34] Because actions consist of a variety of subsidiary or nested actions, and because such nested actions are not pursued or found in every discrete moment that makes up the duration of the more fundamental action (I §26), it is only if we happen upon Hamlet when he is, say, "carrying out revenge" but not "organizing the play" or "investigating the evidence" that we might be led to an artificial language of speaking about his desires, wishes, and so forth.[35] Once we take such a view of action, where what is important is its unfolding temporal process, we should hesitate to think that we always immediately have a grip on what is or counts as an action, or indeed that action is somehow "given" and all we need to do is find the mental state that justifies it.[36] In this way we can banish the specter of "deviant causal chains,"[37] which haunts views of action where mental causation is the means by which actions are actualized. What is important is the *form* of action. What is an action will be settled not by reference to some prior mental state, but through reference to and amid other actions. Anscombe's water-poisoning pumper is an apt example here (I §26). We encounter someone operating a water pump. We ask why he is moving his arms up and down, and he replies that he is operating the pump. We ask why he is operating the pump, and he replies

33. See notably the example of the golfer who cannot help raising her head, even as she desires not to do so, in Richard Shusterman, *Body Consciousness: A Philosophy of Mindfulness and Somaesthetics* (Cambridge: Cambridge University Press, 2008), 21, 122–23.

34. Cf. what is termed "naïve realization" in Thompson, *Life and Action*.

35. Such a story about action and temporality is developed in ibid., 138–46.

36. On this point, see G. E. M. Anscombe, "Practical Inference," in *Virtues and Reasons: Philippa Foot and Moral Theory*, ed. Rosalind Hursthouse, Gavin Lawrence, and Warren Quinn (Oxford: Oxford University Press, 1995), 2ff.; Candace Vogler, *Reasonably Vicious* (Cambridge, MA: Harvard University Press, 2002), 218–19. One of the most elegant justifications for this point is Anton Ford, "Action and Generality," in *Essays on Anscombe's Intention*, ed. Anton Ford, Jennifer Hornsby, and Frederick Stoutland (Cambridge, MA: Harvard University Press, 2011), 76–104. For a good statement of the view being opposed, see Donald Davidson, "Agency," in *Essays on Actions and Events* (Oxford: Clarendon Press, 2001), 43–63.

37. See Roderick Chisholm, "Freedom and Action," in *Freedom and Determinism*, ed. Keith Lehrer (New York: Random House, 1966), 11–44; Donald Davidson, "Freedom to Act," in *Essays on Actions and Events* (Oxford: Clarendon Press, 2001), 63–83.

that he is refilling the water supply. We ask in turn why he is refilling the water supply, and he tells us it is so he can pump poisoned water into the house. We might then ask why he is doing that, and he might respond that it is to poison the men inside. In this way, we have a means-end relation amid the actions; furthermore, all these separable actions stand in a distinct relation to each other: each provides another description of what is going on. The way an action becomes intentional, then, is not through possessing some special quality, but through its *form* (I §47). In the example above, each subsequent description of the action depends on the one before it but is independent of the following one—and this just is another way of proposing what a means-end relation is (cf. I §26). So while the man could not be operating the water pump without moving his arms, there might be a variety of reasons he is moving his arms up and down (he might, for example, be imitating a chicken, signaling an accomplice, or having a seizure). Any particular means is necessary for any particular end, but not vice versa (it is not the case that any particular end is necessary for some particular means). Following Anscombe, we might call this an A-B-C-D structure.

According to this model, successful intentional action will have a distinct formal structure, where the means and ends stand in a proper relation, while unsuccessful or unintentional action will be lacking this form in some particular way. Anscombe imagines two ways this might happen (I §32). The first is a mistake in the performance of an action: I might go to the store buy some butter. I walk into the store, stroll down the aisle, and reach for a package of butter. Not noticing, however, I pull out a package of margarine. Here the A-B-C structure is correct and is performed in order to D (say, "buy butter"), but what is performed instead is E ("buy margarine"). In this way the pieces (A through D) do not stand in the proper relation to each other, because D was replaced by E, and so A-B-C do not fit with E—an error in performance emerges when we examine the relation of the four. Anscombe's second example is an error of judgment,[38] where I might go to a part of town that is guaranteed not to have the product I am looking for (say I go to a Wichita sandwich shop to buy Baltimore crab cakes). I will go through all the requisite actions for buying my product (open the door, walk to the counter, talk to the clerk, and so forth), but my A-B-C-D order is guaranteed to be unsuccessful

---

38. A lot more might be said here about the relation between theoretical and practical judgment. For our purposes, it is important to understand that the two are distinct, and practical reason is not something that occurs *prior to* action, but rather occurs *in* action. On this point, see especially Anscombe, "Practical Inference," and Candace Vogler, "Anscombe on Practical Inference," in *Varieties of Practical Reasoning*, ed. Elijah Milgram (Cambridge, MA: MIT Press, 2001).

because I have fundamentally misjudged the fit between a part of that order (A-B-C) and my end (D). It ought to be apparent, then, that if the form of action is taken to be the salient fact about whether an action is intentional, it will be just as relevant to inquire about possible or potential actions *after* any particular action as to talk about events leading up to that particular action.[39]

Now, Anscombe's examples are not exhaustive, and we can add a few more possibilities for breakdown or alteration in the form of action (in this way what follows is also not exhaustive).[40] Returning to Adorno's own example of the German army officer who participated in the plot to assassinate Hitler (see section 2 above), we might understand the officer's various day-to-day actions (say, filling out a form, filing paperwork, meeting with subordinates, and so forth) as standing in a means-end relation (A-B-C) to "maintaining army order" (D). At the same time, we might take the officer also to have as an end "resist Hitler" (E). On most days the officer will perform (A-B-C-D), but on some days—for whatever reason—he might perform (A-B-C-E), and this will make all the difference in how we understand *what* he is doing, even though for the most part he may be doing exactly the same things (filling out a form, filing paperwork, meeting with subordinates, and so forth). It might make a difference that he does A-B-C on *this* day and in this particular way, since on this day it contributes to E and not D. This is one way to understand why Adorno maintains that with moral actions like resistance (E), it is not so much that they are irrational as that they seem to appear under an "irrational aspect" (PMP 9). How that aspect appears depends on the form through which actions are revealed. Addendum actions, therefore, might appear irrational because they seem to violate a certain currently conscious means-end relation (A-B-C-D), but they need not remain so, because upon reflection they come to be seen as occupying an alternative (whether unconscious, implicit, or unexamined) means-end relation (A-B-C-E). In this way it is not inappropriate to speak of an "irrational aspect" to such actions. That aspect, however, appears or emerges only through a process——through time, and that aspect might also dissipate in time. This is a way of saying that addendum actions have the peculiar place of being both a "failure" within the form of action and also, if that form

39. On this point, see the excellent discussion of patricide and Oedipus in Vogler, "Anscombe on Practical Inference," 445ff.

40. My thinking here has benefited from Charles Norman Todd, "Life Interrupted: Akrasia, Action, and Active Irrationality" (PhD diss., University of Chicago, 2011). Although I do not think Adorno's addendum actions are exactly cases of *akrasia*, and though Todd does not deal with Adorno, Todd's work (which obviously builds on Anscombe and Thompson) first invited me to try broadening the range of variations possible in the form of action.

comes to be expanded temporally, a success. And this is what it means to understand intentional action as conforming to a particular form, a form that unfolds over time and with a certain means-end structure. (What follows is just a suggestion, but apart from what is at stake in reading *Hamlet*, we might in this vein see our propensity to understand action as caused by mental states as being grounded in exactly the sort of mechanized temporality engendered by modernity, late capitalism, and the rise of instrumental thinking.[41] In this way such a view of temporality is the natural counterpart to views of action that conceive of actions in a discrete and inert manner, warping their temporally extended form.)

Framing things with this means-end model of action, it ought to be obvious that Adorno takes Hamlet's revenge still to occur in and originate from within the space of reasons. Although such actions can profitably be described as instances of "absorbed coping,"[42] the idea is not that certain actions are somehow "so responsive to the specific situation that they could not be captured in general concepts"[43] and thereby exist outside the space of reasons. Instead, for Adorno, even though certain actions may not be captured by general concepts, they are not thereby nonconceptual. It is rather that rationality always involves embodied coping and that the content of reason can never be entirely specified "in detachment from the situation."[44] Conceptuality cannot in this way be divorced from particular spatiotemporal embodiment. Rationality, again, cannot be "detached from bodily life" and characterized "in abstraction from the specifics of the situation in which embodied coping is called for."[45] As Adorno puts it, "As an activity, consciousness is never pure . . . but is always actual behavior; it is an ontic reality, or, to put it provocatively, it is always a material reality" (HF 260). In this way, then, immediacy (or having actions "pulled out of us") ought not suggest a lack of conceptuality. Nor is it accurate to say that when "one experiences the environment calling for a certain way of acting" one "finds one's body responding to the call" and "one's body . . . drawn to do what

41. For more on modernity and such a notion of time, see Espen Hammer, *Philosophy and Temporality from Kant to Critical Theory* (Cambridge: Cambridge University Press, 2011).

42. See Hubert Dreyfus, *Being-in-the-World: A Commentary on Heidegger's "Being and Time,"* Division I (Cambridge, MA: MIT Press, 1991), 69ff.

43. Hubert L. Dreyfus, "Overcoming the Myth of the Mental: How Philosophers Can Profit from the Phenomenology of Everyday Expertise," *Proceedings and Addresses of the American Philosophical Association* 79, no. 2 (2005): 51.

44. John McDowell, "What Myth?" *Inquiry* 50, no. 4 (2007): 340.

45. Ibid., 349.

needs to be done."[46] Speaking of my body doing anything in such situations is just as misleading as speaking of a disembodied "I" doing something. Rather, it is me doing the deed (and neither my body nor a disembodied "I"). Speaking of my body as doing something here (or talking as if it "knows" how to do something) can only be a matter of metaphor.[47] This is all another way of saying that addendum actions are crucially distinct from say, nervous twitches, where one's body truly is the nexus of action. To drive this point home, one can imagine the disparate evaluations of behavior that would be proposed between a genuine nervous twitch (my body's action) and one that I feign to garner certain responses (my action).[48] Ultimately, in thinking about action, there is no good reason to restrict our analysis solely to the time frame of discrete actions (especially when actions are generally nested), and it is ultimately this temptation that suggests that instances of "embodied coping" or "addendum actions" might be irrational or nonconceptual.[49] Such actions might appear irrational in a process of reflection immediately following the action, because they seem initially unanticipated from the view of that process, but ultimately they are not irrational, since they still reference a space of reasons (which the agent can later come to acknowledge). Ultimately, any such space is "inscribed within every intentional action" where action "figures in a space of reasons as a region, not as a point."[50] Or as Adorno puts it, "With this impulsiveness, *freedom extends into the realm of experience*" (HF 237; emphasis added; cf. ND 228–29/6:228).

With this broader picture of action in mind, we might wonder whether agents can *fail* to accomplish actions. After all, if the temporal scope of the form of an action can be expanded (seemingly indefinitely, restricted perhaps only by death), then an agent might always come to see any of her actions

46. Hubert L. Dreyfus, "Detachment, Involvement, and Rationality: Are We Essentially Rational Animals?" *Human Affairs* 17 (2007): 104; emphasis added. Cf. Dreyfus, "The Return of the Myth of the Mental," *Inquiry* 50, no. 4 (2007): 352–65.

47. Cf. John McDowell, "Response to Dreyfus," *Inquiry* 50, no. 4 (2007): 368.

48. Relevant here is Anthony Marcel, "The Sense of Agency: Awareness and Ownership of Action," in *Agency and Self-Awareness*, ed. Johannes Roessler and Naomi Eilan (Oxford: Oxford University Press, 2003), 48–94. Marcel describes "Alien Hand" (Hemisomatoagnosia) and "Anarchic Hand." In the former, a patient will not recognize the actions of her hand as her own; in the latter the patient's hand will move on its own, but she will (after the fact) recognize the actions as her own.

49. To co-opt a phrase of Quine's, we might speak here of a "modulus of stimulation" but apply it to actions, where what is important is the "length of stimulations counted as current." See W. V. O. Quine, *Word and Object* (Cambridge, MA: MIT Press, 1960), 28.

50. Thompson, *Life and Action*, 112.

as successful. So, by the standard model, it is clear that if a mental intention is not actualized, the action has failed. By the model being elaborated, since we have jettisoned talk of intentions as mental states causing actions, it becomes difficult to see how failure might occur: if there is allegedly no intention causing the action, I might just say that *anything* I do after the action counts as success (that is, after the fact, I can claim that I had whatever form of action that best rationalizes whatever occurred).[51] One way we might deal with this issue is to propose that in such cases we simply "had not in fact resolved to act, at least not with the degree of commitment . . . assumed."[52] This is largely to cede authority to others in matters of action. And we might be tempted to do so simply because it seems that actions are thoroughly public and thereby in a deep sense not ours. Hannah Arendt puts this point well when she points out that actions always "fall into a predetermined net of relationships, invariably dragging the agent with them, who seems to forfeit his freedom the very moment he makes use of it."[53] My understanding of my own action does not exist in a vacuum, and I may turn out to have been wrong about what I have done. Stressing such a social view of agency and action,[54] then, either pushes us (if in opposition) toward understanding agency as implying a sort of "inner citadel" to which agents might always retreat (opposing whatever was done to whatever was allegedly intended) or, in a radicalizing of the view, toward conceptualizing agency as thoroughly purged of any such citadel, where agents instead come to find that they were not committed to what they thought they were committed to and that their alleged intentions were largely illusory or self-deceived. (I explore this possibility in chapter 4, section 5.)

I take Adorno to be endorsing a view related to the latter, but with an important difference. His broader theory of action suggests that I fail to perform a particular action when my means-end relation (A-B-C-D) is somehow

51. This objection is neatly propounded in Arto Laitinen, "Hegel on Intersubjective and Retrospective Determination of Intention," *Bulletin of the Hegel Society of Great Britain*, no. 49/50 (2004): 54–72.

52. Pippin, *Hegel's Practical Philosophy*, 165.

53. Hannah Arendt, *The Human Condition* (Chicago: University of Chicago Press, 1958), 234. This theme (without reference to Arendt), has also received significant attention from some contemporary Hegelians; see notably Pinkard, *Hegel's Naturalism*, 32ff., and Pippin, *Hegel's Practical Philosophy*, 154ff. Cf. PR §119, where Hegel discusses the proverb that "a stone flung from the hand is the devil's." I §22 is also relevant here.

54. For examples and discussion, see Stanley Cavell, "A Matter of Meaning It," in *Must We Mean What We Say?* (Cambridge, MA: Harvard University Press, 2002), 229ff.; Pippin, *Hegel's Practical Philosophy*, 156ff.

contradictory or out of order.[55] In this way it is not that I find out I was not doing what I thought I was doing; it is rather that I instantiate or realize a distinct practical failure of agency. And such failure can occur by a variety of routes. Actions might be inserted into the A-B-C-D chain that do not belong there (whether intentionally or not), or parts of the chain might turn out to have been pursued for ends they would never achieve, or overlapping sequences within the chain may be pursued for different actions, or some other scenario may occur. The two essential features are that the failure is instantiated and becomes apparent only over time and only amid a teleological relation in the actions of an active and embedded agent. So I might undertake to rob a bank (D). I bribe the security guards and disable the alarm system (A) in order to enter the premises to demand money from the teller (B). I demand the money (B) in order to stuff the money into my bag and make an escape (C). I stuff it into my bag and make an escape (C) in order to rob the bank (D). As I am leaving, a guard emerges, giving me back my bribe and saying, "I can't take this after all . . . we . . . *you* . . . need to stop this right now!" In response, initiating a new teleological chain, I draw my weapon (A) in order to shoot the guard (B) so that I can make my escape (C) in order to rob the bank (D). As we face off, however, I realize that I cannot do (B). Now, we might explain my failure in a variety of ways: I am simply incapable of firing handguns (indeed, I have left the safety on), or I cannot take a human life (I happen to be a doctor and have sworn an oath, which I take quite seriously), or I cannot kill this particular guard (I realize that I know him), or countless other possibilities. What is crucial is that, in failing to shoot the guard, it is not that I did not intend to rob the bank after all. Instead, something went awry in the A-B-C-D chain; something in the means-end teleology does not stand in the requisite relation to everything else. Now I might, especially when on trial, insist that I never intended to rob the bank in the first place, but it would be difficult to square my actions with such a claim. We might imagine other cases where the means-end failures are more difficult to judge, and that reaffirms what it means to exist as a social creature: means and ends are navigated socially and potentially allow for some fluidity.

One way to summarize an implication of this view is to stress that talk of intentions is not always misleading; in fact, we can speak of intentions innocuously enough, without committing ourselves to a causal voluntarist

---

55. Cases of *akratic* actions exhibiting such a defect are excellently proposed and explored in Todd, "Life Interrupted." For an overview of the traditional (causal) views of *akrasia* (generally glossed as "weakness of the will"), see Arthur Walker, "The Problem of Weakness of Will," *Noûs* 23, no. 5 (1989): 653–76.

view of agency, when we understand intentions as linked to a teleological structure that develops over time, and concerned fundamentally with
action.[56] The ends (and the various means) in our means-end chains emerge
through our embodied being in the world, where not only our social and
institutional normative commitments play a part, but also our somatic impulses. (This last point will become increasingly important to understanding how Adorno responds to the damaged state of the world; in other words,
such impulses are exactly what my and Adorno's discussion of the addendum is meant to make plausible and understandable, for such impulses are a
variation on the addendum.) Intentions, then, ultimately are intentions-in-
action.[57] Put simply, for Adorno an intention to do something can be distinguished from what is actually done, but not because they are ontologically
separate types of things (e.g., propositional state versus action); as Adorno
puts it, "the separation of inner and outer . . . cannot be sustained" (HF 185).
Instead, what distinguishes the two is where they stand in the means-end
chain and what *sort* of action they delineate. One way to bring out this
point[58] is to think for a moment about what intentions-in-action express:
they express moments in the means-end chain: I am tilling this ground because I am planting crops. Intentions-in-action, then, are grammatically always imperfective. Notice, however, that when speaking of "wanting" or
"desiring" or "intending," *non*imperfective grammatical constructions appear ("I want to plant these crops"). In such a case the action is presented as
seemingly complete—it is no longer in process. Yet this is not how we talk
about what we are doing when we are doing it; furthermore, given Adorno's
suggestion that we are actively already always in the world, there is just
no space for that sort of nonimperfective grammatical construction to enter *here*, when we are analyzing the justifications behind actions (and this
without denying that speaking of intentions as propositional states might
be a useful way to divvy up or manageably describe failed, interrupted, or
abandoned actions).[59]

56. I am thereby committed only to the epistemic sense of retrospective determination,
which is innocuous (and useful) enough. See Laitinen, "Hegel on Intersubjective and Retrospective Determination of Intention," 65–66.

57. I am drawing on, but not explicitly following, usage by Robert B. Brandom, *Making It
Explicit: Reasoning, Representing, and Discursive Commitment* (Cambridge, MA: Harvard Uni-
versity Press, 1998), 256ff., and John Searle, *Intentionality* (Cambridge: Cambridge University
Press, 1983).

58. The following discussion of imperfective and perfective ways of talking about intentions is based on Thompson, *Life and Action*, 120–49. Making a similar overarching point, but
in a different manner, is Ford, "Action and Generality."

59. On this point, see Thompson, *Life and Action*, 142–46.

To return to Adorno's reading of *Hamlet*, in broad strokes an opposition to a mental causal view of action is central to Adorno's estimation of the philosophical stakes of *Hamlet* (cf. HF 230–33). For Adorno, the play itself ought to be understood as illustrating this attack on such a philosophical view. Hamlet's inaction exactly represents the philosophical dead end presented by the view of intentions causing actions. For Adorno, on such a view it becomes mysterious how we could ever translate certain *inner* intentions into *outer* actions—action thereby becomes so mysterious that it literally turns into its opposite: *inaction*. Hamlet then illustrates the philosophical worries that emerge with such a voluntarist picture (e.g., how might mental acts cause bodily actions, what is the nature of such causation, and so forth). Adorno puts the point like this:

> Wherever the subject wishes to move to action, he finds himself in the grip of a *horror vacui*, unsure about how he will ever succeed in emerging from his own rationality so as to transform into reality what he has perceived to be rational and what actually constitutes the substance of a reflecting subjectivity. For the fact is that this reality whose meaning has been sucked out of it and has become wholly concentrated in the human subject itself no longer provides the basis for an intervention, and, indeed, has become so radically alien and opposed to the human subject that the latter prevaricates while attempting the simplest task and finds himself unable to cope. (HF 233)

Adorno continues, urging that "thus in a philosophical sense Hamlet's feigned madness is also his true madness." Now, my aim here is not to defend this extraphilosophical claim about the symbolic nature of Hamlet's madness (or even his reading of the play more generally). Such claims are useful, however, in showing how deeply Adorno was committed to an alternative to this picture of agency, finding arguments against it even in well-worn works of literature. In rejecting this model, he instead views intentions and actions as two cross sections of the same thing. He calls their unity "impulse" or "will." This unity is, according to Adorno, the "strongest and most immediate proof that there is such a thing as freedom; it is neither blind nature nor suppressed nature" (HF 235).

The two sides of "impulse"—intention and action—are then the two sides of one phenomenon vivisected at varying chronological points of its existence (and the metaphor here can be taken with some plausibility, for actions are best seen organically as opposed to mechanically). Mere "consciousness" (intention, desire, and so forth) is insufficient for an analysis of action. As Adorno puts it in *Negative Dialectics*, any such analysis "requires something other, something that is not exhausted through consciousness, something incarnated, that is mediated into reason [*vermittelt zur Vernunft*] and qualitatively different from reason" (ND 229/6:228; translation modified). None of this is meant to deny that we have a mental life in which we can come to refer to ourselves, and thereby to our beliefs and desires about the world—beliefs and desires that can affect (sometimes in major ways) the affordances for action the world presents to us. (It is only that such beliefs and desires do not play an immediately or directly causal or justificatory role with respect to action.)[60] In this regard, as we saw, Adorno agrees and emphasizes that we have "the capacity for self-reflection," acknowledging that because of this "fact the human subject is liberated from the blind pursuit of natural ends and becomes capable of alternative actions" (PMP 104).[61] With the discussion of chapter 1 in mind, Adorno's well-known fear of a radically administered world is as much that it is entirely determined as that such powers of reflection would be extinguished. As he puts it, in such a case all action would be supplanted by "reflex actions, in other words, by that dreadful realm that was first established by Pavlov's experiments" (HF 235). Impulse actions, however, are distinct from reflex actions in that with the former, actions are solicited from me because I am a distinct sort of *agent*, while with the latter, it is because I am a distinct sort of *organism*.

One way to frame Adorno's broadest worries, then, might be to see him as committed to the idea that late capitalism consistently and systematically deforms possibilities for proper means-end structures. Some examples might include being forced into roles that seem counter to our standing as agents (commodity fetishism), pursuing ends that, in the context of late capitalism, take on destructive hues (self-preservation run amok), carrying out ends that are contradictory (the various aporias of modernity) or simply inserting into the means-end relation actions that muck it up, causing it to become irrational in its form (the compartmentalized and distracted nature

60. See, for example, the discussion of having a chip on your shoulder in Christopher Yeomans, "Hegel and Analytic Philosophy of Action," *Owl of Minerva* 42, no. 1/2 (2011): 51.

61. This is not to suggest any Frankfurt-style commitment to first-order/second-order desires. That conceptualization is still underpinned by a voluntarist picture, with the relation between the first and second order still left mysterious. Frankfurt's recent recourse to all such desires as being unified through self-satisfaction brings him closer—formally—to Adorno's account. See Harry Frankfurt, *Necessity, Volition, and Love* (Cambridge: Cambridge University Press, 1999), 95–108. The earlier view can be found in Frankfurt, "Freedom of the Will and the Concept of a Person," *Journal of Philosophy* 68, no. 1 (1971): 5–20.

of existence in late capitalism). Similarly, the arrangements of late capitalism also make it exceedingly difficult to judge whether we have taken or
even how we would take the correct means toward our end (e.g., we know
we are capable of ending homelessness, but we do not seem to know exactly
how to do it). The dialectic of enlightenment illustrates these same formal
phenomena at the most basic level of our agency: our commitment to autonomous freedom actually dissolves our very standing as agents. And it is
in this sense that we might take Adorno's claim that "there is no right living in false life" (MM §18; translation modified). There is no "right living"
because the means-end relations do not add up to a coherent whole, for as
Adorno tells us, "the whole is the false" (MM §29). In other words, it might
be that the world of late capitalism is inhospitable to proper means-end rationalization and inherently contradictory (cf. PMP 124). As Adorno would
put it, actions in late capitalism might be "tied to a *reality* full of contradiction" (HF 237; emphasis added). Telling *this* story about means-end
relations in late capitalism is beyond my scope here,[62] but I wanted at least
to suggest how the picture of action sketched here might relate to some of
Adorno's other concerns. Instead, I next want to use this theory of action to
turn to Adorno's moral thought, which in turn will allow us to return most
immediately to our broader concerns about freedom and autonomy.

5. THE BACKGROUND TO ADORNO'S MORAL THOUGHT

Indeed, keeping this broader picture of agency in mind will help us make
sense of Adorno's view of morality, for ethical agency will function akin
to agency more broadly. Ethical actions too will be "pulled" out of agents;
the world may come to be imbued with *ethical* affordances.[63] Morality is
a distinct way of being in the world. This picture is what I take Adorno to
suggest when he claims that the "entire sphere" of morality must be conceived of as "permeated [*durchdrungen*] by reason" (PMP 97). Returning
once again to Adorno's initial example of the German officer involved in the
plot to assassinate Hitler, we can now note how Adorno stresses the addendum as well as the officer's most basic view of the world. As he points out,

---

62. I pursue elements of this story in Martin Shuster, "Adorno and Anscombe on the Final
Ends of Life" (unpublished manuscript).

63. In broad strokes, I am drawing on views of ethics found in Sabina Lovibond, *Realism
and Imagination in Ethics* (Minneapolis: University of Minnesota Press, 1983); John McDowell,
Mind, Value, and Reality (Cambridge, MA: Harvard University Press, 1998), 95–167; and David
Wiggins, *Needs, Values, Truth: Essays in the Philosophy of Value* (Oxford: Blackwell, 1987),
59–215.

it was "because of [the German officer's] critical and theoretical insight into the lies and the crimes that he had to deal with that he was brought to the point of action. *If he had not had this insight . . . he would quite certainly never have been moved to that act of resistance*" (PMP 8; emphasis added).

The exact mechanics of how theoretical insight, critical judgment, and the moral addendum connect with each other are my focus in what follows. However, it ought to be apparent already that Adorno's concerns with morality will be quite different from traditional ones, since his interest is beyond any narrow focus on moral judgment (common in contemporary moral philosophy)[64] and is not concerned exclusively with choice as the paradigm of moral action. This is so because Adorno believes morality concerns a person's entire worldview (understood as involving *how* one's distinct embodied existence permeates and structures one's perception of the world and thereby *what* sorts of affordances present themselves). Such a view of morality can be understood as a person's "total vision of life, as shown in their mode of speech or silence, their choice of words, their assessments of others, their conception of their own lives, what they think attractive or praiseworthy, what they think funny: in short the configurations of their thought which show continually in their reactions and conversation."[65] When Adorno claims that "the task of moral philosophy is above all else the production of consciousness," he has in mind precisely this view of morality (PMP 9), which suggests that "moral differences look less like differences of choice, given the same facts, and more like differences of vision."[66]

An issue that still needs clarification, however, is *how* we might come to feel, "bodily, the moment of the moral addendum" (ND 365/6:358). What this question seeks is not how the imperative ought to be justified or grounded, as if the real problem of evil in the modern world occurs at this level of justification. (*That*, to speak with Adorno, truly *would* be an "outrage," for, among other things, it would suggest that the problem could be fixed just with greater philosophical facility.) Instead, the goal is to understand the mechanisms by which the new imperative operates and, perhaps more important, the means by which it *fails* to register for agents. This failure ought be understood not as a failure of justification, but rather as a distinct failure of sensibility—that is, the question might be taken to be,

---

64. A similar approach (without reference to Adorno) is suggested in Crary, *Beyond Moral Judgment*.

65. Iris Murdoch, "Vision and Choice in Morality," in *Existentialists and Mystics* (New York: Penguin, 1997), 81.

66. Ibid., 82.

Why is allegedly "unbearable physical agony" frequently perfectly bearable, indeed, seemingly unacknowledged or even unseen?

Adorno's approach to these issues is best understood as building on several of Horkheimer's essays from the 1930s. It was ultimately Horkheimer "who relentlessly forced Adorno back over and over again to the relationship between philosophy and bodily human suffering."[67] Two essays by Horkheimer are particularly relevant: "Materialism and Morality" (1933) and "The Rationalism Debate in Contemporary Philosophy" (1934). In the latter essay Horkheimer sketches a view of needs that ought to be familiar. For him, all thinking is fundamentally tied to needs (even the notion of truth is wed to material needs). In distinction to certain strands of pragmatism, however, the idea is not that truth is "merely" usefulness,[68] but that, as he puts it, "the theoretical need itself, the interest in truth, is determined by the situation of the knowers" (BPP 242/3:192–93). Horkheimer's suggestion is that the position(s) one stakes out in the world, the parameters by which one measures the criteria for judging one's questions and answers, indeed the practice of giving and taking reasons, are intimately wed to our needs. But all this is so without understanding needs uncritically, since for Horkheimer, as for Adorno, "need is a social category" (AGS 8:392). Horkheimer summarizes this entire line of thinking with a pithy claim: "A god cannot know anything because he has no needs" (BPP 242/3:193; translation modified). Thinking must always be "thinking of something *and for something*."[69] Such a view of needs, in turn, builds on his earlier "Materialism and Morality," where he suggests that "human impulses [*menschlichen Impulse*] which demand something better take different forms according to the historical material [*geschichtlichen Material*] with which they have to work" (BPP 37/3:137). For Horkheimer it is these historically determined, but nonetheless fundamentally constant, impulses that underwrite claims to truth, and thereby not only the claims of traditional morality, but more specifically the various claims by which we judge all present circumstances (we may say here that the traditional scope of morality is being broadened). Such impulses do not "maintain concepts unchanged" but rather aim to "better the lot of the world at large [*Allgemeinheit*]" (BPP 37/3:137).

67. Cf. Simon Jarvis, "Adorno, Marx, Materialism," in *The Cambridge Companion to Adorno* (Cambridge: Cambridge University Press, 2004), 84.

68. William James, "What Pragmatism Means," in *Pragmatism* (New York: Longmans, Green, 1949), 77.

69. Jarvis, "Adorno, Marx, Materialism," 98; emphasis added.

This is so true that Horkheimer ultimately concludes that "all living beings have a claim to happiness [*Glück*]" and that for such a claim we cannot "in the least ask [for] any justification or grounds" (BPP 34/3:134). Much more might be said about this picture,[70] but for the moment I will leave this thread and double back to Adorno's deployment of a similar line of thinking, beginning with a consideration of the relation between freedom and morality.

6. SPECULATIVE SURPLUS AND DEPTH AS FREEDOM

Keeping Horkheimer's picture in mind, we can begin to cement the connection between freedom and morality by working toward the new categorical imperative from the picture of agency sketched in section 4. We can best do that by focusing on a concept that Adorno employs in *Negative Dialectics* and the surrounding lectures—the concept of "depth" (*Tiefe*).[71] Adorno does not provide a formal definition of the concept (for why, see LND 103), but he does link it to speculation, which he describes as a "surplus that goes beyond whatever is the case, beyond mere existence" (LND 108). Concerning "depth," Adorno claims that this concept "is undoubtedly connected to what I described . . . as the speculative element. I believe that without speculation there is no such thing as depth" (LND 107). This speculative surplus,[72] in turn, is linked to freedom. As Adorno puts it, "This speculative surplus that goes beyond whatever is the case, beyond mere existence . . . *it alone does stand for freedom* [*Freiheit*], because it represents the tiny quantum of freedom we possess" (LND 108; emphasis added). In this way it is not too much to say that freedom is at least in part the process of resistance, if resistance is understood as a refusal to acquiesce to things as they are at present. As Adorno puts it, "The element of speculation survives in

70. See Hauke Brunkhorst, "Dialectical Positivism of Happiness," in *On Max Horkheimer: New Perspectives*, ed. Seyla Benhabib, Wolfgang Bonss, and John McCole (Cambridge, MA: MIT Press, 1993), 67–99. For more on Horkheimer's thought in general, see James Schmidt, "The *Eclipse of Reason* and the End of the Frankfurt School in America," *New German Critique* 34, no. 1 (2007): 47–76.

71. Adorno adopts this notion from Hegel; cf. LND 98. For Hegel's use, see PS ¶10.

72. For more on speculative thinking in Adorno, see Deborah Cook, "From the Actual to the Possible: Nonidentity Thinking," *Constellations* 12, no. 1 (2005): 21–35; Simon Jarvis, "What Is Speculative Thinking?" *Revue Internationale de Philosophie* 58, no. 227 (2004): 69–83; Gillian Rose, *The Melancholy Science: An Introduction to the Thought of Theodor W. Adorno* (New York: Columbia University Press, 1978), 44–46; Rose, "How Is Critical Theory Possible? Theodor W. Adorno and Concept Formation in Sociology," *Political Studies* 24, no. 1 (1976): 69–85.

such resistance" (LND 189). But such resistance is *fundamentally* not a reflective attitude (although nothing bars it from becoming one—indeed, Adorno will suggest that it ought to become one). "Resistance" is rather "in the first place instance a category of impulse [*Impuls*], a category of immediate reaction" (LND 102). This reliance on impulse should be understood as referring to the entire theory of action sketched above. Possibilities for moral action and for freedom are tied to these impulses, which are a variation on that picture. Adorno pulls all these elements together in a characteristically stark image: "If thought is not measured by the extremity that eludes the concept, [then] it is from the outset in the nature of musical accompaniment with which the SS liked to drown out the screams of its victims" (ND 365/6:358). All this requires significant elaboration, however, and I especially want to get a grip on the thought that "depth" might be understood as freedom.

After all, seeing freedom as a "surplus" or as "depth" is peculiar, to say the least. Given the picture of agency I have been pursuing, however, it ought to have some plausibility: "surplus" and "depth" are ways our framework for affordances, and thereby the actions available to us, becomes expanded and enlarged. We can see this most clearly if we remember that Adorno's concerns with freedom occur in a very distinct register: his chief example of *un*freedom is an administered world. As Adorno puts it, "In a radically administered world . . . the will would lose all its power" (HF 235; cf. PMP 176). So genocide is the starkest image of administration (AGS 4:287). In an administered world, all human actions become predictable, akin to the ways farms or robots or chemicals might be administered. We can see why this would be so in light of the earlier theory of action: an administered world limits the number of individual affordances available to creatures (that, we might say, is the point of *administration*—the management of possibilities).[73] And this would be true even if the administered world offered a variety of possibilities; the point is about how and where sites of action arise—from the interests of the administrators or the interests of agents. (To illustrate the point most forcefully, having an array of possibilities for property afforded to one is not the same as having the option of organizing the world without property in mind in the first place.) This is the context for Adorno's worries about freedom, much more so than that our actions will turn out, after all, to have been cosmically determined by God or physics. Adorno's worry is that, apart from such cosmic

73. There are analogies here to Arendt's notion of "total domination." See Hannah Arendt, *The Origins of Totalitarianism* (London: André Deutsch, 1986), 437–59.

routes, not only are we turning ourselves into administered creatures but, even more alarmingly, we are becoming unable to even imagine or conceive a different world (HF 203). (And this is one way of understanding why Adorno takes the traditional problem of "free will" to be naïve or irrelevant [HF 221]; another will emerge shortly.) The problem of administration is doubly significant, Adorno thinks, for we ourselves seem to be co-opted in the process of administration.

To lay my cards on the table, I take this issue of modality to be what motivates and underpins Adorno's "negativism."[74] Adorno's worries about the modern world are that, in ways ranging from the pernicious (e.g., mass media) to the radically evil and violent (e.g., genocide), the modern world strangles human possibilities, especially possibilities for novelty and expression, replacing them with administration and integration. This view ought already to have some plausibility in light of my discussion. In the first chapter I showed how the dialectic of enlightenment dissolves one's capacities for practical reason. In this chapter I have been proposing a theory of action that gives pride of place to one's situated context. The dissolution of practical reason therefore becomes a particularly pressing issue in regressive social contexts (and, given the prevalence of suffering in late capitalism, it seems *empirically* true that our current context is such a one). What I aim to pursue in the rest of the chapter, then, is an examination of how agents might be able to engender novel possibilities (especially for social change and progress) even in contexts that are repressive; I see this as intimately related to the new categorical imperative and as a defining mark of Adorno's moral thought. In my view it is not "the form of rationality itself" that is "the underlying cause of radical evil."[75] Rationality (what readers of Adorno typically term identity thinking) does not, in a *strong sense*, somehow

74. See note 9. As Finlayson and Freyenhagen have both suggested, Adorno's negativism raises problems for him about normative grounding, an issue I turn to shortly (see notes 91 and 92). There is also a lot more to be said about "modality" in Adorno; see Iain Macdonald, "Un utopisme modal? Possibilité et actualité chez Hegel et Adorno," in *Les normes et le possible: Héritage et perspectives de l'École de Francfort*, ed. Pierre-François Noppen, Gérard Raulet, and Iain Macdonald (Paris: Maison des Sciences de l'Homme, 2013).

75. Finlayson, "Adorno on the Ethical and the Ineffable," 2. Cf. Raymond Geuss, "Art and Theodicy," in *Morality, Culture, and History: Essays on German Philosophy* (Cambridge: Cambridge University Press, 1999), 78–116. For a more temperate view, see Freyenhagen, "Moral Philosophy," 100–103. In other places, where he is directly critiquing Finlayson, Freyenhagen also seems to affirm Finlayson's more radical reading; see, e.g., Freyenhagen, "Adorno's Ethics without the Ineffable."

cause or ground the various ills of the modern world.[76] While Adorno certainly sometimes talks in this way, I see this route as a philosophical dead end[77] and opt instead to stress elements within Adorno's thought that require us to see the evils of the modern world as distinct problems tied to particular social, economic, and political conditions. Distinct from (though not *divorced* from) such empirical inquiries, we might also pursue a philosophical inquiry into agency. Such an inquiry is what I take *Dialectic of Enlightenment* to be concerned with, and what I have reconstructed in the first chapter, where the dialectic of enlightenment was shown to dissolve agency, producing agents incapable of opposing suffering and evil, even rationally (see chapter 1, especially section 10). I take such a view of things to be in play when Adorno claims that Auschwitz *confirms* (*bestätigen*) the philosophy of pure identity (ND 362/6:355). With the conditions of the camps, where victims are no more than specimens of death, the dissolution of agency that the dialectic of enlightenment engenders is confirmed—presented in ghastly flesh. In other words, I take the estimation of the world as "radically evil" and the statement that "there is no right living in false life" (MM §18) to be empirical claims about present society. So, the problem of rationality, as traced throughout this book, is not that the form of rationality engenders evil, but rather that a type of autonomous reason dissolves itself. (And I want to stress now, as I did earlier, that this would remain a problem even if the material conditions of the modern world were suddenly devoid of suffering.) In the rest of this chapter, the locus for these issues is the worry that, because of the dialectic of enlightenment, we seem unable even to imagine alternative ways of structuring our world so that suffering would not exist (or would at least be minimized or reduced). This withering of imaginative capacities is thereby a serious problem for any discussion of freedom, but especially for one where the central problem is the dissolution of agency. The guiding thread moving forward, then, is that reigniting the spark of such imaginative capacities will also jump start possibilities for practical reason and thereby open new regions for action. And this is the goal toward which my discussion of the addendum has moved.

---

76. Finlayson clearly makes this move in justifying the claim cited in the note above. Cf. Finlayson, "Adorno on the Ethical and the Ineffable," 3.

77. This point is hammered home in Pippin, "Negative Ethics."

7. FREEDOM AND EXPRESSION, HAPPINESS AND SUFFERING

To begin to elaborate all this, let me first stress that, for Adorno, "reflex actions" (HF 235) within an administered world are distinct from the sort of "impulse" actions that I have glossed as "addendum" actions. As I suggested earlier, impulse actions are attributable to agents, while "reflex actions" are attributable to organisms. To expand this point, the former neglects that addendum actions can be explained only from a first-person perspective, with recourse to reasons, not causes.[78] Such neglect threatens to mangle the nature of addendum actions: that even given their initial "irrationality," they fundamentally express *who* an agent is. At the same time, Adorno recognizes that the actions that come to define agency occur, first and foremost, amid a situated and embodied environment (see especially section 3 above). So, for example, in relating action to responsibility, Adorno thinks that what is at stake is the extent to which *society* is free, that is, how much one's environment draws out of one actions that can then be understood as expressing who one is (cf. HF 203, 221). This is so true that when thinking about evil, Adorno claims that "evil, unfreedom, is not to be found where old metaphysicians of the satanic looked for it, namely in the idea that some people use their freedom of choice to choose evil" (HF 206; cf. ND 243/6:241). For Adorno, the horizon where actions occur is of greater significance than the distinct actions that occur there (without implying that the latter are unimportant or that responsibility is *solely* about the horizon). Adorno's theory of expressivity, then, takes seriously the agent's social context (although, as will soon forcefully emerge, it is not a theory that reduces expressivity *solely* to social contexts). This theory of expressivity, in turn, forms the core of Adorno's notion of freedom. As Adorno puts it, "Freedom follows the subject's urge [*Drang*] toward expression" (ND 17/6:29; translation modified).

Expression (*Ausdruck*), in turn, is tied to "the need to give voice to suffering," which Adorno terms "a precondition [*Bedingung*] for all truth" (ND 17–18/6:29; translation modified; cf. LND 190). How the "urge toward expression" and "the need to give voice to suffering" relate to each other is essential for understanding Adorno's view of freedom. This is especially

---

78. For two different approaches to "cashing out" the importance of such a perspective, see Robert B. Pippin, "Natural and Normative," *Daedalus* 138, no. 3 (2009): 35–43, and Dan Zahavi, "Subjectivity and the First-Person Perspective," *Southern Journal of Philosophy* 45, no. S1 (2007): 66–84. See also section 10 of chapter 1.

obvious when he all but equates the two, seeing both as preconditions for truth. As he claims in his lectures on *Negative Dialectics*, freedom "is grounded in the human subject's urge to express itself, a precondition for all truth; in the need to lend a voice to suffering" (LND 189–90; translation modified; cf. ND 17/6:29).[79] We can work our way into the relation between "urges" and "truth" by seeing them as modeled on the relation between needs and truth proposed by Horkheimer (see section 5 above). The picture will come to be this: The acknowledgment of suffering is an important element to freedom. *Which* and *whose* suffering registers is expressive of agency (as is which and whose *does not*). Truth, in turn, is necessary to *staking* such expressive claims, and the paradigm of truth in this context is a concern with the conditions of when it is appropriate to say someone is in pain or suffering. (Of course, truth is not *solely* to be concerned with this, for there are conditions—albeit, not general ones—for the appropriateness of any particular claim.) Two separate issues, then, require clarification. The first is what such a view of truth looks like (pursued in the next section), and the second is what it means to see the registering of suffering as bound up with expressivity (pursued in the rest of this section).

To take up this latter point, I introduce another comparison with Cavell, since it helps clarify Adorno's position. This comparison becomes clearest and most suggestive if we take stock of Cavell's discussion of J. S. Mill's *On Liberty* (1859). Mill writes:

> In our times, from the highest class of society down to the lowest, every-
> one lives as under the eye of a hostile and dreaded censorship. Not only
> in what concerns others, but in what concerns only themselves, the in-
> dividual or the family do not ask themselves, what do I prefer? Or, what
> would suit my character and disposition? Or, what would allow the best
> and highest in me to have fair play and enable it to grow and thrive?
> They ask themselves, what is suitable to my position? What is usually
> done by persons of my station and pecuniary circumstances? or (worse
> still) what is usually done by persons of a station and circumstance supe-
> rior to mine? I do not mean that they choose what is customary in pref-
> erence to what suits their own inclination. *It does not occur to them to*

---

79. In the lectures Adorno is concerned with "speculative freedom," but given how closely the published text of *Negative Dialectics* (which mentions only "freedom") follows this material, I do not think it is inappropriate to use the two interchangeably here; in any case, I will argue why "freedom" and "speculative freedom" are intimately related.

have any inclination except for what is customary. Thus the mind itself
is bowed to the yoke: even in what people do for pleasure, conformity
is the first thing thought of; they like in crowds; they exercise choice
only among things commonly done; peculiarity of taste, eccentricity of
conduct, are shunned equally with crimes: *until by dint of not following*
their own nature, they have no nature to follow: their human capacities
are withered and starved; they become incapable of any strong wishes
or native pleasures, and are generally without either opinions or feelings
of home growth, or properly their own. Now is this, or is it not, the desirable condition of human nature?[80]

In his analysis,[81] Cavell stresses that Mill describes a situation where
questions about what is desirable no longer arise. The analogy between this
and an administered world is striking; with an idea now familiar from the
discussion of the first chapter, Cavell suggests that "Mill now finds that it
is we who are . . . the threat to our own liberty" (CW 97). Cavell takes Mill's
aspiration here to be fundamentally "to show us that we have a right to our
own desires, to have them recognized as touchstones for social criticism
and reform" (CW 97). Keeping this point in mind, compare Cavell and Mill's
account to what Adorno writes in a relatively late piece, "Society" (1963):

> That adaption of men to social relationships and processes which consti-
> tutes history . . . has left its mark on them such that the very possibility
> of breaking free . . . even breaking free mentally—has come to seem a
> feeble and distant one. Men have come to be—triumph of integration!—
> identified in their innermost behavior patterns with their fate in modern
> society.[82]
>
> Men must act in order to change the present petrified conditions
> of existence, but the latter have left their mark so deeply on people,
> have deprived them of so much of their life and individuation, that they
> scarcely seem capable of the spontaneity necessary to do so.[83]

80. John Stuart Mill, *Essays on Politics and Society*, ed. J. M. Robson, vol. 8 of *Collected*
Works of John Stuart Mill (Toronto: University of Toronto Press, 1977), 265; emphasis added.
Quoted in CW 96–97.

81. For a broader discussion of Cavell's ambitions with this essay, see Paola Marrati, "Political Emotions: Stanley Cavell on Democracy," *Revue Internationale de Philosophie* 2, no. 256
(2011): 167–82.

82. Theodor W. Adorno, "Society," *Salmagundi* 10/11 (1969/1970): 152. The German is in
AGS 8:5–20.

83. Ibid., 153.

Similarly in *Negative Dialectics*, Adorno writes that "the fixation of one's own need and one's own longing deforms the idea of a happiness that would only arise when the category of the individual is no longer shut off from itself. Happiness is not invariant" (ND 352/6:345–46; translation modified).

I take Adorno to be diagnosing the same problem that Cavell and Mill elaborate. Strikingly, such claims—whether by Mill, Cavell, or Adorno—are not grounded with reference to utility (cf. CW 93–95). Instead, "what is coming into play here is the difficult notion of, if one can express it so, the rights of desire itself" (CW 182). This amounts to a stress both on individual expression and on the way such a failure of expressivity is not just a matter of conformity, and thereby a failure of self-creation, but even more worrisomely, a failure of imagination, an inability even to *imagine* "that different desires could be available to us, that we can and should experiment with ourselves."[84] Adorno takes an analogous line of thought when he points out, in a passage already cited, that it is exactly our speculative surplus that "represents the tiny quantum of freedom we possess, it also represents the *happiness [Glück]* of thought" (LND 108; emphasis in the original). It is with respect to this point, to the idea that such expressivity is essential, that that our institutions must "be responsive to human preferences (what we may call desire)" (CW 90). (And it is possible that such institutions might need to be reworked altogether—this is an empirical question.) Another way to frame matters here is to understand that the dialectic of enlightenment, in dissolving agency, dissolves freedom, leaving agents in conformity and the world as it is. Perniciously, the dialectic of enlightenment also produces agents incapable even of imagining the world differently (and it is in this sense that a bridge to Emerson's "secret melancholy" or Thoreau's masses "leading lives of quiet desperation" might be pursued; cf. CW 97). As Cavell points out, such a view suggests that whereas for Kant freedom depended on "freedom from desire," for Mill it depends on "the freedom for desire" (CW 182). Furthermore, Cavell also takes it that "passion, and a happy life, is threatened by *unrestrained reason—a change brought about by whatever has brought about rationalized, commodified, mass societies*" (CW 182; emphasis added). And *this* point should by now be familiar. These are all bold claims, and the claim that desire or happiness is *necessary* to freedom is one I will return to when considering Adorno's mature position in light of Kant's rejoinder as found in the previous chapter (see section 10 below).

84. Marrati, "Political Emotions," 173; emphasis added.

The desire for something better is an impulse that expresses a speculative surplus, and for Adorno it is both essential to our freedom and *expressive* of that freedom (LND 90–91; cf. ND 17/6:29). Such speculative impulses potentiate reality, suggesting routes of salience and lines of action that otherwise would be absent: impulses "spark" reality.[85] Impulses, Adorno suggests, can take at least two forms. The first is a speculative playfulness that goes beyond whatever is (LND 90–91); this side of speculation implies that personal experimentation potentially always is just a feature of self-expression. (The importance of such experimentation raises political questions centering on the allocation of resources, but they are not fatal to such a theory; [on this point see CHU xi–33, 101–27 and also CW 164–89]). I leave this element of freedom aside, however, since it is not the centerpiece of Adorno's account. The second form these impulses take is the expression of an acknowledgment of suffering. But what does it mean to see such impulses both as registering suffering *and* as a form of expression? Adorno portrays them in this fashion with statements like this:

> Suffering is objectivity that weighs upon the subject, what it experiences as most subjective; its expression, is objectively mediated. (ND 18/6:29; translation modified)
>
> What I am describing is philosophical depth regarded subjectively—namely, not as the justification or amelioration of suffering, but as the *expression of suffering*, something which understands the necessity of suffering in the very act of expression. (LND 108)
>
> The most subjective thing, expression, objectively mediated, viz. by suffering, in which the shape of the course of the world is contained. (LND 110)

I take Adorno's claims here to center on the idea that our world is structured and permeated by a plethora of "objective" normative commitments and stances. How far our actual world and experience fall short of the ideals behind those commitments, however, ought "subjectively" to be understood as suffering. The German word for "suffering" (*Leiden*) originates from an Old German root meaning "to go" or "to journey."[86] We can riff on

85. Cf. the idea of "reckoning with the possible" found in Maurice Merleau-Ponty, *Phenomenology of Perception*, trans. Colin Smith (London: Routledge, 2002), 125; Komarine Romdenh-Romluc, "Merleau-Ponty and the Power to Reckon with the Possible," in *Reading Merleau-Ponty: On "Phenomenology of Perception*," ed. Thomas Baldwin (London: Routledge, 2007).

86. Jacob Grimm and Wilhelm Grimm, *Deutsches Wörterbuch* (Leipzig: Hirzel, 1885), 658.

this meaning if we understand suffering as the gap represented by the conceptual distance traveled from our commitments to our actual practices—between what *ought* to be and what actually is. That is, what is at stake here is the normative gap that emerges between the standards we propose and how far our experience, in revealing that gap, falls short of such proposals and ideals.

Importantly for Adorno (and for Cavell), however, the contours of this gap are not fixed *solely* through reference to universal standards or preexisting rules,[87] but as much through reference to "the expression of a conviction whose grounding remains subjective—say myself—but which expects or claims justification from the (universal) concurrence of other subjectivities, on reflection" (CHU xxvi), that is, a reflective judgment.[88] The notion of a reflective judgment ought to be understood, formally, in its Kantian context (but only formally; neither Adorno nor Cavell is committed to Kant's broader philosophical picture). Judgment, according to Kant, is the "faculty for thinking . . . the particular as contained under the universal" (3C 5:179). This might be accomplished in two ways: the universal concept might be present to us, so our search consists of finding the particular to be subsumed under that universal; or the particular might be present and our search consists in finding the universal for it (3C 5:179).[89] The latter notion of judgment is no less normative for Kant, and is not "merely" subjective but also demands universal agreement (cf. CHU xxvi).[90] Adorno is thereby committed to what might be called a "context-dependent" view of normativity; claims are grounded in and through particular contexts.[91]

A way to understand Adorno's position here is to stress that there are cases where suffering registers in a way that is not merely formal—that is, not justifiable through reference to an established rule or norm or concept.

87. I would take the chief contemporary example of such a position to be John Rawls, *A Theory of Justice* (Cambridge, MA: Harvard University Press, 1971).

88. For Adorno and reflective judgment, see Bernstein, *Adorno: Disenchantment and Ethics*, 306ff. See also Lars Rensmann and Samir Gandesha, "Understanding Political Modernity: Rereading Arendt and Adorno in Comparative Perspective," in *Arendt and Adorno: Political and Philosophical Investigations*, ed. Lars Rensmann and Samir Gandesha (Palo Alto, CA: Stanford University Press, 2012), 11–12.

89. The literature around this notion is immense—for a good starting point, see Bernstein, *Adorno*, 309n56.

90. This, then, is a response to worries about the normative grounding of Adorno's theory. See James Gordon Finlayson, "Morality and Critical Theory: On the Normative Problem of Frankfurt School Social Criticism," *Telos* 2009, no. 146 (2009): 7–41, and Freyenhagen, "No Easy Way Out."

91. Freyenhagen, "Adorno's Ethics without the Ineffable," 145. Freyenhagen attributes a similar view to Raymond Geuss, whose company I am happy to be in.

To illustrate, think of a formal case where a prisoner might plead: "You *can't* execute me yet! I was told I'd have *three* chances for an appeal, but I've only had two." Distinct from this case, there might be cases where suffering registers solely through recourse to my sensibilities, to *who I am*. In such a case, the search for the rule in question cannot be divorced from *my* subjective capacities (hence the suitability of Kant's notion of reflective judgment and the reference to *my* desires; and I should note that this is also exactly the issue that Cavell's dispute with Rawls centers on; see CHU xi–33, 101–27, and also CW 164–89). As Cavell puts it, "A moral judgment of a state of affairs . . . has a perceptual dimension and assesses pleasure and pain, and because it is informed by sensibilities in various stages of perceptiveness or impressionability" (CHU xxvi). Such a stress on reflective judgment mitigates worries about the suitability of immanent critique as a justification for criticism (where the norms of society are invoked to criticize that society).[92] Adorno seems to express this worry when he wonders whether our social space and norms might be so meager that "there is not [even] a crevice in the cliff of the established order into which the ironist might hook a fingernail" (MM 211/4:241). What is true of the ironist would also be true of the immanent critic.[93] Conceiving of such impulses as grounded in reflective judgment allows for the possibility that there may not as yet exist a rule or norm or concept for the impulse coming into play: the norm might have to be invented or proposed.

While the notion of reflective judgment mitigates worries about the potential paucity of social norms, there are concomitant worries about our physical capacities. For example, present forms of social configuration might affect our very capacities as embodied creatures, where our capabilities for such impulses are being *physically* undermined or destroyed (by means of say, mass media, pharmaceuticals, or socioeconomic conditions more generally). This is the sense in which I would read Adorno's worries about our imaginative capacities being undermined in the modern world (ND 352/6:345). These concerns are also expressed in "Resignation" (1969) when he points out that "the administered world has a tendency to strangle all spontaneity" (CM 292). I take such worries to fundamentally require investigations beyond my scope here (investigations that would span disciplines like neurobiology, cognitive science, pharmacology, psychology, and

92. For an expression of this worry, see Freyenhagen, "No Easy Way Out," 46, and Jaeggi, "'No Individual Can Resist.'"
93. Cf. Freyenhagen, "No Easy Way Out," 49n42.

so forth).[94] And I think at present we have to say that it might turn out that our physical capacities are capable of being destroyed. (Note that this is a different point than that our physical capacities are being trained or coarsened so that the registering of suffering suggests inflicting more suffering, that is, when the impulse might be to respond to suffering with violence, to "polish the victim off." This objection is one I address shortly.)[95] My gambit is to forge ahead with Adorno's theory. I take this to be both currently justifiable and reflective of Adorno's own views. On the former, it is not settled whether resistance as speculative surplus is capable of being entirely undermined physically (here it is striking that even the most forceful fictional conceptualizations of such possibilities, say *1984* or *Brave New World*, require ideological methods of repression as much as physical ones). Concerning the latter, and given his conceptualization of the interpenetration of the mental and the somatic, Adorno appears hopeful that reflection might spark somatic capacities as much as vice versa. We can see this in his stress on reflection, as when he claims that we must "refuse resolutely to remain satisfied with the surface, and . . . insist on breaking through the façade" (LND 107). Adorno continues, charging that we should place our "trust only in the ruthless power of reflection" (LND 107).[96] In "Resignation" Adorno is starkly realistic, but nonetheless hopeful about our reflective capacities. He writes that "such an emphatic concept of thinking admittedly is not secured, not by the existing conditions, nor by the end yet to be achieved, nor by any kind of battalions. Whatever has once been thought can be suppressed, forgotten, can vanish. *But it cannot be denied that something of it survives*" (CM 293; emphasis added). My procedure, then, is to note this danger while moving forward with an elaboration of the rest of Adorno's account.

To summarize what I have presented thus far, Adorno takes the registering of suffering to express the capacity for speculative freedom. When and what suffering registers always has recourse to a state of affairs where that suffering does not exist. Suffering, then, delineates what ought not to be. This "ought" is grounded in the gap that emerges between what should be and what is, but without any necessary recourse to a universal rule as

94. For an attempt in this vein see John Protevi, *Political Affect: Connecting the Social and the Somatic* (Minneapolis: University of Minnesota Press, 2009).

95. For expressions of this worry, see Espen Hammer, "Review of *Adorno: Disenchantment and Ethics*," *Notre Dame Philosophical Reviews* (2002), and Nick Smith, "Making Adorno's Ethics and Politics Explicit," *Social Theory and Practice* 29, no. 3 (2003): 493–95. I pursue this point at the end of the next section.

96. An allusion to Marx; cf. CM 393n2.

justification. What justifies my estimation is a reflective judgment. Freedom involves expression, and such expression implicates my desires insofar as such desires are linked to the registering of suffering. I desire that things not be so *because* I register certain forms of suffering. This need not imply that all desires are of this sort—the "need to give suffering a voice is a precondition for all truth" is a species of the idea that "the subject's desire to express herself is a precondition for all truth." For Adorno the registering of suffering is the paradigmatic site of such expression, and the one that is most immediately and alarmingly threatened "after Auschwitz." But it is not the sole site of such expression, and we do Adorno's thinking no injustice if we gloss the statement, as he himself does in parts of *Negative Dialectics* and his lectures, as the more general idea that the precondition for all truth is the subject's desire to express herself (ND 17/6:29; LND 189–90). Finally, note that Adorno *does* connect expression to truth, which implies that there is a stake in getting things right. Adorno is not merely propounding narcissism. How truth serves this function and how self-expression is intimately tied to relations with others is taken up in the next section.

8. EXPRESSIVITY, LANGUAGE, AND TRUTH

One way to broach this point is to note that any talk of expressiveness ultimately suggests a consideration of language. *Human* expressivity is in large part linguistic (although not exclusively so). If speech is to be expressive of me, it will reflect my take on the world, my distinct "being in the world," which is expressive of me in that it reveals my freedom–that is, my speculative capacities. In turn, such claims are as much claims about myself (*who* I am and *what* registers for me and why) as they are about others (whom I am claiming *to speak for* and to and why). We might put this point by stressing that *I* am essential to my speech, my language. Adorno seems to stress this point in a notoriously maligned passage in the introduction to *Negative Dialectics*. There he writes that "immediate communicability [*unmittelbare Kommunizierbarkeit*] to everyone is not a criterion of truth" (ND 41/6:51; translation modified). In this passage (called the "privilege of experience") Adorno outlines what is allegedly a problematic elitist position.[97] He admonishes readers to "resist the all but universal compulsion to confuse the communication of knowledge with knowledge itself," while insisting not only that "philosophical experiences [are] . . . not equally accessible to ev-

---

97. Cf. Lambert Zuidervaart, *Social Philosophy After Adorno* (Cambridge: Cambridge University Press, 2007), 96–100.

eryone," but that "it would be fictitious to assume that all men might understand, or even perceive [bemerken], all things" (ND 41/6:51). Given such passages and Adorno's personal preferences (e.g., his artistic tastes), it is not surprising that these passages have been taken as expressions of questionable elitist sentiments. After all, given the earlier discussion of how modern agency seems to be dissolving our capacities for expressiveness and for registering suffering, we might wonder how we can even begin to develop such capacities. And with such passages, Adorno seems to throw up his hands, suggesting at best that it is a matter of chance or luck, but at worst that we must just be resigned to elitism. (And something like "Education After Auschwitz," despite its intent, largely repeats such worries instead of dispelling them.) Adorno seems to confirm this suspicion when he refers to individuals who possess or acquire such insight as having acquired "undeserved happiness" (unverdiente Glück) (ND 41/6:51).

To see how this is not the case, let me highlight again a point of convergence between Adorno and Cavell. We can do this (and work toward understanding Adorno's views of truth) if we stress a few other elements of Adorno's conception of language. To begin with, here is how Cavell, in *The Claim of Reason*, describes the very notion of having a voice:

> I do not know in advance how deep my agreement with myself is, how far responsibility for the language may run. But if I am to have my own voice in it, I must be speaking for others and allow others to speak for me. The alternative to speaking for myself representatively (for *someone* else's consent) is not: speaking for myself privately. The alternative is having nothing to say, being voiceless, not even mute. (CR 28)

Cavell's point is that any claim is always a claim *to* community. It is a claim to speak for others, and thereby for myself amid others.[98] He points out that "the philosophical appeal to what we say, and the search for our criteria on the basis of which we say what we say, are claims to community" (CR 20). In light of this we might say that the "wish and search for community are the wish and search for reason" (CR 20). This is so much so that the alternative to such speech is not some sort of "private" speech, but speech that does not reach anyone, speech that is *mute* (CR 28). In a different tenor, Cavell puts this point like this:

---

98. Cf. Richard Eldridge, "The Normal and the Normative: Wittgenstein's Legacy, Kripke, and Cavell," *Philosophy and Phenomenological Research* 46, no. 4 (1986): 571.

What I am suggesting is that "Because it is true" is not a *reason* or basis
for saying anything, it does not constitute the point of your saying something; and I am suggesting that there must, in grammar, be reasons for
what you say, or be point in your saying of something, if what you say
is to be comprehensible. We can understand what the *words* mean apart
from understanding why you say them; but apart from understanding
the point of your saying them we cannot understand what *you* mean.
(CR 206)

This is Cavell's version of the point that Horkheimer stressed (see section 5 above) and Adorno seemed also to acknowledge: that our speech is
tied to concrete needs. Our claims (particular claims by particular people
at particular times) occur based on our desires, needs, and wants (particular desires by particular people at particular times). Claims and desires are
inseparable.[99] So Cavell describes his project as the attempt to "put the human animal back into language and therewith into philosophy" (CR 207).
We might take all this as saying that expressive claims are lodged *from a
perspective within a world*—like actions (see section 4 above); the entirety
of our being is implicated in every claim. Divorced from such a context—
from a world—we might perhaps register your words (by, say, consulting
a dictionary), but we would not understand what *you* mean by them. We
might say that it "is a matter of seeing through" the meaning of the words
"to their point."[100]

On this view there is a responsibility for our words, which it would
not be too much to call *moral*. Our words determine *who* we are; they also
determine who the others are in relation to us, and what the relation between us will be and can be. Individuals, then, give an expressive voice
to suffering when they register suffering through their claims. We can see
Adorno subscribing to an analogous view of language when he points out
that in staking claims about suffering, it is up to agents to "make the moral
and, as it were, representative effort to say what most of those for whom
they say it cannot see or, to do justice to reality, will not allow themselves
to see" (ND 41/6:51). In such cases truth "will lose the privileged character that resentment holds against it through the fact that it no longer
makes excuses for the experiences to which it owes itself, but [rather] gets

---

99. Cf. Avner Baz, "On When Words Are Called For: Cavell, McDowell, and the Wording of
the World," *Inquiry* 46 (2003): 473–500.

100. Avner Baz, *When Words are Called For: A Defense of Ordinary Language Philosophy*
(Cambridge, MA: Harvard University Press, 2012), 189.

involved in configurations and logical connections [*Konfigurationen und Begründungszusammenhänge*] that help it to evidence itself or to convict it of its shortcomings" (ND 42/6:52; translation modified). Adorno adds that thereby "elitist arrogance [*Hochmut*] would be the last thing to befit philosophical experience" (ND 42/6:52; translation modified; cf. MM §1.6). What is emerging here, then, is a certain sort of elitism: it just is the case that suffering might register only for some, and this is largely a matter of chance.[101] How far such elitism should be seen as a problem is mitigated through reference to an unpublished essay of Adorno's from the 1930s, "Theses on the Language of the Philosopher" ("Thesen über die Sprache des Philosophen"). There Adorno writes:

> The language of philosophy is prefigured by material content [*Sachhaltigkeit*]. The philosopher does not have elective thoughts to express, but must find the words, that are alone legitimized by the state of truth in them. The words are to bear the intention the philosopher wants to articulate and cannot otherwise articulate than by hitting upon the word in which such truth dwells at the historical hour. (TLP 36/1:366; translation modified)

The connection to Cavell is striking. We must *find* the words, and in turn these words are legitimized by the use we put them to, all within the context of a particular form of life. Adorno makes this explicit: "The ruin of words are his [the philosopher's] material, to which history binds him; his freedom is solely the possibility of their configuration according to the force of truth in them. He is as little permitted to think the word as pregiven as to invent a word" (TLP 37/1:368–69). This last sentence can best be understood as analogous to Cavell's notion of "word projection." He stresses that although "we learn the meaning of words and what objects are," such "learning is never over, and we keep finding new potencies in words and new ways in which objects are disclosed" (CR 180). Again, for Adorno and for Cavell, language is defined by the possibility of putting words to new uses, contexts, and purposes. Such novelty hinges on and exposes the fragility of language, and thereby the frailty of community and our contextualized existence as individuals. Since word projection intimately involves

---

101. It is not inappropriate to speak here of "moral luck" (especially "constitutive moral luck"). See Thomas Nagel, "Moral Luck," in *Mortal Questions* (Cambridge: Cambridge University Press, 1979), 24–38, and Bernard Williams, "Moral Luck," in *Moral Luck* (Cambridge: Cambridge University Press, 1981), 20–40.

others, new uses of words might be accepted or rejected. It is in this context that we should understand Adorno's stress on humility and modesty, as when he claims that "we need to hold fast to moral norms, to self-criticism, to the question of right and wrong, *and at the same time to a sense of the fallibility of the authority that has the confidence to undertake such self-criticism*" (PMP 169; emphasis added). At the same time, exactly in light of such fallibility, we must also understand that we are *all* masters of language (CR 166ff.). New projections may fail for a variety of reasons—some good, some bad, some extraordinary, and some banal. Both Cavell and Adorno realize the various difficulties involved in word projection and its moral implications.[102] This mitigates (but again, does not entirely resolve) the elitism worry in that any such moral luck is not permanent, finding the right words is an *imperative*, and one's constitution is neither fixed nor fixable, "right" once and for all, for every occasion. (Again, I say this does not "resolve" the elitism issue insofar as it is a species of a much more nefarious issue: it may be possible that modern conditions are such that we are becoming *entirely* inexpressive and thereby incapable of finding the right words for *any* occasion—see the end of section 7 above).

With this view of language in mind, a basic question arises about truth (including moral truth): What does it mean to say something is true? Answering this allows us to see that Adorno's theory is not just a theory of narcissism. In response to the broader question of the nature of truth, I want to stress that any case of word projection, and thereby any case of speech that reveals suffering, must rely on *some* notion of truth. For a new projection to take hold, the possibility of argument about its veracity must exist. We must be able to ask whether it captures the object(s) it purports to reference. A notion of truth and the possibility of error are therefore both required for us even to make sense of the notion of word projection.[103] We might say that

> different strategies of description, on this view, are ways of bringing salience to different causal patterns in the world, patterns with which we engage. And that is just the great ability that language brings, this ability to reprogram our causal dispositions through salience-alteration . . .

102. A similar picture of Adorno (without reference to Cavell) can be found in Judith Butler, "Adorno on Becoming Human," in *Giving an Account of Oneself* (New York: Fordham University Press, 2005).

103. Bjørn Ramberg makes an analogous point in defending Davidson against Rorty's insistence that Davidson drop a notion of truth. See Ramberg, "Post-ontological Philosophy of Mind: Rorty versus Davidson," in *Rorty and His Critics*, ed. Robert B. Brandom (Oxford: Blackwell, 2000), 363.

by changing our causal dispositions, redistributing significance across kinds, we affect how we engage with the world, and thus also the world.[104]

I take Adorno to propose something analogous when he claims that "in order to posit a new truth, there remains for the philosopher no hope other than to place the words in a new configuration, which would itself yield such a new truth" (TLP 38/1:369). Any procedure of elaborating truth "is not to be identified with the aim of "expounding" new truth through conventional words" (TLP 38/1:369). In opposition to such an extrahistorical or extrasocial notion of truth, for Adorno "configurative language will instead have to completely avoid the explicit procedure that presupposes the unbroken dignity of words" (TLP 38/1:369). Language brings to the fore new objects and thereby new possibilities for moral action within the world. It is in this way that "configurative language represents a . . . dialectically intertwined and explicatively indissoluble unity of concept and thing" (TLP 38/1:369). Indeed, "It is to be asked of the words themselves how far they are capable of bearing the intentions attributed to them, to what extent their power has been historically extinguished, how far they can somehow be configuratively preserved" (TLP 38/1:369). Any such deployment of language is linked to a notion of truth. It is in this sense, then, that the "human subject's desire to express itself" is a "precondition for all truth" (LND 189–90). To be saying anything at all, we must be expressing our own take on the world, one filled with our own distinct needs and desires.[105] And to the extent that suffering and expressivity come to be linked (see section 7 above), "the need to give voice to suffering is a condition for all truth" (ND 17–18/6:29; translation modified). Ultimately *any* expressive procedure presupposes a notion of truth, albeit one that is akin to (a certain understanding of) the truth of mathematics, where the "continuing cumulative process of making or constructing can amount to the creation of a shared form of life that is constitutive of rationality itself, furnishing proofs that are not compulsions but procedures to guide our conceptions, explaining, without explaining away, our sense that sometimes we have no alternative but to infer this from that."[106] It is in this sense that we should understand

---

104. Ibid.; emphasis added. In this context, see also 367. Also relevant is Andrew Bowie, "Adorno, Pragmatism, and Aesthetic Relativism," *Revue Internationale de Philosophie*, no. 227 (2004): 41.

105. One of the clearest recent elaborations of such a view is Baz, *When Words Are Called For*.

106. David Wiggins, "Truth, Invention, and the Meaning of Life," in *Needs, Values, Truth: Essays in the Philosophy of Value* (Oxford: Blackwell, 1987), 128.

Adorno's claims not to know the "absolute," where the absolute is under-stood as something that is true *irrespective* of a shared form of life.

Adorno presents this idea in the claim that "we may not know what the absolute good is or the absolute norm, we may not even know what man is or the human or humanity—but what the inhuman is we know very well indeed" (PMP 175). We can perceive suffering in that such perception does not necessarily rely on an absolute divorced from a particular form of life. In this way our perception of suffering is based on a perception of something now in the world, on something *there*, "to be found by anyone, or by anyone who is sufficiently attuned to what bears upon the matter."[107] And here we can profitably compare the experience to understanding 4 + 4 = 8, also avail-able to anyone who has been properly attuned.[108] Of course this raises the elitism worry, this time in a different register. As one commentator puts it, "The smell of blood may always be a call for help, but those answer-ing may be responding to less benevolent, but nonetheless object-oriented, motivations."[109] The smell of blood might just call for us to "polish off" the victim instead of helping her. This, however, *is* a description of how morality functions. It is essential "to the form of life we call morality" that "no one can settle a moral conflict in the way umpires settle conflicts" (CR 296), that is, definitively and with a clear view of the rules. Instead, it is constitutive of morality that "our way is neither clear nor simple; we are often lost. What you are said to do can have the most various descriptions; under some you will know that you are doing it, under others you will not. What alternatives we can and must take are not given, but must be created in what we care about" (CR 324).

Furthermore, we must realize, then, that

> morality must leave itself open to repudiation; it provides *one* possibil-ity of settling conflict, a way of encompassing conflict which allows the continuance of personal relationships against the hard and apparently in-evitable fact of misunderstanding, mutually incompatible wishes, com-mitments, loyalties, interests and needs, a way of mending relationships and maintaining the self in opposition to itself or others. Other ways of settling or encompassing conflict are provided by politics, religion, love and forgiveness, rebellion, and withdrawal. Morality is a valuable

---

107. Wiggins, "Truth as Predicated of Moral Judgments," in *Needs, Values, Truth: Essays in the Philosophy of Value* (Oxford: Blackwell, 1987), 157.

108. Ibid.

109. Smith, "Making Adorno's Ethics and Politics Explicit," 494.

way because the others are so often inaccessible or brutal; but it is not everything. (CR 269)

This view of morality, and the possibility of alternative responses to objective conditions, is no objection to Adorno's understanding of freedom, action, and moral life. It just means that he fashions his morality in response to the concrete events of the Nazi genocide and related cases of suffering. And this is neither surprising nor problematic, given that Adorno, like Hegel, views morality as a historical achievement (PMP 98–99). Furthermore, on such a view of morality, it is a fact that any particular view is open to repudiation. Nonetheless, even though morality relies not on a priori principles, but on somatic and perceptual capacities and powers for reflective judgment, morality is still more than mere opinion.[110] Morality still *demands* universal agreement in ways that other opinions might not.

Nonetheless, there may be a worry here that has less to do with worries about the nature of morality and more with the fact that even in light of such a connection between sociality and objectivity, when attuned in similar ways, we might come to overestimate our own suffering and underestimate or even entirely ignore the suffering of others.[111] As Adorno's conceptualization of the relation between subjectivity and objectivity in relation to expression makes clear, however, what is striking about *any* expressive communication is how far it exactly converts a particular subjective stance into something objectively accessible. More strikingly, such objectivity *potentially* appears to others, even if they have tried to inoculate themselves against it (through, say, bigotry or racism; and this point will apply to ourselves as much as to others). Emmanuel Levinas captures a similar thought well with the metaphor that "language" is *"like a battering-ram, it is the power to break through the limits of culture, body, and race."*[112] In being so objectivated, expressions take on a life of their own, and this is what it means to see suffering as objective. Adorno makes an analogous point when in his posthumous *Aesthetic Theory* he writes that when a claim of suffering is staked, when it "is spoken . . . distance is . . . won from the

110. Adorno is not thereby "amoral," as pictured in Giuseppe Tassone, "Amoral Adorno: Negative Dialectics outside Ethics," *European Journal of Social Theory* 8, no. 3 (2005): 251–67.

111. Cf. Raymond Geuss, "Suffering and Knowledge in Adorno," *Constellations* 12, no. 1 (2005): 18.

112. Emmanuel Levinas, "Language and Proximity," in *Collected Philosophical Papers* (Dordrecht: Martinus Nijhoff, 1987), 122; emphasis added. Cf. the metaphor of a "grappling iron" in Rush Rhees, "'What Is Language?'" in *Wittgenstein and the Possibility of Discourse*, ed. D. Z. Phillips (Oxford: Blackwell, 2006), 27.

trapped immediacy of suffering," thereby "transform[ing that] suffering just as screaming diminishes unbearable pain. Expression [*Ausdruck*] that has been objectivated as language *endures* [*persistiert*]."[113] This is why in *Negative Dialectics* Adorno will write that "even in an age when they fall silent, great works of art express hope" (ND 397/6:389). So we may overestimate our own suffering or ignore the suffering of others, but this need not remain our fate. The registering of suffering, when *expressed*, endures in spite of being ignored or overlooked (and this might be true even if such an expression is quickly extinguished, as when the possibility for conversion through guilt or acknowledgment remains open by means of memory). In so enduring, relations to such expressions are always open to modification. Many new issues arise here about the possibilities of and sites for expression; I cannot go into them here, but I do want to underscore how the acknowledgment of suffering then becomes the locus of any discussion.[114] This suggests the importance of truth for such acknowledgment (this ought to be obvious from the preceding discussion), and the importance of others (thereby offering a plausible rejoinder to narcissism, although not a dissolution of its possibility). (As I will show, it is crucial to understand that acknowledgment, though involving truth, is *not* just about truth. As Cavell puts it, acknowledgment is "an interpretation of knowledge.")[115]

We can see how others are at the center of acknowledgment when we stress that acknowledgment is "evidenced equally by its failure as by its success."[116] Cavell underscores this element of our relation to others when he points out that "only I could reach to the other's (inner) life. My condition is not exactly that I have to *put* the other's life there; and not exactly that I have to *leave* it there either. I (have to) *respond* to it, or refuse to respond. It calls upon me; it calls me out. I have to acknowledge it" (CR 84). Refusal is always a possibility. In such a case, with a failure of acknowledgment it is not that something is *absent*; rather, there is "the presence of something, a confusion, an indifference, a callousness, an exhaustion, a

---

113. Theodor W. Adorno, *Aesthetic Theory*, ed. Gretel Adorno and Rolf Tiedemann, trans. Robert Hullot-Kentor (Minneapolis: University of Minnesota Press, 1997), 117; emphasis added. AGS 7:179.

114. In this context it is worth thinking about Rorty's liberal ironist and his insistence on the importance of "*notic[ing]* suffering when it occurs." Richard Rorty, *Contingency, Irony, and Solidarity* (Cambridge: Cambridge University Press, 1989), 93.

115. Stanley Cavell, *In Quest of the Ordinary: Lines of Skepticism and Romanticism* (Chicago: University of Chicago Press, 1994), 8.

116. Stanley Cavell, "Knowing and Acknowledging," in *Must We Mean What We Say?* (Cambridge, MA: Harvard University Press, 2002), 263.

coldness."[117] These are all practical stances I take *toward* the other. Even in murder, I acknowledge the other.[118] Or as Cavell puts it, "The question is still why my hand is ever stretched out, even in the form of a fist. It shows that I want something of another. It shows that I am exposed to my humanity" (CR 439). Here we can see that even when particular expressive claims might be repudiated or ignored, they are repudiated or ignored in a distinct register, one where they are still *acknowledged*. There just is something "that is simply *there*."[119] (This is one way, for example, to understand the significance of Himmler's famous Posen speech.)

9. MORALITY AND THE NONIDENTICAL

Keeping in mind this broad picture of morality, language, and truth, I will complete my sketch of Adorno's mature theory by briefly discussing a notion taken to be central to his project: the nonidentical. My discussion of this term is cursory, since it is meant only to fill in the contours of the broader picture about freedom that I have been proposing. On my reading, Adorno's notion of nonidentity is intimately wed to, but not exhausted by, his notion of freedom—what earlier was termed the "speculative element," the "surplus that goes beyond whatever is the case" (LND 108). It is in this sense that we must understand Adorno's suggestion that "the only kind of philosophy for which, in the face of despair, responsibility could be assumed, would be the attempt to contemplate all things the way that they would present themselves from the standpoint of redemption. Cognition has no light other than the one that shines onto the world from redemption: everything else exhausts itself in reconstruction and remains a piece of technique" (MM 247/4:281; translation modified).[120]

The standpoint of redemption is anchored to a somatic origin and proposed by means of this speculative element. Adorno, then, is not committed to any dogmatism about nonidentity—to some sort of bald realism. The point is rather to *contemplate* things from such a standpoint. This stance is suggested by the idea that "one cannot peer out. What would be

117. Ibid., 264.

118. For a great illustration of this point, see Emmanuel Levinas, *Totality and Infinity: An Essay on Exteriority*, trans. Alphonso Lingis (Pittsburgh, PA: Duquesne University Press, 1980), 198–99; Michael Morgan, *Discovering Levinas* (Cambridge: Cambridge University Press, 2007), 72ff.

119. Wiggins, "Truth as Predicated of Moral Judgments," 157.

120. My translation of this passage is indebted to Gerhard Richter, "Aesthetic Theory and Nonpropositional Truth Content in Adorno," *New German Critique* 33, no. 1 (2006): 119–35.

beyond appears only in the materials and categories of what is within"
(ND 140/6:143). Adorno continues, pointing out that "this is where the
truth and the untruth of Kantian philosophy divide. It is true in destroy-
ing the illusion of an immediate knowledge of the Absolute; it is untrue in
describing this Absolute by a model that would correspond to an immediate
consciousness, even if that consciousness were the *intellectus archetypus*"
(ND 140/6:143–44). The heart of things could no more be apprehended by
an understanding different from ours (e.g., some divine or intuitive understanding) than it could be immediately grasped by an understanding like
ours. I take this point as a guiding thread to understanding Adorno on
nonidentity.[121]

From a bird's-eye view of things,[122] we might envision Adorno interpreters as impaling themselves on one of two poles: as either critiquing
conceptual knowing *as such*, thereby implicitly or explicitly referencing
something that conceptual knowing cannot capture, or critiquing *our* brand
of conceptual knowing, thereby aiming to correct it with some other. I
take the latter to be mistaken because it aspires to somehow "fix" identity
thinking; I take the former to be mistaken because it takes the nonidentical as some sort of ineffable ground. Concerning identity thinking, let me
stress again that not even the *intellectus archetypus* could capture what we
also seem unable to grasp: there is no "failure" on the part of the *subject*,
or if a failure can be said to be happening, it is not *that* sort of failure (i.e.,
there may be an ethical failure, but not an ontological or metaphysical).
While Adorno does insist on trying to "use the strength of the subject to
break through the fallacy of constitutive subjectivity," he intends this to
occur *not* by means of some more robust notion of subjectivity, if that is
understood—even logically—as imagining the nonidentical as "graspable"
(ND xx/6:10). With respect to any sort of grounding for cognition, he repeatedly points out that he "does not aim at another ontology," not even a
"nonontological" one (ND 136/6:140). Going that route "would be merely
positing another downright first," just this time "not absolute identity . . .
but nonidentity" (ND 136/6:140). Adorno instead insists that "the nonidentical is not to be obtained directly," nor "is it obtainable by a negation of the
negative" (ND 158/6:161).

---

121. I greatly expand this point in Martin Shuster, " 'Nothing to Know': Framing Adorno's
Moral Perfectionism" (unpublished manuscript).

122. For overviews of Adorno scholarship, see Hammer, *Adorno and the Political*, 5–8, and
Yvonne Sherratt, *Adorno's Positive Dialectic* (Cambridge: Cambridge University Press, 2002),
8–16.

I take Adorno's position to be that the nonidentical is the *result* of the friction between mind and world—it is a distinct way of being in the world. We might link the procedure intimately to a "concern for possibility, for the individual nature of things as being always *not yet*."[123] When an object proposes its utopian picture through either its own normative claims (say, what the Supreme Court *ought* to be according to its own standards, broadly speaking) or our reflective judgment about those claims (say, what I judge the Supreme Court *ought* to be in light of my subjective capacities in the face of its own standards, broadly speaking), we can judge how far the present state of affairs falls short of that utopian picture. This is why dialectics is ultimately "the ontology of the wrong state of things" (ND 11/6:22). Only in a fundamentally damaged world is dialectics necessary; only in such a world does the nonidentical exist. In this way, dialectics might begin with determinate negation (*bestimmte Negation*),[124] or it might begin with a somatic impulse bound to a reflective judgment. In either case, however, an object that lacked deficiency would not—even potentially—invite any dialectical speculation of that sort; dialectics would be unnecessary. The nonidentical is the chafing that arises when mind and world rub against each other.[125]

In such a case the procedure always begins with the object (taken in the expansive sense of section 2; that is, as opposed to the subject). It is the object that either proposes a determinate negation (through normative commitments proposed by the object's own standards) or produces a reflective judgment. (It is important to see that such judgments are anchored in the object in a way that regulative judgments are not—something *outside us*

123. Ståle Finke, "Between Ontology and Epistemology," in *Adorno: Key Concepts*, ed. Deborah Cook (Stocksfield, UK: Acumen, 2008), 91.

124. For an overview of this notion, see PS ¶79 and Jon Stewart, "Hegel's Doctrine of Determinate Negation: An Example from Sense-Certainty and Perception," *Idealistic Studies* 26, no. 1 (1996): 57–78. In Adorno's eyes, the debate between him and Hegel is whether such negation can terminate in anything positive (M 144). I return to this point in the next chapter.

125. Such mind/world phrasing invites dialogue with John McDowell. See Bernstein, *Adorno*; Bernstein, "Re-enchanting Nature," in *Reading McDowell: On Mind and World*, ed. Nicholas H. Smith (London: Routledge, 2002), 217–46; Bernstein, "Mimetic Rationality and Material Inference: Adorno and Brandom," *Revue Internationale de Philosophie* 58, no. 227 (2004): 7–25; Ståle Finke, "Concepts and Intuitions: Adorno After the Linguistic Turn," *Inquiry* 44 (2001): 171–200; Espen Hammer, "Minding the World: Adorno's Critique of Idealism," *Philosophy and Social Criticism* 26, no. 1 (2000): 71–92. For hesitations, see Roger Foster, *Adorno: The Recovery of Experience* (Albany: State University of New York Press, 2007), 167–95; Hammer, "Minding the World," 87; Jonathan Short, "Experience and Aura: Adorno, McDowell, and 'Second Nature,'" in *Adorno and the Need in Thinking: Critical Essays*, ed. Donald A. Burke et al. (Toronto: University of Toronto Press, 2007), 181–203.

necessitates the judgment, not the constitution of our reason.)[126] Ultimately, for Adorno, we are "to gain such perspectives without arbitrariness [*Willkür*] and violence [*Gewalt*], wholly from one's contact with objects—this alone is what matters to thinking" (MM 247/4:281; translation modified). The nonidentical emerges from the relation between subject and object (taken in broad terms), that is, from being in the world in a particular way. In this way, as I already hinted above (see section 6), the nonidentical forms the backdrop to moral action; the notions of "nonidentity" and "depth" are two sides of the same coin. This is what I take Adorno to suggest when he proposes that there is a "reciprocal criticism [*Reziproke Kritik*] of the universal and of the particular; identifying acts of judgment that judge whether the concept does justice to what it covers and whether the particular fulfills the concept—this is the medium of thinking about the nonidentity of particular and concept" (ND 146/6:149). Again, in the right state of things, dialectics would not exist: "The right state of things would be free of dialectics: neither a system nor a contradiction" (ND 11/6:22).

But such flashes of the nonidentical are always intimately connected to the needs they arise from. It is in this context that we should take Adorno's comments about any thinking of utopia. Such thinking ultimately "is entirely impossible, because it presupposes a standpoint removed, even if only by the most minuscule degree, from the sphere of the spell of being, whereas every possible cognition, *in order to become binding*, not only must first be wrested from what is, but for this very reason is itself stuck with the same disfiguration and neediness from which it intends to escape" (MM 247/4:281; translation modified and emphasis added).

Adorno's point is that *because* any such speculative surplus (i.e., any thought of utopia) is tied to the expression of suffering (see sections 7–9 above), then it is impossible to imagine such a speculative surplus arising *without* such concrete ties. And this point ought to be fairly plausible from our discussion of language and of forms of life: claims are tied to distinct needs and are meaningful only by virtue of the same. Now, here we might stress the other element of speculation that Adorno mentions—the element of speculative playfulness (LND 90–91). This would not be in tension with this account, for there would be no reason to call the results of such speculation *utopian*. To make them so would still require a need in the present moment. Sometimes dreams might just be dreams and play just play.

126. For how reflective judgments differ from other sorts of judgments in being so tied to the object, see Eckart Förster, *Kant's Final Synthesis* (Cambridge, MA: Harvard University Press, 2000), 8–9.

In this way Adorno's notion of the nonidentical is immediately moral (and this without suggesting that it is thereby not also epistemological). Insofar as the standpoint of redemption arises from the need to give suffering a voice, a need in the present world, Adorno's concerns are with *how* any such content arises. As he puts it,

> The need is what we think from, even where we disdain wishful thinking. The motor of the need is the effort that involves thought as action. The object of critique is not the need in thinking, but the relationship between the two. The need in thinking . . . however, demands its negation through thinking, it must disappear into thinking, if it is really supposed to be satisfied, and in this negation it continues to exist. (ND 408/6:399–400; translation modified)

Negative dialectics describes this movement: a flash of utopia (a pursuit of happiness, a desire for more, a somatic need) arises because of a particular way of being in the world (cf. Cavell's description of this friction as a "curb . . . we forever chafe against" [CHU 9]). Claims are lodged and suffering is registered. All such claims, however, modify one's being in the world; they alter the points of salience and trajectories of possible action. Since our world is not perfect, the process continues in "an infinite movement."[127] The more powerful the voice given to suffering, the more elaborate is the utopian picture, and the more we move away from our present world, threatening to leave it altogether. It is in this sense that we ought to understand Adorno's claim that "in philosophy we experience a shock: the deeper, the more vigorous its penetration, the greater our suspicion that philosophy removes us from things as they are" (ND 364/6:357). Similarly, Adorno suggests that "the more passionately thought seals itself off from its conditionality [*Bedingtsein*] for the sake of the unconditional [*Unbedingten*], the more unconsciously, and therefore the more disastrously, it falls toward the world" (MM 247/4:281; translation modified). The nonidentical reflects what Cavell says of the self, that it "is always attained, as well as *to be* attained" (CHU 12). It is in this sense that when pressed in lectures to make a list of cardinal virtues, Adorno responds that he "could think of nothing except for modesty" (PMP 169). Modesty—for no self is final. In this way moral conversion need not rely solely on the possibility of *deliberating* correctly, that is, on rational argument or didactic

127. Hent de Vries, *Minimal Theologies: Critiques of Secular Reason in Adorno and Levinas*, trans. Geoffrey Hale (Baltimore: Johns Hopkins University Press, 2005), 297.

instruction (although conversion is not prohibited by these routes). One's somatic standing is equally a feasible site for conversion. In fact, in that it does not rely on one's motivational makeup (say, intellectual background),[128] as much on one's embodied nature, conversion remains generally an open possibility (but keeping in mind the worries about this point at the end of section 7). In this way, particular moral possibilities can be understood as a "transition *to* deliberating correctly, not one effected *by* deliberating correctly; effecting the transition may need some non-rational alternation such as conversion."[129]

10. CONCLUSION: KANT AND FREEDOM

Given this picture of Adorno's mature project, we can return to our discussion from the previous chapter and tease out another essential piece of Adorno's engagement with Kant. In chapter 2 we saw that Kant *does* have a plausible rejoinder to the worries of the dialectic of enlightenment. But this rejoinder requires a rational theology. This, then, is the register in which Adorno's response to Kant is couched. Adorno's basic contention is that reconciliation with our present world is prohibited.[130] The discussion above (especially sections 6–8) ought to make it clear *why* he adopts this stance: reconciliation would forfeit any voice given to suffering (a necessary site for expression would be destroyed). It is in this context that we must understand the claim that "as long as the world is as it is, all pictures of reconciliation, peace, and quiet resemble the picture of death" (ND 381/6:374). (And note again the intermixing of an empirical assessment—how the world is—with a normative stance.) In refusing suffering a voice, the dialectic of enlightenment reigns supreme, agency is dissolved, and even death—arguably the last remaining site of expression available (as, say, *my* expressive death)— now becomes merely the death of a specimen.[131] This is the force of thought behind one of Adorno's most powerful passages:

128. For such phrasing, see Bernard Williams, "Internal and External Reasons," in *Moral Luck* (Cambridge: Cambridge University Press, 1981), 101–14.

129. John McDowell, "Might There Be External Reasons?" in *Mind, Value, and Reality* (Cambridge, MA: Harvard University Press, 1998), 107.

130. For a different reading, see Christoph Menke, "Critical Theory and Tragic Knowledge," in *Handbook of Critical Theory*, ed. David M. Rasmussen (Oxford: Blackwell, 1996), 78–119.

131. Lengthier discussions of death in *Negative Dialectics* are Bernstein, *Adorno*, 423–26; Espen Hammer, "Adorno and Extreme Evil," *Philosophy and Social Criticism* 26, no. 4 (2000): 75–93; and Michael Marder, "*Minima Patientia:* Reflections on the Subject of Suffering," *New German Critique* 33, no. 1 (2006): 66.

The feeling [*Gefühl*], which after Auschwitz bristles against [*sträubt*] any claim for the positivity of existence [*Positivität des Daseins*] as preachy yammering [*Salbadern*], as injustice [*Unrecht*] toward the victims, which balks, as a mockery [*Hohn*], at the thought of squeezing any kind of meaning, no matter how utterly depleted [*noch so ausgelaugter*], from their fate, has its objective moment [*objektives Moment*] after events in condemning the construction of a meaning to immanence, which radiates from an affirmatively posited transcendence. (ND 361/6:354; translation modified)

For Adorno, whatever positivity might be imputed to events retroactively, such events could *never redeem* the suffering of the individuals who underwent the horrors of the camps or any of the genocides that followed. (And with Kant's notion of the highest good, it must be stressed that no matter *how* bad events get in the present, they could always potentially be "redeemed" later, through the achievement of the highest good as the final end of creation.) This is what I take Adorno to mean by his claim that even in Kant, the great all-destroyer, "the ontological proof of the existence of God, which Kant himself subjected to withering criticism, continues to live on" (PMP 151).

One way to make this worry plausible is to see that, while the highest good as the final end of creation is fundamentally a social problem, and so can be achieved only by *humankind* (R 6:97–98), Kant also takes it that "the history of mankind can be seen, in the large, as the realization of Nature's secret plan" (8:27). This teleological core to history seems necessary to Kant's picture.[132] God and nature are linked in that the latter is a unified whole under the purview of the former (cf. chapter 2). It is in this context that Adorno claims that the "secret [*Geheimnis*] of Kant's philosophy is the unthinkability of despair [*Unausdenkbarkeit der Verzweiflung*]" (ND 385/6:378). One strategy that can be teased out of Adorno's writings, therefore, is the aim to pit Kant against Kant on this point. In the "World Spirit and Natural Section" model of *Negative Dialectics*, Adorno takes Hegel to task for conceiving of a historical progress where individuals are both subsumed under a universal and allegedly also understood only "through themselves" (ND 326/6:320; for a more nuanced discussion, see HF 49ff.). I take Adorno's argument against Kant to rely implicitly on a

132. See Robert S. Taylor, "Kant's Political Religion: The Transparency of Perpetual Peace and the Highest Good," *Review of Politics* 72 (2010): 9ff. For reasons that this may not be essential to Kant's mature picture, see Förster, *Kant's Final Synthesis*, 133ff.

similar move. Adorno's claim can be understood as the idea that Kant's notion of the highest good as the final end of creation in an ethical commonwealth (R 6:94ff.) is fundamentally in tension with the *Groundwork*'s formula of humanity, which demands that all human beings be treated as "an end and never as a means only" (G 4:429).[133] Such a suggestion requires significantly more force to be effective, since Kant claims it is problematic to treat individuals as "means *only*," not that it is problematic to treat individuals as means. The question, then, must be a question of *theodicy*: the point must be that the notion of God at the heart of the highest good is problematic insofar as God thereby violates "the dignity of the earlier age" when its unhappiness is used as a means to the happiness of a later one."[134]

And that line of thinking ultimately harks back to the issue of happiness raised earlier (see section 7 above). Kant argues in *The Metaphysics of Morals* that happiness cannot be a duty because duties cannot consist of "mere gifts" for which we are "indebted to nature" (MOM 6:386). In this way it might be said that "because happiness is not an unconditioned good, it is entirely consistent with God's benevolence and wisdom" that the "unhappiness of an earlier generation can be used to promote the happiness of a later one."[135] This cuts to the heart of the debate between Kant and Adorno. In the *Metaphysics of Morals*, Kant presents a rubric for what our duties as rational agents consist of, and these break down into duties of right and duties of virtue (the former can be enforced externally, while the latter are proposed internally because we are the sorts of agents we are). For Kant, the "supreme principle of the doctrine of virtue is to act in accordance with a maxim of *ends* that it can be a universal law for everyone to have" (MOM 6:395). He continues, pointing out that "a human being is an end for himself as well as for others, and *it is not enough* that he is not authorized to use either himself or others merely as means . . . *it is in itself his duty to make the human being as such his end*" (MOM 6:395; emphasis added). I take Kant's point to be that, given the *Groundwork*'s formula of humanity, there emerge certain ends that we *must* have by virtue of being an end ourselves—it is our duty to have such ends (MOM 6:394–95). And this is true because if there were no such ends, then "all ends would hold for practical reason only as means to other ends; and since there can be no action without an end, a *categorical* imperative would be impossible" (MOM

---

133. This objection has a long history, originating from Herder. See Allen W. Wood, *Kant's Ethical Thought* (Cambridge: Cambridge University Press, 1999), 389n4.

134. My understanding of Kant in what follows has been enriched by ibid., 390.

135. Ibid.

6:385). As Kant puts it, "This would do away with any doctrine of morals" (MOM 6:385). He suggests that there are two such ends, "one's own perfection and the happiness of others" (MOM 6:385). I ignore the latter for this discussion and instead note that, for Kant, the most basic element to one's own perfection must be what "can result from [one's] *deeds*, not in mere *gifts* . . . indebted to nature; for otherwise it would not be a duty" (MOM 6:386–87). Thus one's own happiness is eliminated as a necessary end (MOM 6:386), since what one "already wants unavoidably, of his own accord, does not come under the concept of duty" (MOM 6:386).

What I take Adorno (and Cavell and perhaps Mill) to suggest is twofold. First, at the very least, that Kant is mistaken about this *empirical* point and that this, then, has certain consequences for his ethical theory (and we must note that Kant's theory is in this respect not entirely a priori, but rather is wed to certain empirical theses).[136] If pursuits of happiness *can be extinguished* (see the discussion of section 8 above) and also define our ability to pursue even the sorts of moral ends that Kant himself envisions, then it may be that pursuits of happiness thereby fall within the scope of Kant's own theory. This would be a way of confronting him through his own premises and would perhaps then allow us simply to modify Kant's theory without further dispute. I have my doubts about this strategy, but I do not pursue *that* point because I take a second, deeper worry about the formula of humanity to emerge. Can respect for humanity be determined without reference to history or empirical facts? Even Kant already seems to suggest it cannot, in that empirical details bleed into the a priori theory. The worry is, as one commentator puts it, that "there is no such thing as a half-hearted Hegelianism."[137] That is, it is hard to see how "rational human freedom" can be understood without reference to history. This is the worry I take Adorno to express when he asks whether freedom "might not be essentially historic [*geschichtlichen Wesens*], and . . . *not just as a concept but in its experiential content [Erfahrungsgehalt]*" (ND 218/6:217; emphasis added). What does it mean to value *humanity*? Adorno puts this worry as the idea that Kant wants neither "to cede the idea of humanity to the existing society nor to vaporize it into a phantasm," as a concept that has no empirical instantiation (ND 258/6:256). It is in this sense that we might

136. This latter point is raised in ibid., 70ff.

137. Robert B. Pippin, "Kant's Theory of Value: On Allen Wood's '*Kant's Ethical Thought*,'" *Inquiry* 43, no. 2 (2000): 258. My second point is indebted to Pippin's discussion, especially 258ff. I have also greatly benefited from Nancy Sherman, *Making a Necessity of Virtue: Aristotle and Kant on Virtue* (Cambridge: Cambridge University Press, 1997).

take Adorno's injunction that "reality today is so overpowering that it calls for agility, flexibility and adaptation [*Anpassung*]—qualities that rule out action in accordance with principles. Kant's principles are predicated on a strong, stable self, something that no longer exists" (PMP 124; translation modified). The unfolding of rationality and the valuing of humanity is itself a historical project. Here we can see how this worry connects to the earlier questions raised about suffering: perhaps who (and what) comes to count as human is an evolving question. (We have seen this again and again with our discussion; especially see section 10 of chapter 1, Cavell's example at CR 468, and the worries expressed at sections 7 and 8 in this chapter.) And this seems to be a question that is fundamentally *empirical*, worked out over time. The task is to comprehend one's own moment in time.

This, however, raises fundamentally Hegelian questions about the nature of history, and especially about the relation between such a Hegelianism and the story I have told thus far. These worries particularly arise in light of the idea that the dialectic of enlightenment produces individuals who no longer are *expressive*, for whom language may be nothing; that is, we may be entering an administered world (and it is in this context that we should take Adorno's talk of "bourgeois coldness" in MM §1.6).[138] In this chapter I have suggested that impulses for something better might combat this threat. An important element of that project, however, is the availability of reflection. Reflection seems both constitutive of our present agency and (in addition to speculative impulses) an important possibility for any modification of our agency. As we saw earlier, Adorno speaks of the necessity of trusting "only in the ruthless power of reflection" (LND 107). But what might this mean when such a capacity for reflection is seemingly left largely to chance (see section 8 above)?

One way to sharpen this question is to take a step back from my broader argument. We seem to have bypassed one worry about the dialectic of enlightenment: we have a means for understanding ourselves as free individuals in that an alternative notion of freedom has been proposed (sections 2–9 above) and reasons have been advanced for rejecting Kant's rational theology as conceptually unsatisfactory (and as operating upon a mistaken view of agency—see section 2 and the present section). Nonetheless, it seems that part and parcel of our new notion, given its stress on "depth" and "expression," must be a concomitant desire to understand our *history*—how we came to be so situated, how we came to occupy the sort of being in the

---

138. On this notion, see Bernstein, *Adorno*, 410ff.

world that we do, not only personally, but also socially (not to mention economically and politically). Doing so would give our current being in the world a greater vivacity and would allow for more elaborate projects for expression and action. Furthermore, given how closely our understanding of ourselves is tied (but, again, not *reducible*) to our embodied, social existence (see especially sections 3 and 7 above), such a procedure already seems necessitated by the account developed thus far. I take Adorno to make an analogous point when he claims that "the individual who cultivates himself as an absolute and as the guarantor of depth, and who imagines that he can discover meaning in himself, is a mere abstraction, a mere illusion vis-à-vis the whole" (LND 107). We must come to reflect upon ourselves in order, ultimately, "not to be irrational and hence ephemeral or even false" (LND 102).

In response, I suggest that we might use the German philosophical tradition to help Adorno's theory here. Hegel is the philosopher of reflection par excellence, and if the procedure of the *Phenomenology* (as a reflective exercise in the genesis of our historically situated agency) could somehow be available to Adorno, then Hegel might be able to offer a valuable resource to the theory of freedom and agency being developed here.[139] Such a task requires understanding elements of the relation between Hegel and Adorno, a task I turn to in the next chapter.

---

139. For the idea that Hegel is intimately concerned with "reflection" (his criticisms of Fichte on the notion notwithstanding), see H3S 71ff.

CHAPTER FOUR

Reflections on Universal Reason:
Adorno, Hegel, and the Wounds of Spirit

1. INTRODUCTION

In the previous chapter it emerged that an elaboration of Adorno's notion of freedom relies on constitutive moral luck, what Adorno terms *"undeserved* happiness" (ND 41/6:51; emphasis added). By itself this need not be a problem, since it closely approximates what happens in late capitalism, where not only through genetic differences, but also through social and economic differences, agents start with widely varied affordances for action and reflection. Where a tension emerges is in Adorno's own account of the *necessity* of reflection. As he points out, "While this element of resistance yields the idea or the impulse, . . . *resistance must not only reflect on itself, if it is not to be irrational and hence ephemeral or even false, it must develop within a theoretical framework"* (LND 102; emphasis added; cf. ND 398/6:391).[1] At the same time, Adorno is clear that such reflection is not part of moral *action.* He makes this explicit with an example in his moral lectures, where he asks us to consider

> the moment when a refugee comes to your door and asks for shelter.
> What would be the consequence if you were to set the entire machinery
> of reflection in motion, instead of *simply acting* and telling yourself that
> here is a refugee who is about to be killed or handed over by some state

---

1. I am using reflection in a fairly narrow sense, as reflection on our normative commitments. The broader theme of reflection has been a constant theme for Adorno since even *Dialectic of Enlightenment;* on this point see especially Hauke Brunkhorst, "The Enlightenment of Rationality: Remarks on Horkheimer's and Adorno's *Dialectic of Enlightenment,"* *Constellations* 7 (2000): 133–40; Pierre-François Noppen, "Reflective Rationality and the Claim of *Dialectic of Enlightenment,"* *European Journal of Philosophy* (forthcoming): 11ff.

police in some country or other, and that your duty there is to hide and protect him—*and that every other consideration must be subordinated to this? If reason makes its entrance at this point then reason itself becomes irrational.* (PMP 97; emphasis added)

And this ought to be fairly plausible from the earlier discussion of addendum actions, moral and nonmoral (see sections 4–8 of chapter 3). The issue, then, is not that an account of freedom or moral action has not yet been given. We *do* have a way to navigate between the Scylla of Kant's rational theology and the Charybdis of the dialectic of enlightenment. The worry instead might be put as the idea that we might still languish on the isle of Ogygia, enchanted by the affordances around us but unable to reflect on them in any critical fashion, and thereby incapable of a robust understanding of ourselves and our freedom. It is in this sense that our actions, perhaps morally commendable, may yet come to be irrational. Talk of a "responsiveness to reasons as such" is apt here, that is, talk of grasping reasons as reasons,[2] and a suggestion of John Dewey's summarizes the desideratum plainly as the idea that "what was won in a more or less external and accidental manner must now be achieved and sustained by deliberate and intelligent endeavor."[3] I take Adorno to be after something similar.

One way to understand the task before us is to systematically develop the specific historical, social, economic, political, religious, cultural, and aesthetic dimensions of our contemporary form of life, especially its relation to and even proclivity toward the production of suffering. Adorno's own work on authoritarianism, the culture industry, fascist propaganda, anti-Semitism, and "education after Auschwitz" might play a crucial role in any such study and would have to be supplemented by a variety of other inquiries. As a frame of reference or model, we might point to Horkheimer and Adorno's original research plan into anti-Semitism, as outlined in the *Zeitschrift für Socialforschung*,[4] where they called for

a study of selected historical events (the First Crusade, the crushing of the Albigensian heresy, "Jew baiting" in 12th and 13th century England,

---

2. John McDowell, "Conceptual Capacities in Perception," in *Having the World in View: Essays on Kant, Hegel, and Sellars* (Cambridge, MA: Harvard University Press, 2009), 128ff.

3. John Dewey, *The Later Works, 1925–1953*, ed. Jo Ann Boydston (Carbondale: Southern Illinois University Press, 1988), 13:185. Adorno was sympathetic to Dewey; see LND 237–38.

4. On this program, see Rolf Wiggerhaus, *The Frankfurt School*, trans. Michael Robertson (Cambridge, MA: MIT Press, 1994), 275–77.

the Reformation, the French Revolution, and the German war of resistance against Napoleon) that would explore the link between attacks on
other social groups and attacks on Jews in each of these periods.[5]

Here, however, the scope and frame of reference would be remarkably expanded, centering on an even broader and fundamentally global framework.[6]
That would be one path, and one I consider a necessity.

That is not the path I pursue here, however, in part because of its required scope, but also because what I take to be equally necessary is a more
robust understanding of what it means to see our agency as historically
situated and realized. This is related to that project in that details of the former might become essential to the latter, but it is distinct in that the latter
can nonetheless be understood formally, as an elaboration of the picture of
agency sketched in the previous chapter. Understood in this (still general)
way, Hegel then might be taken to plug a hole in Adorno's own account.
For if Hegel's account, especially in the *Phenomenology of Spirit* (1807),
does anything, it presents ourselves as historically situated agents who can
then grasp ourselves as such—that is, seemingly exactly the desideratum
before us.

This suggestion is not without its worries, and the chief of these is that,
for all his praise of Hegel, Adorno seems equally antagonistic to him, especially Hegel's philosophy of history (see, e.g., the "World Spirit and Natural
History" model in *Negative Dialectics*). In this chapter, then, I pursue three
tasks. First, I present Hegel's philosophy as a means for supplementing a
desideratum that emerged with Adorno's conception of freedom. Second,
I do so while presenting a reading of Hegel that casts him as a thinker neither of teleology nor of totality. Hegel thereby does not succumb to criticisms (launched by Adorno himself) that his view of history is redemptive
or constitutes a theodicy. Third, I accomplish both these tasks while presenting a view of Hegel on agency that is compatible with Adorno's own,
especially the latter's stress on our embodied nature and sensibility. And I
accomplish all three of these tasks by focusing chiefly on Hegel's account
in the *Phenomenology of Spirit* (1807). To accomplish these goals, we have
to go deep into Hegel's text, especially with an eye toward what he took as

5. Quoted in James Schmidt, "Genocide and the Limits of Enlightenment: Horkheimer and
Adorno Revisited," in *Enlightenment and Genocide, Contradictions of Modernity*, ed. Bo Strath
(Brussels: Peter Lang, 2000), 96.

6. The only study I know of that comes anywhere near this scope is Mark Levene, *Genocide in the Age of the Nation State*, 4 vols. (London: I. B. Tauris, 2005).

his overarching goal in the text. Once that goal is understood, we can see whether Hegel achieves it and to what extent such an achievement fits with our present concerns. At the same time, owing to the massive project that is the *Phenomenology*, in many regards my account here must be somewhat programmatic and sketchy, incapable of dealing with the entirety of the text in the proper depth. The contours of such a sketch, however, should be enough to achieve these basic goals.

2. THE METHODOLOGY OF THE *PHENOMENOLOGY OF SPIRIT*

To understand Hegel's chief aspiration with the *Phenomenology*, it is essential to understand his method. And the method is most fully on display in the transitions between the *Phenomenology*'s various shapes, first of "consciousness" and then of "spirit." The transitions starkly reveal how these various shapes succumb to breakdown and how they allegedly lead to their subsequent shapes. In this way the transitions form the locus for judging claims about teleology and totality: if the transitions are somehow progressive, then the story about teleology and totality gains plausibility. I will come back this issue. For now I want to stress a more basic fact about the transitions. They reveal a breakdown, and one feature of all such breakdowns is that the failure always stems from the normative commitments a particular shape has proposed and the sorts of problems that emerge for it *because* of *those commitments*.[7] In light of such breakdowns (in light of determinate negation) there emerge new sets of commitments, and thereby new objects. The question, then, is in part about the status of these objects and about the sense in which they do or do not hang together.

Before getting into that question, owing to the abstract nature of the discussion, I will illustrate the point with an example from Hegel's text. Beginning with the opening of the *Phenomenology*, with "Sense Certainty," the shape under consideration proposes certainty of its object by means of immediate knowledge through the senses. This immediate knowledge is nothing more than knowledge of the *being* of the object, since anything more (say, any predicate) would make it somehow *mediate* (and also would void its certainty, since the predicate could be wrong). In Hegel's words, "In *ap*prehending the object, we must refrain from trying to *com*prehend it"

---

7. Cf. William Bristow, *Hegel and the Transformation of Philosophical Critique* (Oxford: Oxford University Press, 2007), 213–18, and Terry Pinkard, *Hegel's Phenomenology: The Sociality of Reason* (Cambridge: Cambridge University Press, 1996), 12–13.

(PS ¶91, 58/3:82). As Hegel demonstrates, the only way to "cash out" what such a proposal might mean (to achieve immediate sense certainty) is with the idea that there is no expressible difference between the object we are conscious of and our consciousness. To elaborate such claims, consciousness uses indexicals (e.g., this, here, now). Indexicals offer a means of making good on the hopes of consciousness: they give us a means for grasping an object in its *immediacy* and *entirety*. In this way "sense certainty appears to be the *truest* knowledge; for it has not as yet omitted anything from the object, but has the object before it in its perfect entirety" (PS §91, 58/3:82). Such a reliance on "this" or "here" or "now" begins to break down, however, since it must always be mediated by a specific context.[8] Not only does the content of "here" change for me (as I shift my vision from here to *here*), it also changes from me to you (not to mention him or her). In contextualizing, we already always mediate our alleged immediacy. As Hegel points out, "The self-preserving Now is . . . not immediate but mediated; for it is determined . . . *through* the fact that something else, namely, day and night, is *not*" (PS §96, 60/3:84). What is worse is that such mediation is unavoidable. *Anything* we say about the object will inevitably be mediated. Since the objects of sense certainty cannot *in any way* be described (not even described as indescribable, since that too would *somehow* mediate them), we find that sense certainty breaks down, given its own criterion (¶97 and ¶99). (This procedure is then repeated for two additional ways of understanding sense certainty, showing how they fail in similar ways.)

The conclusion of "Sense Certainty" is that our knowledge is already always somehow mediated, and the "Perception" chapter proposes a way of understanding such mediation, initially without the input of a subject. This too is shown to fail (as is the even more complex attempt in the "Force and Understanding" section), ultimately illustrating that *any* knowledge must account for the role of the subject in the production of that knowledge (i.e., the shift to *self*-consciousness). What is significant for our discussion is that in all such failures the concluding moment of any prior shape is maintained in the opening moment of the shape following it (as, for example, when "Perception" maintains the insight from "Sense Certainty" that all knowledge is mediated). In this way we can see that the shift or breakdown or

---

8. Cf. Willem DeVries, "Hegel on Reference and Knowledge," *Journal of the History of Philosophy* 26, no. 2 (2008): 297–307. For a different, transcendental reading, see Charles Taylor, "The Opening Arguments of the *Phenomenology*," in *Hegel: A Collection of Critical Essays*, ed. Alasdair MacIntyre (Garden City, NY: Doubleday, 1972).

dialectical transition is necessary, in that the claims of any particular shape break down *of their own accord*; but at the same time this transition is, in an important way, *forgotten* by the subsequent shape. So the shape involved in "Perception," although retaining the insights of "Sense Certainty," has no knowledge of how it attained those insights. Indeed, in a very deep sense it never did *attain* them, but only inherited them. The individual shapes of the *Phenomenology* have no *explicit* knowledge of each other. The analogy to our position as agents ought to be obvious. With our discussion in section 1 in mind, we might say that, formally, what is at stake in the discussion of this chapter is how we might *attain* the moral insight that we seem to have acquired already.

Keeping such a formal aspect of Hegel's method in mind allows us to stress another feature of the text. In following these shapes, *we* track the entire procedure; we pursue the same path as consciousness. Consciousness breaks down and begins upon another path, and so do we as we follow it. In doing this, however, we can do something that the shapes of consciousness are unable to do: we can grasp several shapes at once. Hegel thereby sets his readers this task: "In every case the result of an untrue mode of knowledge must not be allowed to run away into an empty nothing, but must necessarily be grasped as the nothing *of that from which it results*—a result which contains what was true in the preceding knowledge" (PS ¶87, 56/3:79–80). This entire procedure is famously characterized by Hegel as "the pathway of *doubt*, or more precisely as the way of despair" (PS ¶78, 49/3:72). In this context, the reference to doubt and despair has a dual significance. First, it describes the various breakdowns the shapes of consciousness succumb to. Second, it also describes us as the observer, since we witness these continuous breakdowns. If we simply observe them, following along with the experience of consciousness, then our experience is no different than that of consciousness. But if we instead attempt to hold on to each shape of consciousness as it breaks down and then attempt to consolidate the various shapes into some greater unity, then we produce an entirely *different* object. Hegel is explicit about this when he stresses that with *determinate* negation (a negation where one form collapses into another, as opposed to one form's merely following another), "a new form has thereby immediately arisen, and in the negation the transition is made through which the progress through the complete series of forms comes about of itself" (PS ¶79, 51/3:74). If we undertake this procedure, then "the series of configurations which consciousness runs through along its way is the varied history of the *education* [*Bildung*] of consciousness to the standpoint of Science" (¶78,

50/3:73; translation modified). In this sense, it truly is a *pathway* of doubt
or despair.[9] Through failure and despair, we are able to achieve something
the shapes of consciousness cannot: a path. It is up to us, however, to make
a path as opposed to just a series of steps, that is, to make this negation
determinate as opposed to contingent. It is up to us to undertake the experiment Hegel proposes: to try to keep the various shapes together *in light
of the transitions between them*. Because of the importance of this to the
success of the argument of the *Phenomenology*, Hegel laments, in response
to early reviews of the book, the way readers consistently missed or ignored
the transitions, which were, according to him, key to the whole project.[10]

Hegel claims we can attain insight into a *transition* between the shapes.
By holding them together in our consciousness, we retain the previous
shape, the breakdown, and the new shape. We can perceive a transition between them because the new shape retains elements of the old shape. It
is up to us to see what those elements are and how they came about by
retaining the path of the former shape in light of the new shape. For Hegel,
however, there is no fixed or established goal for *our* experiment. His claim
is more modest: there is no guarantee that this procedure will succeed (another way this truly is the pathway of doubt and despair). Rather, *if* the procedure succeeds, its success will be measured by something that originates
within the consciousness under observation (within the shapes we are ob-
serving). We can grasp this point if we remember that for Hegel as much as
for Adorno (on this point, see section 9 of chapter 3), there is a *restlessness*
to critique (dialectics just *is* restlessness, without implying that dialectics
cannot *come* to a rest).[11] Hegel puts this point a couple of ways:

> Consciousness is something that goes beyond limits, and since these
> limits are its own, it is something that goes beyond itself. (PS ¶80,
> 51/3:74).
>
> Thus consciousness suffers this violence at its own hands: it spoils
> its own limited satisfaction. When consciousness feels this violence,
> its anxiety may well make it retreat from the truth, and strive to hold

9. The best recent exposition of Hegel's approach is Bristow, *Hegel and the Transformation
of Philosophical Critique*.

10. See the letter to van Ghert, October 15, 1810, in Johannes Hoffmeister, ed., *Briefe von
und an Hegel* (Hamburg: Felix Meiner, 1952), 1:328–31.

11. Hegel's notion of "bad infinity" just confirms the idea of dialectics as restlessness,
for the "bad infinite" proposes an *artificial* end to dialectical inquiry (by positing an unconditioned), which then engenders an infinite regress. Cf. Pinkard, *Hegel's Naturalism*, 46.

on to what it is in danger of losing. But it can find no peace. (PS ¶80, 51/3:74–75)

The movement of the shapes is a *self-movement*. Hegel's gambit is that *our* procedure will be complete when the "last" shape under consideration (say, the "final" shape) *ceases moving of its own volition*. This is what he means in paragraph 80 when he points out that "the *goal* is as necessarily fixed for knowledge as the serial progression; it is the point where knowledge no longer needs to go beyond itself, where knowledge finds itself, where Notion corresponds to object and object to Notion" (PS 51/3:74). The process reaches completion when there is no further movement to be made by consciousness. We can see, then, how no teleological conclusion is presupposed—the only thing presupposed is that there *may* be a point at which self-movement ceases. Or there may not be. Hegel's sole claim is that *if* consciousness is to have what he terms "satisfaction," it is to be found only when consciousness cannot proceed further. In this sense there is no plan by which we match up our segments to some completed whole, determining where they fit and how. Rather, we observe the shapes in question, keeping them together through the course of the experiment. If we are lucky, the experiment ends. It is in this sense that Hegel characterizes the *Phenomenology* as a "self-completing skepticism" (*vollbringende Skeptizismus*) (PS ¶80). The pathway of despair will complete itself (or it will not). We cannot determine *before* undertaking such an experiment what will happen. Even *we* as the observers must bring into question *our* norms when we refuse to decide beforehand whether such a procedure can attain success; a willingness to observe is the expression of such openness.[12] It is in this sense that we should stress again that this is the alleged "*education of consciousness*" (¶78, 50/3:73; translation modified).

3. FROM THE *SCIENCE OF THE EXPERIENCE OF CONSCIOUSNESS* TO THE *PHENOMENOLOGY OF SPIRIT*

That said, however, a different worry about the *Phenomenology* arises, and this is the worry that is most central to our broader discussion of what the *goal* of the *Phenomenology* might be. One goal, obviously, is to see whether the "standpoint of Science" might be achieved (in more neutral, less "science-centered" parlance, to see what the aforementioned education

---

12. Cf. Bristow, *Hegel and the Transformation of Philosophical Critique*, 234–44.

amounts to). Taking this idea seriously, however, it becomes obvious that the goal of a "self-completing skepticism" is reached *midway* through Hegel's book. Indeed, as any careful reader of the text will notice, the *Phenomenology* reads like *two separate books*. In broad strokes, one half deals with consciousness (and is perhaps comparable to a peculiar sort of philosophy of mind), and the second half deals with history (and perhaps with something like an even more peculiar philosophy of history). This is so much so that one of the earliest commentators said the *Phenomenology*'s two halves consisted of a "transcendental-psychological deduction" and a "historical construction."[13] And the halves are seemingly split off by the transition to "Spirit."

In fact, we can clearly see that Hegel's statements in this chapter exactly match up to the criterion he had proposed in paragraph 80, that consciousness is to reach "the point where knowledge no longer needs to go beyond itself, where knowledge finds Itself, where Notion corresponds to object and object to Notion" (PS ¶80, 51/3:74). In the transitional chapter to "Spirit," "Individuality Which Takes Itself to Be Real in and for Itself" ("Die Individualität welche sich an und für sich reell ist"), he writes:

> With this Notion [the present one], self-consciousness has returned into itself out from both the opposed determinations that the category had for self-consciousness and from the opposed determinations in the relation of self-consciousness to the category, as observing and then as active self-consciousness. *Self-consciousness has the pure category itself for its object, or it is the category, which has become conscious of itself. The account [Rechnung] self-consciousness has with its previous forms is now closed; they lie behind it, in oblivion, and they no longer confront it as its given world, rather they develop themselves only through themselves as transparent moments.* (PS ¶395, 236–37/3:293; translation modified and emphasis added)

Hegel makes the same point explicitly several times in the opening lines of the "Individuality" chapter:

> Self-consciousness has now grasped the Notion of itself which, first, was only our Notion of it, namely that in the certainty of itself it is all reality; and end [*Zweck*] and essence [*Wesen*] are for it now the moving

---

13. Rudolf Haym, *Hegel und seine Zeit: Vorlesungen über Entstehung und Entwicklung, Wesen und Werth der Hegel'schen Philosophie* (Berlin: Rudolph Gaertner, 1857), 236.

permeation [*Durchdringung*] of the universal—of gifts and capabilities—
and of individuality. (¶394, 236/3:292; translation modified)

Since end [*Zweck*] and being-in-itself have proved to be the same
as *being-for-another* and *found reality*, truth and certainty no longer
separate themselves, whether the set end is taken as certainty of itself
and the realization for truth or whether the end is taken for truth and
the realization for certainty. To the contrary, essence [*Wesen*] and end
[*Zweck*] in and for itself is the certainty of immediate reality itself, the
permeation [*Durchdringung*] of itself and for-itself, the universal and the
individuality. (¶394, 236/3:292; translation modified)

We can see, then, that in a very deep sense some sort of conclusion has
been reached in this chapter—a certain account within the *Phenomenology*
has come to a close.[14] In epistemological terms, subject and object are mediately involved with each other, and following the section called "Virtue
and the Way of the World," the consciousness under discussion, and not just
we readers, realizes this point. Both we and the shape in question realize
that our world is spiritual, permeated by a "social space."[15] What then does
Hegel mean to accomplish with the second half of the book? What does the
transition to spirit accomplish? In this way, given that some sort of completion is reached in the "Individuality" section, the transition to spirit must
especially be explained. Now, one option might just be to deny any unity
to the *Phenomenology*,[16] but if this option is refused, then the function of
sections VI ("Spirit"), VII ("Religion"), and VIII ("Absolute Knowing") of
the *Phenomenology* must be disclosed. It is, then, a striking defect of Hegel
scholarship that this is one of the most neglected sections in the entire
book (with even the often maligned "Phrenology" section receiving more
attention).[17] Putting all this another way, since we know that the original

14. Cf. Jon Stewart, *The Unity of Hegel's "Phenomenology of Spirit": A Systematic Interpretation* (Evanston, IL: Northwestern University Press, 2000), 267. Stewart calls this section
the "absolute knowing of the Reason chapter."

15. For this term, see Pinkard, *Hegel's Phenomenology*, 7ff. Pinkard appropriates it from Jay
F. Rosenberg, *The Thinking Self* (Philadelphia: Temple University Press, 1986), 191ff.

16. See, e.g., Otto Pöggeler, "Die Komposition der '*Phänomenologie des Geistes*,'" in
Materialien zu Hegels "Phänomenologie des Geistes," ed. Dieter Henrich and Hans Friedrich
Fulda (Frankfurt am Main: Suhrkamp, 1973), and Pöggeler, *Hegels Idee einer Phänomenologie
des Geistes* (Munich: Karl Alber, 1993), 170–231.

17. I am aware of only three pieces dedicated to it: André Kaan, "L'honnêteté et l'imposture
dans la société civile (à propos du chapitre V.C. de la *Phénoménologie*: La règne animal de
l'esprit)," *Hegel Jahrbuch* (1971): 45–49; Gary Shapiro, "Notes on the Animal Kingdom of the
Spirit," in *The "Phenomenology of Spirit Reader*," ed. Jon Stewart (New York: State University

title of Hegel's book was the *Science of the Experience of Consciousness* (*Wissenschaft der Erfahrung des Bewusstseins*), determining the import of this section will help us understand how we ended up with the *Phenomenology of Spirit* (*Phänomenologie des Geistes*).[18]

4. SPIRIT

One way we can begin to address the issue is by seeing what Hegel himself took to be behind the "Individuality" transition to "Spirit." While doing this we can also look ahead to his later works in order to understand how Hegel understood the concept of "spirit" (*Geist*), and therefore what might have been at stake in changing the *Science of the Experience of Consciousness* to the *Phenomenology of Spirit*. Beginning with the former point, if we turn back to paragraph 395, we can see that while Hegel does believe self-consciousness has somehow "closed" the account with its previous shapes, the account is still considered deficient because the shapes "fall apart within . . . consciousness as a *movement* of distinct moments which have not yet been integrated [*zusammenfaßen*] into their substantial unity. In *all* of these moments, however, self-consciousness clings to the simple unity of being and self which is its genus [*Gattung*]" (PS ¶395, 237/3:293; translation modified). Before I analyze this sentence in greater detail, I will quote the next paragraph at length, since it is essential to any understanding of what is going on here. There, in paragraph 396, Hegel writes this:

> Consciousness hereby has thrown away all opposition and every condition of its action; it starts afresh from itself and not from another, but solely of itself. Since individuality is in its own self an actuality, the material of its actions [*Wirkens*] and the end [*Zweck*] of its actions [*Tuns*] is in the action itself. Action [*Tun*] has, hence, the appearance of the movement of a circle, which moves freely in its own self in a void, unhindered,

---

of New York Press, 1998); Donald Phillip Verene, "Hegel's Spiritual Zoo and the Modern Condition," *Owl of Minerva* 25 (1994): 235–40.

18. There are many interesting historical details about the composition of the book, and also a reconstruction of the importance of this section, in Eckart Förster, "Hegels 'Entdeckungsreisen': Entstehung und Aufbau der '*Phänomenologie des Geistes*,'" in *Hegels "Phänomenologie des Geistes": Ein kooperativer Kommentar zu einem Schlüsselwerk der Moderne*, ed. Klaus Vieweg and Wolfgang Welsch (Frankfurt am Main: Suhrkamp, 2008), 37–57; Förster, *The Twenty-Five Years of Philosophy: A Systematic Reconstruction* (Cambridge, MA: Harvard University Press, 2012), 301ff. Förster's reconstruction is invaluable, and I am greatly indebted to it. Förster also clearly and importantly shows how Hegel's method is indebted to Goethe's experiments and methodology.

now extended, now constricted, and plays perfectly contently only in and with itself. The element, wherein individuality displays its shape, has the significance of a pure gathering [*Aufnehmen*] of this shape; it is actually the day when consciousness wants to show itself. Action [*Tun*] changes nothing and goes against nothing; it is the pure form of a translation [*Übersetzen*] from not-being-seen to being-seen, and the content, which is brought forth and which displays itself, is none other than what this action already is in itself. It is in itself: this is its form as a thought unity, and it is actual, this is its form as an existent [*seiende*] unity; it [action] itself is content only in this determination of simplicity against the determination of its change and its movement. (PS ¶396, 237/3:293; translation modified)

Many issues are compacted into these two paragraphs,[19] but I will focus on two. First, it is crucial to realize that, in some as yet to be determined sense, Hegel sees this chapter as a sort of "new beginning." He is explicit about this in several places, most clearly with his claim that consciousness "starts afresh." (Incidentally, this point allows us to make sense of the peculiar beginning to the "Spirit" section of the *Phenomenology*: a beginning that takes us *back* in time to ancient Greece.) At the same time, any talk of a "new beginning," again suggests the presence of *some* sort of completion (something *from which* we can begin anew). Second, in paragraph 395, Hegel also points out that the impetus for such a new beginning is the fact that a yet higher level of unity might still be achieved. (This is what I take to be the import of his claim that the moments the *Phenomenology* has thus far presented "have not been integrated into their substantial unity.") This higher unity, however, raises questions not only about what such a unity can mean, but about what it can mean in the *context* of the *Phenomenology*. It is also the wedge by which we can feel the teleology creeping back in. Are we not assuming that there *is* such a unity? Addressing these concerns requires understanding, at least in broad sketch—what Hegel means by "spirit."

In this regard it is useful to look ahead to Hegel's *Encyclopedia of the Philosophical Sciences* (*Enzyklopädie der philosophischen Wissenschaften*

19. One is the way it centers on action; cf. Jean Hyppolite, *Genesis and Structure of Hegel's "Phenomenology of Spirit"* (Evanston, IL: Northwestern University Press, 1979), 296. For a reconstruction of Hegel's philosophy of action, see Michael Quante, *Hegel's Concept of Action*, trans. Dean Moyar (Cambridge: Cambridge University Press, 2004). See also Robert A. Pippin, *Hegel's Practical Philosophy: Rational Agency as Ethical Life* (Cambridge: Cambridge University Press, 2008).

im Grundrisse) (1817). There, in the *Philosophy of Spirit*, Hegel writes that
"the essential, but formally essential, feature of spirit is freedom" (E §382,
15/10:25). In the Addition (*Zusatz*), Hegel elaborates by pointing out that
"the substance of spirit is freedom, i.e., the absence of dependence of an
other, the relating of self to self" (E §382, 15/10:26). He presents a similar
point in the *Phenomenology* when he writes, "Reason is Spirit when its
certainty of being all reality is raised to truth, and it is conscious of itself as
its own world and of the world as itself" (PS ¶438, 262/3:324; translation
modified). I take these sorts of claims by Hegel to be asserting that not only
does "spirit" denote a sort of self-relation (albeit one that, as the master/
slave dialectic section of the *Phenomenology* makes clear,[20] presupposes
an other), but "spirit" also describes a condition in which one is manifestly
aware of such a relation, taking it as mediately structuring one's experience.
On such a view, "spirit" is not meant to denote a *redemption* of the entirety
of one's world, but rather a basis for attempting to understand it as constituted in social space (a space that, I hasten to add, can be warped through
a variety of means, from market forces in late capitalism to the dialectic of
enlightenment). In understanding the spiritual nature of our world, we do
not posit some object, "spirit," that is out there; rather, we acknowledge
how far this world is *our* world. To return to the *Phenomenology*, in "Individuality Which Takes Itself to Be Real in and for Itself," consciousness
has grasped this point: it has seen that its own activity anchors the mediate
distinction between subject and object, and it has grasped itself as grasping
this point.

In light of this, it is important to stress that "spirit" is an achievement.[21]
In the *Philosophy of Subjective Spirit*, Hegel writes this:

> If we ask what spirit is, the immediate answer is that it is this motion,
> this process of proceeding forth from, of freeing itself from nature; this
> is the being, the substance of spirit itself. Spirit is usually spoken of as
> subject, as doing something, and apart from what it does, as this mo-
> tion, this process, as still particularized, its activity being more or less

20. For more on this section and this point, see Robert A. Pippin, *Hegel on Self-
Consciousness: Desire and Death in the "Phenomenology of Spirit"* (Princeton, NJ: Princeton
University Press, 2011).

21. Cf. Terry Pinkard, *Hegel's Naturalism: Mind, Nature, and the Final Ends of Life* (Ox-
ford: Oxford University Press, 2012), 194ff.; Robert A. Pippin, "Naturalness and Mindedness:
Hegel's Compatibilism," *European Journal of Philosophy* 7, no. 2 (1999): 194–212; and Pippin,
"What Is the Question for Which Hegel's Theory of Recognition Is the Answer?" *European
Journal of Philosophy* 8, no. 2 (2000): 155–72.

contingent; it is of the very nature of spirit to be this absolute liveliness, this process, to proceed forth from naturality, immediacy, to sublate, to quit its naturality, and to come to itself, and to free itself, it being itself only as it comes to itself as such a product of itself; its actuality being merely that it has made itself into what it is.[22]

While there are many threads to pull here,[23] the one I want to tease out is how far spirit takes itself to be "a product of itself." I take the implication to be that the spirit relation is fundamentally a *historical* process. If this is the case, then it may be plausible, retrospectively, to see how the various pieces in the process hang together. But this need not imply that they were taken to do so before such a retrospective procedure, *or* that they will continue to hang together in the same way in the future, with additional "links" continually being added to the conceptual chain. This suggestion has a direct bearing on reading the *Phenomenology*, since this is exactly the feature that Hegel highlights as distinguishing the second half of the book from the first. He points out: "These shapes [the shapes discussed in the "Spirit" section], however, distinguish themselves from the previous ones in that they are real spirits, proper actualities [*eigentliche Wirklichkeiten*], and instead of being shapes merely of consciousness, they are shapes of a world" (PS ¶441, 265/3:326; translation modified). A "shape of a world," in turn, according to Hegel, is "the *ethical life* of a nation [*Volk*], insofar as it is the *immediate* [*unmittelbare*] *truth*; the individual, that is a world" (PS ¶441, 265/326).[24]

Hegel's claims here, then, are as much about our agency as about the backdrop to that agency. The chief claim is that our agency *exactly is* the way we navigate any such historical backdrop, that is, social space. Shapes of spirit (or "shapes of a world") are *not* a *worldview* (a "mere *Weltanschauung*") through or by means of which one sees the world. A "shape of spirit" *just is* the world in the sense that "a shape of spirit forms the attunements in terms of which those distinctions between subject and object are drawn in the first place."[25] And "attunement" here should be understood exactly

---

22. G. W. F. Hegel, *Hegels Philosophie des subjektiven Geistes/Hegel's Philosophy of Subjective Spirit*, trans. Michael Petry (Dordrecht: Riedel, 1978), 1:7.

23. Especially Hegel's philosophy of nature; see Sebastian Rand, "The Importance and Relevance of Hegel's Philosophy of Nature," *Review of Metaphysics* 61, no. 2 (2007): 379.

24. This need not imply racism or nationalism; cf. Terry Pinkard, *Hegel: A Biography* (Cambridge: Cambridge University Press, 2001), 176.

25. Terry Pinkard, "What Is a Shape of Spirit?" in *"The Phenomenology of Spirit": A Critical Guide*, ed. Dean Moyar and Michael Quante (Cambridge: Cambridge University Press, 2008), 114.

in the sense that Cavell gives to Wittgenstein's notion of "*Übereinstim-mung*" (CR 31ff.). In this sense it is as apt to use Wittgenstein's notion of "form of life" here as it was for Adorno (see section 3 of chapter 3). For Hegel, as for Adorno, a "form of life," or a "shape of spirit," is the "whirl of organism" that makes up our world.[26] Hegel, like Wittgenstein after him (and I would add, though in a different way, Adorno), is interested in the ways and moments when such reasons give out, when reasons come to an end—when "our spade is turned." For Hegel, these might be claims like, "We fight because he is the king" or "I am a sister and I cannot thereby do that." Meaning, then, is neither mere interpretation nor entirely capricious or nonexistent; it is tied to concrete practices.[27] As Wittgenstein puts it, "giving grounds, however, justifying the evidence, comes to an end;—but the end is not certain propositions striking us immediately as true, i.e. it is not a kind of *seeing* on our part; it is our *acting*, which lies at the bottom of a language-game."[28]

The significance of such a comparison for the second half of the *Phenomenology* can be brought out by something Cavell says about Wittgenstein. In "The Argument of the Ordinary," Cavell writes, "It is exactly as important to Wittgenstein to trace the disappointment with and repudiation of criteria . . . as to trace our attunements in them" (CHU 92). The same is true of Hegel. The entire project of the *Phenomenology* from the "Spirit" section onward is to trace our history, to trace the ways various shapes of spirit break down, collapse, and ultimately fail. Only in looking at such shapes of spirit do we present an account that is ours. (And for Hegel this admittedly means "Western," although he did famously—and unsuccessfully—try to present an account of "World Spirit." The project failed, however, because of Hegel's clear lack of an equally intimate understanding about cultures besides the European, not because of any immediately obvious limitation in the method.)[29]

26. Stanley Cavell, "The Availability of Wittgenstein's Later Philosophy," in *Must We Mean What We Say?* (Cambridge, MA: Harvard University Press, 2002), 52.

27. Neither a "super rigid machine" nor a completely individual affair—see John McDowell, "Wittgenstein on Following a Rule," in *Mind, Value, and Reality* (Cambridge: Cambridge University Press, 1998).

28. Ludwig Wittgenstein, *On Certainty* (New York: Harper and Row, 1969), ¶204, 28. See also Jonathan Lear, "Transcendental Anthropology," in *Open Minded: Working Out the Logic of the Soul* (Cambridge, MA: Harvard University Press, 1998), 280.

29. Terry Pinkard, *Hegel's Naturalism: Mind, Nature, and the Final Ends of Life* (Oxford: Oxford University Press, 2012), 194–95.

Hegel's goal is to map out how we might understand ourselves to have come to be who we are, not just as a particular consciousness (no longer just a "science of the experience of *consciousness*"), but rather as a *concrete* consciousness permeated by a shape of spirit. In this sense the first half of the book (the formerly titled *Science of the Experience of Consciousness*) shows the various options, failures, and progressions in conceptualizing the subject/object divide, while the second half (in every regard the distinguishing feature of the "Phenomenology of *Spirit*") shows something similar, but with shapes of spirit, as opposed merely to the consciousness of subject and object. In this way, then, the necessity of reflection is already implicit in Hegel's account at the conclusion of the "Individuality" section. Furthermore, what Hegel realizes with the dawning of the necessity of the second half is that shapes of consciousness are already always part of a more fundamental shape, namely, a "shape of spirit."[30] (In Wittgensteinian terms, we can think of a "shape of spirit" exactly as *bedrock*.) Hegel makes this explicit when he writes: "Spirit is the substance and the universal, constant, equal only to itself essence [*sichselbstgleiche Wesen*]—it is the unshakeable and indissoluble *ground* and *point of origin* for the action of all and it is their *purpose* and *goal* as the *in-itself* of all self-consciousness as rendered into thought" (PS ¶439, 264/3:325; translation modified). Hegel then adds: "This substance is by the same token the universal work, which produces itself through the *action* of all as their unity [*Einheit*] and parity [*Gleicheit*], for this substance is *being-for-itself*, the self, the action" (PS ¶439, 264/3:325; translation modified). Hegel's project in the second half, then, is to reconstruct the historical experience of such a self-education of *spirit* while keeping open the possibility of reaching a sort of conclusion to such a procedure (the idea of a "self-completing skepticism" is not abandoned here).

In this way, paragraph 28 of the preface to the *Phenomenology* is a crucial passage. There Hegel points out that "the task of leading the individual from his uneducated [*ungebildeten*] standpoint up to and into knowledge [*Wissen*] had to be grasped in its universal sense, and the universal individual, the self-conscious spirit, had to be examined in its formation [*Bildung*]" (PS ¶28, 16/3:31; translation modified). The crucial question is what cultural education can amount to "in its universal sense." Again, one easy way to make sense of this idea in Hegel is by stressing an analogy to Wittgenstein.

---

30. Cf. Pinkard, "What Is a Shape of Spirit?" 114.

In a remarkable passage in the *Philosophical Investigations*, Wittgenstein asks, "If the formation of concepts allows itself to be explained by facts of nature, should we not be interested, not in grammar, but rather in that in nature which is the basis of grammar?" (PI 230e). Wittgenstein answers that while we should be interested in the correspondence between concepts and "very general facts of nature" (facts like we die, we breathe, we have sex, we must eat and drink, sleep, and so forth), our interest cannot "fall back upon these possible causes of the formation of concepts" (PI 230e). This is because "we are not doing natural science; nor yet natural history—since we can also invent natural history for our purposes" (PI 230e). Wittgenstein continues::

> I am not saying: if such-and-such facts of nature were different people would have different concepts (in the sense of a hypothesis). But: if any-one believes that certain concepts are absolutely the correct ones, and that having different ones would mean not realizing something that we realize—then let him imagine certain very general facts of nature to be different from what we are used to, and the formation of concepts dif-ferent from the usual ones will become intelligible to him. *Compare a concept with a style of painting. For is even our style of painting ar-bitrary? Can we choose one at pleasure? (The Egyptian, for instance).* (PI 230e; emphasis added)

Stressing this train of thought in the *Investigations* allows us to see Hegel as exactly affirming the possibility of the procedure Wittgenstein de-scribes. In looking at our concepts, at the ways they have changed, evolved, and failed, we can see how they have been informed by history (taking stock of our "natural history") and how they have been informed by and them-selves informed our various institutions, whether social, political, scientific, religious, or artistic (to name just a few). Furthermore, and most controver-sially, Hegel's idea is that we can examine such a story about our concepts and our various complex normative claims *in order to* derive certain con-clusions from that story about how and why various failures occurred, ulti-mately situating these various claims amid each other. Wittgenstein never undertakes such a procedure, opting instead just to test particular failures of criteria so as to draw our attention to the historical nature of our agency (and thereby our philosophical problems), but Hegel undertakes the more ambitious task of trying to do that while telling a broader story about our-selves. The second half of the *Phenomenology* is this project. In turn, this is what Hegel has in mind with the idea that knowledge must be grasped in its "universal sense" and that in doing so we understand "the universal individual, the self-conscious spirit . . . in its formation." I take Hegel to suggest this view of things explicitly when he suggests in paragraph 28, a particularly colorful passage, that

> the particular individual is incomplete spirit, a concrete shape in whose whole existence *one* determinateness is dominant and other determinations are present only in blurred ways. In any spirit that stands higher [*höher*] than another, the lower concrete existence [*Dasein*] has been reduced to an inconspicuous [*unscheinbaren*] moment; what was most at stake is now only a trace [*was vorher die Sache selbst war, ist nur noch eine Spur*]; its shape has been covered over and has become a mere shade [*Schattierung*]. The individual whose substance is spirit standing at the higher level runs through this past in the way that a person who takes up a higher science goes through preparatory studies that he has long ago internalized in order to make present their content; he calls them to mind without having his interest linger upon them. Every individual must also run through the content, through the education level of universal spirit [*Bildungsstufen des allgemeinen Geistes*]. Such an individual, however, runs through them as shapes that spirit has already laid aside, as levels on a path that has been worked out and smoothed; so we see in fragments of knowledge that what in earlier ages engaged the men of ripened spirit has been reduced to the level of facts, exercises, and even games for children, and in this pedagogical progression we recognize the history of the formation [*Bildung*] of the world traced in silhouette. This past existence is already the acquired possession [*erworbenes Eigentum*] of universal spirit; it forms the substance of the individual and hence appears to him as his external, inorganic nature. In this respect education [*Bildung*], regarded from the side of the individual, consists in acquiring [*erwerbe*] what is before him, living off [*zehre*] his inorganic nature and seizing it for his possession [*Besitz*]. Regarded from the side of universal spirit as substance, this is nothing other than its giving itself self-consciousness, its coming-to-be and its reflection into itself. (PS ¶28, 16–17/3:32–33; translation modified)

The purpose of the second half of the book, then, is to allow for the intellectual possession, in reflection, of what is already implicitly ours: our spiritual landscape. As Hegel puts it, consciousness turns "to itself, because the overcoming of alienation is none other than the return to self-consciousness, in its individual world and present time, discovering it as its possession

[*Eigentum*]" (PS ¶803, 488/3:586; translation modified). Furthermore, in doing so we not only acquire it, but also *seem to actualize it*, in that the second half *concludes*, and thereby somehow *also closes*, the narrative in the way the first half did. Allegedly, and this is how the teleology story starts, as the shapes of spirit progress, their perspective gets closer to our own perspective as readers. As Hegel puts the point in paragraph 805, ultimately in such absolute knowledge, "spirit has concluded the movement in which it has shaped itself" (PS 490/3:588). Likewise, "when it has done this, it will have taken the first step to climb down [*herabsteigen*] from the *intellectual world*, or in fact it will have spiritualized [*begeisten*] the abstract element of this intellectual world with the actual self" (PS ¶803, 488/3:586; translation modified). In this way the movement of the shapes of spirit ceases of its own volition (the second half's "spiritual" version of the "self-completing skepticism" of the entire book), and the shape of spirit under consideration (at the end of the *Phenomenology*) is recognized to be the same as the shape of spirit of the reader.[31] Hegel confirms this point in the "new" "Absolute Knowledge" section when he writes that "the movement of producing the form of its knowledge of itself is the work that spirit achieves as *actual history*" (PS ¶803, 488/3:586; translation modified).

Such a progression is essential to understanding Hegel's often cited, often puzzling, and often maligned remark in the preface: "In my view, which must be justified only in an exhibition of the system itself, everything depends on grasping and expressing the true, not only as *substance*, but equally as *subject*" (PS ¶17, 9–10/3:22–23; translation modified). Grasping the progression of spirit as substance means understanding that spirit is exactly the immediate backdrop to all our actions (i.e., a form of life), while grasping the progression as subject means understanding that all such forms of life *just are* us and our actions understood as concrete historical actualizations, held together by what, with Cavell, we can call a "whirl of organism." What Hegel realizes with the necessity of the *Phenomenology of Spirit* is that the *Science of the Experience of Consciousness* is at best a manual of how potential cognition might work. It is, however, a rubric: it is not obvious how it is to apply to us as concrete agents; but even were we to find that it applies, it would do so only accidentally. Hegel realizes that a full account of our agency requires a historical ("spiritual") dimension, and that without a proper accounting of this aspect of our agency (and the stress must be *our* agency, as opposed to our *agency*), we have a sort of dogmatism,

---

31. Cf. David M. Parry, *Hegel's Phenomenology of the "We"* (New York: Peter Lang, 1988), 227–28.

or at the very least a lack of critical reflection. In other words, Hegel's realization centers on the importance of a procedure exactly like the sort I have claimed Adorno requires (see section 1 above). A mere formal project (as in the *Science of the Experience of Consciousness*) cannot be the whole story, since nothing has been concretely grasped. This is what I take Hegel to mean when he writes, "But the actuality of this simple whole consists in those various shapes and forms *which have become* its moments, and which will now develop and take shape afresh, this time in their new element, in their newly acquired meaning" (PS ¶12, 7/3:19; emphasis added). Hegel's argument is that to truly understand ourselves as the *actual* agents we are, we must undertake such a spiritual procedure or a phenomenology of *spirit*. Indeed, without this latter procedure, ultimately we cannot even properly ground the first half, since *The Science of the Experience of Consciousness*, is a compendium of formal moves *abstracted* from a spiritual landscape. Hegel makes this point explicit: "All previous shapes of consciousness are abstract forms of spirit. They result from Spirit analyzing itself, distinguishing its moments, and dwelling for a while with each. This isolating of those moments *presupposes* Spirit itself and subsists therein; in other words, the isolation exists only in Spirit which is a concrete existence" (PS ¶440, 264/3:325).

In this way Hegel's account, with its stress on "education," provides a plausible model of understanding how we come to be the sorts of agents we are. In this way, in seeming anticipation of the problem that has emerged for us in this chapter, Hegel writes that, without the second half, the standpoint of science would "lack universal intelligibility" and would give "the appearance of being the esoteric possession of a few individuals" (PS ¶13, 7/3:19–20).

5. UNIVERSAL REASON AND FORGIVENESS

Given this gloss on the "Individuality" section as providing a transition to a way of concretizing our agency and of viewing the different moments of that agency as somehow interconnected, it is striking how far Adorno himself *agrees* with such a picture. For example, in *Negative Dialectics* he points out that

> *universal history must be construed and denied.* After past catastrophes and in view of future ones, the assertion that an all-encompassing world-plan for the better manifests itself in history would be cynical. This however is *not* a reason to *deny* the unity that welds together the

discontinuous, chaotically splintered moments and phases of history—
that of the control of nature, progressing into domination over human
beings and finally over inner nature. No universal history leads from
savagery to humanity [*Humanität*], but there is one indeed, from the
slingshot to the megaton bomb. It ends in the total threat of organized
humanity against organized human beings, in the epitome of discon-
tinuity. *Hegel is thereby verified by the horror and stood on his head.*
(ND 320/6:314; translation modified and emphasis added)

Here it seems obvious that Adorno is *not* opposed to the procedure I
have sketched in the last section, but rather is opposed to drawing any positive conclusions from it (and this already ought to have been obvious since
Adorno's own procedure, notably in *Dialectic of Enlightenment*, relies on a
similar stance toward history). His objection, instead, is about the *redeeming power* that any such account might come to have: how far it seems to
mollify or somehow make acceptable the breakdown of the earlier accounts.
Indeed, in the passage above Adorno clearly seems to think that such an account constructs a history of (human) horror. It is therefore possible, even
according to Adorno, to construct *some* version of an account that critically
links the pieces of our history together.

Nonetheless, worries about the redemptive features of Hegel's account
certainly seem justified given Hegel's own talk of completion and "overcoming of alienation" (PS ¶803). In response, I want to make two points.
First, we have good evidence that, certainly by the 1820s, Hegel was dis-
abused of such thoughts. The lectures on art seem to demonstrate that he
was quite aware not only of the contradictions of modern life, but also of
its fragmentation, not to mention its irrationality.[32] In the lectures Hegel
plainly points out that "spiritual culture, the modern intellect, produces
this opposition in man which makes him an amphibious animal, because
he now has to live in two worlds which contradict one another. The result
is that now consciousness wanders about in this contradiction, and, driven
from one side to the other, *cannot find satisfaction for itself in either the
one or the other*" (LA 1:54). Second, however, even within the *Phenomenology*, no redemptive story is necessary. With the *Phenomenology*, there is
equally good reason to think that any such redemptive move is barred.

That point can begin to be demonstrated if we take stock of what happens in the *Phenomenology* after the "Individuality" section. At the most

---

32. Cf. Pinkard, *Hegel's Naturalism*, 174ff.; Benjamin Rutter, *Hegel on the Modern Arts*
(Cambridge: Cambridge University Press, 2010).

basic level of description, the *Phenomenology* proceeds to examine the evolution of *our own particular* spiritual landscape. Hegel moves through various periods of history, showing how various normative commitments at distinct points in time broke down and led to new sets of such commitments (from Greece to Rome to the French Revolution, and so on). In examining such various forms of giving and taking reasons, Hegel is not suggesting that one shape *had* to follow another, only that one shape *can be seen* as arising because of a deficiency in a preceding one. In other words, he wants to tell a story about how we came to be the sorts of agents we are, not about how we were fated or destined or determined to become these sorts of agents. And in telling this story Hegel reveals how certain "shapes of spirit" had self-defeating commitments (but again, such commitments do not somehow historically *necessitate* collapse, only rationally exhibit it—in the way I may continue to insist, out of stubbornness, that my particular behavior was right even though to a neutral observer it is obvious that it was wrong). Furthermore, in telling this story Hegel also wants to argue that our understanding of ourselves as moderns and as free agents is explicitly tied to such a story. Who we are as agents is best explained by such a spiritual structure, as opposed to anything like a metaphysical or biological fact of the matter or any sort of transcendental argument about our abstract faculties.[33]

And putting things this way seems to raise again Adorno's charge and the specters of teleology, totality, and theodicy (the last need not imply any overt religious stance).[34] Hegel's structure allegedly swallows up particular individuality or prohibits a genuine elaboration of difference[35] and so is ultimately implausible (one might marshal figures as diverse as Foucault or Rorty) or simply a joke.[36] Answering these questions one by one is far beyond my scope here.[37] Instead, I suggest that if we examine Hegel's actual transition to "Absolute Knowledge," we realize that all such claims

33. Cf. Robert A. Pippin, *Modernism as a Philosophical Problem: On the Dissatisfaction of European High Culture*, 2nd ed. (Oxford: Blackwell, 1999); Pippin, *Hegel's Practical Philosophy*.

34. On the parenthetical, cf. Richard J. Bernstein, *Radical Evil: A Philosophical Interrogation* (Cambridge: Polity Press, 2002), 46–76.

35. Among others, see Gilles Deleuze, *Difference and Repetition*, trans. Paul Patton (New York: Columbia University Press, 1994).

36. Cf. Søren Kierkegaard, *The Kierkegaard Reader*, trans. Jonathan Rèe and Jane Chamberlain (London: Blackwell, 2001), 18.

37. For accounts that tackle this challenge, see Pinkard, *Hegel's Phenomenology*, 331–43; Pippin, *Modernism as a Philosophical Problem*, 160–79; Jon Stewart, *The Hegel Myths and Legends* (Evanston, IL: Northwestern University Press, 1996); and Allen W. Wood, *Hegel's Ethical Thought* (Cambridge: Cambridge University Press, 1990), 36–77, 92–93.

are dubious. And that is because the transition to "Absolute Knowledge" is radically different from all the other transitions in the *Phenomenology*. Indeed, it is ultimately no transition at all and is left that way intentionally.

To see this, we can pick up the thread of Hegel's dialectical progression in the last section of the "Morality" chapter of the *Phenomenology* (itself the last chapter of the "Spirit" section), since this offers the surest route to understanding Hegel's notion of absolute knowledge. In the beginning of this section we find consciousness with a new notion: conscience. In an earlier section, "The Moral View of the World" (¶¶599–616), Hegel elaborated a view in which the natural world was enlivened by the moral world. For this earlier shape, the world possessed a teleological moral order where every natural occurrence carried with it a moral standing. In a by now familiar story Hegel showed, through the reemergence of the natural world, how such a shape experienced a breakdown when it found itself continually unable to divorce its human rationality from its human desires and impulses. This failure, in turn, prompted the emergence of a view of the world akin to Kant's highest good, where human desires and impulses are acknowledged while being incorporated into an overarching moral order. Any such proposal, however, according to Hegel, is merely a restatement of the problem, not a solution to it. Hegel makes this point in *The Encyclopedia Logic*:

> If this contradiction seems to be palliated by transferring the Idea into *time*, into a future where the Idea also *is*, [we must say that] any such sensible condition, as time, is really the opposite of a solution of the contradiction; and the representation of the understanding that corresponds to this, i.e., the *infinite progress*, is simply nothing but the contradiction itself posited as forever recurring. (E §60, 105/8:143)

Keeping this point in mind,[38] what occurs with the shape termed "conscience" is a sketch of the various dialectical reactions to the problems of the earlier section on morality.[39] In response to those failures, conscience ultimately organizes itself around its potential for negativity, chiefly its ability to take itself as an object. Furthermore, this shape rejects the earlier idea that the object of morality is to be found somehow "outside itself" (PS ¶632, 383/3:464). This shape, rather, strives to mediate between the universal aspirations of morality (say, the giving of universal reasons) and

---

38. A more elaborate and accessible critique of Kantian morality can be found in PR §§129–40. Cf. Wood, *Hegel's Ethical Thought*, 154–74.

39. Cf. Dean Moyar, *Hegel's Conscience* (Oxford: Oxford University Press, 2011), 64–66.

the particular desires implicit to his own person (say, concrete agency), and all without reference to anything outside itself. The former point is worth stressing: in this model, conscience is not mere whim, if that is taken to be action without reason; rather, conscience is a distinct form of giving reasons, where one's reasons are the same as one's desires or passions. Action, then, serves as the expression of this unity (as opposed to, e.g., the manifestation of some inner particularity into an external universality—and this picture ought to be somewhat familiar from the discussion of section 4 in chapter 3). This is what I take Hegel to mean when he writes that in such a case "action is thus only the translation of its individual content into the objective element, in which it is universal and recognized, and it is just the fact that it is recognized that makes the deed a reality" (PS ¶640, 388/3:470).

To lay out Hegel's proposal in this section all at once, according to Hegel all such deeds will require recognition for their actuality. In order to "translate" a deed in this way, it must be understood by someone apart from its originator as this deed instead of that deed. Mutual recognition will serve as the glue holding together any such translation or expression. For this reason, recognition is Hegel's central theme. To see why this is true, we can follow Hegel's presentation of the dialectic between inner and outer. The shape in question is confronted with a certain problem of knowledge: its relation to universal moral duty may be immediate (it knows that this is moral) and thereby one of immediate knowledge, but its relation to its action is not immediate. Every action is a complex amalgam of contingencies, which not only precludes any sort of comprehensive knowledge before the act, but also precludes any comparable knowledge of eventual consequences. Hegel puts the point this way:

> In so far as this knowing has in it the moment of *universality*, conscientious action requires that the actual case before it should be viewed unrestrictedly in all its bearings, and therefore that all the circumstances of the case should be accurately known and taken into consideration. But this knowing, since it *knows* the universality as a *moment*, is at the same time aware that it does not know all the circumstances, or, in other words, that it does not act conscientiously. (PS ¶642, 389/3:471)

This lack of knowledge does not prove fatal in this case, however, since the shape in question can simply convince itself that it *does* possess comprehensive knowledge because the knowledge it possesses is still entirely its "own," not belonging to or originating from or through anyone or anything else (PS ¶642). On such a proposal, it is not the empirical contingencies of a particular action that are important, but rather the self-generated (albeit allegedly universal) convictions behind it. Nonetheless, such a retreat is in reality no solution, since even on this rubric, consciousness ultimately requires action to give such conviction concrete instantiation: consciousness ultimately *must* choose between various empirical possibilities (and inaction too is such a choice). And so there is a potential regress here. As Hegel describes this scenario, "conscience knows that it has to choose between them, and to make a decision; for none of them, in its specific character or in its content, is absolute; only pure duty is that" (PS ¶643, 390/3:472). In such a case, paralleling the earlier dialectic of "Sense Certainty" (see section 2 above), the shape in question ends unable to choose anything because it cannot rely on universal reason to make a choice, since such "universality" or "purity" exactly precludes (or at the very least does not mandate) any *particular* empirical duty (PS ¶643). Owing to this predicament, consciousness falls back on its own impulses and inclinations in order to carry out its actions. As Hegel states, in such a case "as a determination and content," it "is the *natural* consciousness, i.e., impulses and inclinations" (PS ¶643, 390/3:472–73). Such a reliance on impulse, however, raises a question about the ultimate relation of such impulses to anything universal or moral. Not only does this raise again a view of ourselves where a wedge is driven between impulses and desires on the one hand and reasons on the other, but such content also appears to be little more than "caprice" (*Willkür*), and the consciousness in question realizes this. Hegel is clear about this when he points out that in such a case "*every* content . . . stands on the same level as any other" (PS ¶645, 392/3:474; emphasis added).

If we take this point seriously, then with this shape the consciousness in question appears bound by nothing: it no longer happens to be giving *reasons*. It is mere whim. In this way, not only is consciousness not bound to any particular content, but, perhaps more important, consciousness seems not even to be bound to its own natural inclinations, since it can take a negative relation even to them (e.g., I do not eat the ice cream even though I want to). The shape that is conscience, then, is *equally free* from reasons and from desires. Formally, then, such caprice is *exactly* in conformity with universal duty, since it fundamentally cannot be tied to any particular content. As Hegel points out, "This *self-determination* is therefore immediately the simple conformity with duty. Duty is knowledge itself; this simple selfhood is nothing but the in-itself, for the *in-itself* is the pure self-identity, and this is in this consciousness" (PS ¶646, 393/3:476; translation modified). Consciousness acts. And that's it.

Once consciousness acts, however, its action enters social space, where it is inevitably subject to the assessments of others. As Hegel points out, by recognizing the action in a particular way, others take the consciousness to have given "being to a specific content; others hold to this *being* as this Spirit's truth, and are therein certain of this Spirit; it has declared therein *what* it holds to be duty" (PS ¶648, 394/3:477). The potential for two distinct perspectives on the *same* action emerges, and these two perspectives might not ever overlap. The shape of conscience might try to retain an element of privacy by refusing any particular ascription to *its* action. This is so much the case that conscience may use such alleged privacy to undermine any judgment about its actions: conscience will claim that what *really* matters is the intent, which is fundamentally inaccessible to others. In this way a possibility emerges where consciousness takes whatever it introduces into social space and displaces or dissembles it (PS ¶648, 394/3:477). According to Hegel, language, or the formal communication of one's intentions (and hence the very possibility of their publicity), reveals this state of affairs (¶653). This is what I take him to be after when he writes that language mediated "between independent and acknowledged self-consciousness . . . is the true actuality of the act, and the validating of the action" (PS ¶655, 396/3:479). What I take Hegel to be arguing here is *not* that language is somehow *inherently* problematic because it is, for example, a fleeting medium and thereby unstable,[40] but rather that recognition functions in light of a dependence on the medium of language (PS ¶650–54), which requires for its functioning that all be masters (cf. CR 166ff.).[41] On this view, language allegedly delineates the bounds of recognition while also highlighting the possibilities for the failure of the same. (And since there is always a normative surplus within language,[42] this need not imply that the limits of my language are the limits of my world; in this sense Hegel's view of language has significant overlap with the view of language I attributed to Adorno in the previous chapter.)

The problem that surrounds recognition emerges here because of the way the public nature of action and the seemingly private nature of intentions are connected through language. Language is malleable in that words

40. As in Drew Milne, "The Beautiful Soul: From Hegel to Beckett," *Diacritics* 32, no. 1 (2002): 63–82.

41. Cf. Ludwig Siep, *Anerkennung als Prinzip der praktischen Philosophie: Untersuchungen zu Hegels Jenaer Philosophie des Geistes* (Freiburg: Alber, 1979), 129–30.

42. Cf. Pinkard, "What Is a Shape of Spirit?" 125.

gain a meaning only mediately. On one hand consciousness, either because of its own caprice or because of the estimation of another, cannot garner any sort of recognition for its inner being (recognition by another). On the other hand, again because of its capricious nature, consciousness may not be able to determine *for itself* what it has done in light of the estimations of others (self-recognition). The common theme between these worries is that the shape in question cannot manifest its inner being into a lasting outer being without others. Whether consciousness cannot find itself in a particular description or cannot find a particular description for itself, consciousness cannot, in a deep sense, *be* something, or more accurately, *someone*. In Hegel's terminology, consciousness "lacks the power to externalize itself, the power to make itself into a Thing, and to endure being" (PS ¶658, 399–400/3:483). In light of this, consciousness attempts to understand itself without the need for such a possibility; this is precisely what Hegel calls the beautiful soul.[43] He writes:

> The beautiful soul lives in fear [*Angst*] of staining the glory of its insides [*Innern*] by action and existence [*Dasein*]; and in order to retain the purity of its heart, it flees from contact with reality and persists in its self-willed powerlessness to renounce its self, which is reduced to the extreme of ultimate abstraction, and to give itself a substantial existence, or to transform its thought into being and put its trust in the absolute difference [between thought and action]. (PS ¶658, 400/3:483–84; translation modified)

The shape of the beautiful soul will ultimately be untenable. We can begin to see this by realizing that, in an important sense, it is exactly *not a position*, since it cannot occupy any position within social space. Hegel captures this point with a striking image: "In this transparent purity of its moments, it is an unhappy, so-called *beautiful soul*, whose light slowly fades, and who vanishes like a formless vapor dissolving into thin air" (PS ¶658, 400/3:484; translation modified). Because the beautiful soul cannot recognize *itself* as occupying a social space, or be recognized by another, the beautiful soul "vanishes like a formless vapor dissolving into thin air."

43. For an overview of this figure, see H. S. Harris, *Hegel's Ladder* (Indianapolis, IN: Hackett, 1997), 2:467–520; Robert Norton, *The Beautiful Soul: Aesthetic Morality in the Eighteenth Century* (Ithaca, NY: Cornell University Press, 1995); and Allen Speight, *Hegel, Literature, and the Problem of Agency* (Cambridge: Cambridge University Press, 2001), 94–121.

Given such a shape of *spirit*, we can ask how the relation between two such consciousnesses might play out (PS ¶659, 400/3:484). Here the two consciousnesses are alike in that they both have the universal aspirations of morality but nonetheless maintain complete subjective sovereignty over what counts as satisfying that universal. Hegel's point is that when one of the two consciousnesses acts, the other will judge its actions, claiming to be judging them according to a universal standard. As Hegel puts it, "For the consciousness which holds firmly to duty, the first consciousness counts as *evil*, because of the disparity between its *inner being* and the universal" (PS ¶660, 401/3:485). Nonetheless, at the same time, the (now) so-called evil consciousness will claim also to be acting according to the universal (for that is how *any* action gains any concrete standing, where this means essentially that any action is *public*—allegedly universal insofar as it can be understood by everyone). So this consciousness is judged both evil and hypocritical (PS ¶660). At the same time, however, Hegel points out that *this* judgment itself can *ultimately* be justified only by caprice, for the judging consciousness also *does not have access* to the universal *unless* it actualizes its judgment in an *act*, but that exactly will be to make it public, and thereby susceptible to disagreement on the part of evil consciousness. Hegel makes this clear when he claims that "in denouncing hypocrisy as base, vile, and so on, it is appealing in such judgment to its *own* law, just as the evil consciousness appeals to *its* law" (PS ¶663, 402/3:487). Furthermore, in doing so—in judging the consciousness evil—it grants it standing within social space; it "legitimizes it" (PS ¶663, 402/3:487). And this would be true even if the two consciousnesses "*agreed*," that is, if the former judged the latter as "good" instead of "evil." Hegel's point is about the status of norms and the phenomenology of action in light of normativity, and I take the value terms to be used merely for effect. Any judging on the part of one consciousness can be a real judgment only if it is actualized in an act, but any such act requires the other's recognition for its ultimate universal standing and actualization (these form the worries Hegel expresses in paragraph 664 about the beautiful soul's inactivity). Such a recognition, however, could be granted only if the evil consciousness is taken to be capable of granting such recognition, that is, as universal (PS ¶663). Yet this is exactly what the judging consciousness refuses to do, lest it give up *its own* particularity, which it cannot do. (Again, even if it judged the first consciousness as "good" instead of "evil," doing so would mean ceding *its standing as an agent*.) This is the issue Hegel summarizes with the idea that "no man is a hero to his valet":

No action can escape such judgment, for duty for duty's sake, this pure purpose, is not actual. It becomes actual in what individuality does, and as a result, the action has the aspect of particularity in itself. No man is a hero to his valet; not, however, because the man is not a hero, but because the latter—is a valet, a person with whom the man deals not as a hero, but as one who eats, drinks, and wears clothes, i.e., the valet, in general, deals with him in the individuality of his needs and views. Thus, for that kind of judgment, there is no action in which the side of the particularity of individuality cannot be opposed to the side of the universality of action—there is no action in which it cannot play the part of the moral valet toward the actor. (PS ¶665, 404/3:449; translation modified)

In this way hypocrisy comes to be the defining feature of *both* subjectivities. But this just amounts to the point that both subjectivities cannot relinquish being subjectivities, and that both of them are embodying the basic issues surrounding self-determination.

Hegel reinforces this point and attempts to show a path beyond it by suggesting what might happen if one of the consciousnesses realizes its predicament. For this reason Hegel suggests that, in the beautiful soul's judgment and implicit legitimizing of the evil consciousness, the latter recognizes its ultimate "parity with" (*Gleicheit*) the beautiful soul and comes to "an intuition [*Anschauung*] of itself in this other consciousness" (PS ¶664, 403/487).[44] Because the beautiful soul is the mirror image of the evil consciousness, the latter sees—*intuits*—itself in the former (PS ¶665–66). Hegel dramatically elaborates the way this encounter plays out:

He [the "evil" consciousness] intuits [*anschauend*] this parity [*Gleich-heit*], *articulates* it, *confesses* it to the other consciousness, and anticipates that just as much, the other, who indeed had made the two of them equal [*gleich*], will also reciprocate [*erwidern*] his *speech*, and will

44. The use of "intuit" is significant here, and it has been highlighted by Pinkard, "What Is a Shape of Spirit?" 126–29; J. M. Bernstein, "Confession and Forgiveness: Hegel's Poetics of Action," in *Beyond Representation: Philosophy and Poetic Imagination*, ed. Richard Eldridge (Cambridge: Cambridge University Press, 1996), 44. Other discussions include Speight, *Hegel, Literature, and the Problem of Agency*, 117–21; Robert Williams, *Recognition: Fichte and Hegel on the Other* (Buffalo: State University of New York Press, 1992), 206–21; J. M. Bernstein, "Conscience and Transgression: The Persistence of Misrecognition," *Bulletin of the Hegel Society of Great Britain* 29 (1994): 55–70; and Moyar, *Hegel's Conscience*, 166.

also articulate his parity and that ultimately the being of recognition [*anerkennende Dasein*] will arrive. (PS ¶666, 405/3:489–490; translation modified)

Unfortunately, the beautiful soul does not reciprocate this speech. Instead, it maintains a "hard heart" [*harte Herz*], and as a result "the situation is reversed" (PS ¶667, 405/3:490). The beautiful soul retains, in the face of this confession, what Hegel calls a "noncommunicative being-in-itself" [*nicht mitteilendes Fürsichsein*]. Such stubbornness, however, involves the beautiful soul in a contradiction. It can acquire genuine content only through social standing, yet it denies any such possibility by repudiating the other; the beautiful soul denies the conditions of its own possibility. The sort of privacy the beautiful soul imagines simply does not, indeed cannot, exist. This is what I take Hegel to suggest when he claims that the beautiful soul "reveals itself as a consciousness which is forsaken by and which itself denies spirit" (PS ¶667, 406/3:491). The best the beautiful soul can achieve is a negative relationship with the other—what Hegel, in paragraph 668 calls a "spiritless unity of being" (*geistlose Einheit des Seins*). Its sole and defining act is to deny the other. Such an existence drives it to "the point of madness," where it "wastes itself in yearning and pines away in consumption" (PS ¶668, 407/3:491).

In a possible glimmer of hope, however, Hegel points out that the model for reconciliation is "already contained in the foregoing" (PS ¶669, 407/3:491–92). In fact, the model just *is* the action of the evil consciousness. The beautiful soul need only follow suit and renounce its own "being-for-itself" (PS ¶670). It performs such a deed by *intuiting itself* in the evil consciousness (PS ¶670). Hegel points out, somewhat anticlimactically, maybe even unconvincingly, that

the forgiveness [*Verziehung*] it extends to the first [the evil consciousness] is the renunciation [*Verzichtleistung*] of itself, of its *nonactual* essence [*unwirkliches Wesen*], an essence it equated with the *actual* action of the other, and it recognizes as good what it had in thought determined to be bad, namely action. (PS ¶670, 407–8/3:492; translation modified)

This, then, is "absolute spirit" (PS ¶670). In turn, it may be unconvincing exactly in that it appears once again to reaffirm all the worries that opened the discussion of this section. After all, Hegel even explicitly states that "the wounds of the spirit heal and leave no scars behind" (PS ¶669,

407/3:492). Adorno's worries seem to materialize straight out of the vapor in which the beautiful soul languished. "Parity" seems to be achieved all too easily.[45]

This is not an idle worry, but neither is it a fatal one. In response, I want to stress Hegel's use of "intuit" (*anschauen*). The deployment of this term suggests that any reconciliation, and thereby redemption, occurs not because of universal reason, or any logically or teleologically required progression, but rather solely because of a distinct *sensibility*.[46] Forgiveness, and thereby *any transition* to Absolute Knowledge,[47] is a process that cannot be captured or mapped by any economy of sufficient conditions (although it does require the necessary condition of language). The intuition involved in forgiveness is a sort of *immediacy*, albeit one, as the course of the *Phenomenology* demonstrates, that is reached by a complex process of mediation. In this sense it is perfectly in line with Hegel's standard critique of immediacy (as of, e.g., Jacobi's "faith"). As Hegel points out in *The Encyclopedia Logic*, "Not only does the immediacy of knowing *not* exclude its mediation in all of these cases, but they are so far connected that the immediate knowing is even the product and result of the mediated knowing" (E §66, 115/8:156; emphasis added). Attempting to retain itself as the sole conception and arbiter of reality (PS ¶671), each of these consciousnesses can proceed only by renouncing itself before the other. Hegel makes this point explicit, writing that "each self, *for itself*, sublates [*aufheben*] itself in itself through the contradiction of its pure universality, which at the same time strives against and separates itself from its parity with the other" (PS ¶671, 409/3:494; translation modified). And Absolute Knowledge just is this process. This is what I take Hegel to mean when he writes: "Absolute spirit steps into existence *only* at the peak where its pure knowledge of itself is the opposition and the variation of itself with itself" (PS ¶671, 408/3:493; translation modified). In this way, since it is exactly *not* a historical moment, "Absolute Spirit" is fundamentally distinct from the other moments in the

---

45. Cf. Bernstein, *Radical Evil*, 46–76.

46. Albeit one that is *informed* by conceptuality—cf. Pinkard, "What Is a Shape of Spirit?" 126–29.

47. I realize that the transition to "Absolute Knowledge" does not occur immediately after this section, but only after the "Religion" section. My reading, which I cannot defend in detail here, is that the "Religion" section traverses the same dialectical ground that the "Spirit" section presented, except this time from the "pictorial" thinking of religion. In this sense, "Absolute Knowing" is already *formally* arrived at here, with the "Religion" section contributing further *content* but not adding anything formally to the account at the end of the "Morality" section. For an overview of Hegel's conception of the relation between "Spirit," "Religion," and "Art" (as the three parts of "Absolute Spirit"), see LA 1:101–5.

Phenomenology.[48] So forgiveness is "exceptional and extraordinary," interrupting "the ordinary course of historical temporality."[49]

We can return to our broader issue of the redemptive power of Hegel's dialectic if we turn to something Adorno says about Hegel in his lectures:

> Instead of concluding that what we have is a state of non-reconciliation, he behaves a little like a senior church official or a judge, at any rate like some high-up bureaucrat or other, who sees only the limited outlook of the lower orders who are unable to recognize the higher meaning in all of this. He is not deterred in this by the consideration that it is unreasonable to ask the victim, the individual who has to put up with the consequences, to find comfort in the circumstance that the irreconcilable principle of the way of the world should govern his own private fate. (HF 42)

My suggestion, however, is exactly the opposite. Hegel is just as sensitive to this issue as Adorno is, and he recognizes, certainly by the 1820s, but seemingly also as early as the *Phenomenology*, that modern life may simply be irreconcilable—it may be impossible to "redeem" all the moments of spirit (although it may be possible, as Adorno himself admits, to see them as interconnected). Indeed, here Hegel seems exactly to *exhibit* the dignity and importance of the other[50] and firmly opposes any sort of *easily* achieved parity. For Hegel, for spirit to exist, the self in question must "empty" itself before the other. In theorizing forgiveness in this way, Hegel is not outlining the forgiveness of any *particular* action; he is dialectically sketching what it might mean to be a modern agent at all.[51] The two consciousnesses see in each other the possibility and capability of denying themselves by denying the other, and thereby denying their own *concreteness*. Cavell makes an analogous point when he writes that

48. Cf. Fredric Jameson, *The Hegel Variations: On the "Phenomenology of Spirit"* (London: Verso, 2010), 131.

49. Jacques Derrida, *On Cosmopolitanism and Forgiveness*, trans. Michael Hughes and Mark Dooley (London: Routledge, 2001), 31–32. Where Hegel and Derrida differ is that Derrida refuses forgiveness any "normative" or "normalizing" role (31), where for Hegel forgiveness can serve this function (although it cannot *originate* in the same).

50. This is so true that one might draw a connection to Levinas on this point; cf. Robert Bernasconi, "Hegel and Levinas: The Possibility of Forgiveness and Reconciliation," *Archivio di Filosofia* 1, no. 3 (1986): 325–46.

51. Cf. Bernstein, "Conscience and Transgression," 67.

it is nothing, as it were . . . that causes what we can perhaps call . . .
forgiveness . . . and the absence of any sufficient expiation or recom-
pense . . . seems the point . . . as if nothing but *a recognition of common
humanity is sufficient to achieve this virtue, as if each instance of forgiveness constitutes in small a forgiveness for being human, a forgiveness of the human race.* (CHU 120; emphasis added)[52]

6. CONCLUSION

In conclusion, I must stress above all that Hegel is not committed to some
sort of historical teleology where one historical event follows from another.
His procedure is retrospective and looks *back* at history, reconstructing
the ways earlier shapes of spirit ("social spaces") failed. These failures,
however, are connected not causally, but philosophically. In this way such
"philosophical history is concerned not with what caused one form of life
to supplant another (what caused Rome to supplant Greece) but with the
ways in which what a later form of life takes to be authoritative for itself
can be understood only in terms of how it came to see the accounts given
by earlier forms of life as insufficient."[53] Hegel's account is not predictive,
nor is it teleological.

More important to our discussion, the standpoint of Absolute Knowing[54]
is not guaranteed and thereby is not necessarily redemptive. The transition
from "Morality" implies no necessity, and movement forward occurs *only*
by virtue of an *intuition*, that is, a somatic response. In this way Hegel's
argumentative thrust in the *Phenomenology* falters, and even the "philosophical" connectivity of the two moments of "Morality" breaks down; the
transition from "Morality" thus is unlike any of the other transitions in the
Phenomenology. In fact, it is not really a transition but is more a sketch of
a possible one.

Now, perhaps Adorno was nonetheless right, and Hegel still held on to
the redeeming power of reason. Indeed, because Hegel *does* ultimately write
a section called "Absolute Knowing," maybe he was convinced that it could
and would be achieved. I claim, however, that Hegel's philosophy need not
suggest its achievement, or require it. In fact, it may be a feature of modern life, as Hegel seemed to think later, that perhaps "now consciousness
wanders about in this contradiction, and, driven from one side to the other,

52. Jay Bernstein draws the same analogy with Cavell in "Confession and Forgiveness," 63.
53. Pinkard, *Hegel's Phenomenology*, 333.
54. In this context, see note 47 above.

cannot find satisfaction for itself in either the one or the other" (LA 1:54). Or perhaps, more hopefully but equally opposed to complete redemption, any such satisfaction is fleeting, undermined from moment to moment, perpetually yet to be achieved. As Hegel puts it, perhaps "freedom and satisfaction remain *restricted*" and "opposition and contradiction always break out again afresh, and satisfaction does not get beyond being relative" (LA 1:99). Whatever the case, Hegel's account need not imply that all human actions after or even up to the writing of the *Phenomenology* may be dialectically worked into a redemptive story (i.e., that all is ultimately—at least potentially—forgivable). On this point, then, Hegel and Adorno are in agreement.

Instead, with Hegel we can stress that looking at history this way may be beneficial to understanding the commitments we find ourselves with; furthermore, it may serve a therapeutic and then even critical function by allowing us to realize that our "rigidified institutions, the relations of production, are not Being as such, but even in their omnipotence are man-made and revocable" (CM 156).[55] Therapy, however, is not exorcism, nor is analysis theodicy. In this way Hegel's method might allow us to deepen our understanding of ourselves, which, with Adorno, we can see as deepening and expressing our freedom. But such depth does not redeem or actualize that freedom; it only makes our happiness less undeserved. And we can say all this without in any way denying any part of Adorno's critical stance or in any way curbing or dampening his deepest ethical sensitivities and aspirations. In fact, it is striking how both Hegel and Adorno agree that however we do move forward, that movement will be a factor as much of our conceptual capacities as of our somatic intuitions.

---

55. For such a reading of Hegel, see especially Axel Honneth, *Pathologies of Reason: On the Legacy of Critical Theory* (New York: Columbia University Press, 2009), 44–45.

MODEL

Conclusion

A salient feature of the previous two chapters is the idea that the notion of freedom that Adorno endorses is perpetually incomplete, in danger, as much a task as an achievement. Part of such freedom and agency is a capacity for reflection, the possibility of taking one's reasons *as* reasons,[1] with the requisite possibility that what we have taken as a reason was not a reason after all. We might express two related worries about the horizon of the modern world for such reflection, and both revolve around the fact that reflection is, perhaps for the first time, now genuinely possible for large masses of people. (In part this is surely the instantiation of Aristotle's and Hegel's observation that philosophy requires "leisure," but in part it is just that reflection emerges as a serious possibility insofar as various forms of authority have faded or disappeared.) The first worry focuses on the material conditions of our world, especially late capitalism and the social, political, and economic arrangements it fosters. Here the problem is that, just as during Aristotle's time, it appears that for some people to have the leisure necessary for reflection, others have to exist under conditions of poverty, slavery, or domination. Although I have not particularly dealt with this worry, one could imagine a different book, one that explores Adorno's numerous sociological and theoretical texts on late capitalism in order to present a striking picture of this fact. That book would have much more to say about this issue (presumably in dialogue with a variety of other political and economic thought). I have opted to focus on a second worry, the idea that even when conditions are conducive to it, reflection either simply does not occur or, even more perniciously, occurs uncritically. As Adorno puts it

---

1. For a compact discussion of this point, see John McDowell, "Autonomy and Its Burdens," *Harvard Review of Philosophy* 17 (2010): 1–15.

in a slightly different context, even our "free time" appears to be "shackled to its contrary" (CM 167).

This latter worry requires some clarification, which is also a good way to situate Adorno within a strand of contemporary philosophy. Contemporary thinkers have evinced a robust interest in Kantian and post-Kantian philosophy, with Kant, Fichte, Hegel, Nietzsche, and Heidegger (among others) having their day. Adorno has largely remained absent from this renewed interest in German philosophy.[2] One way to see why this is unfortunate is to take up contemporary discussions about the space of reasons. A variety of options are on the table at present. Notably, for many there just is no genuine space of reasons, and suggesting that there is, is just telling, as Rorty might say, a "Whiggish" story that is better understood as the history of power, natural science, or chance (or some combination of these). An alternative option is to suggest that there is a genuine space of reasons, best understood as a space where "in making a claim, one undertakes the conditional task responsibility to demonstrate one's entitlement to the claim, if that entitlement is brought into question."[3] On such a view, in a severely condensed sketch, the space of reasons amounts to an intersubjective space where commitments and entitlements are to be hashed out. For some claims I might hold the necessary entitlements, but for others I might only get the entitlement from someone else; similarly for other persons. The issue with this view of things is that it is a mystery how *any* of the agents involved *get* their authority (and it cannot be that they get it from others, for then certainly there appears to be a regress). After all, what if, in entitling you to your claim, I am merely doing what I have been taught or trained to do, without having examined *why* I ought to recognize your claim, and vice versa.[4] We might therefore view the space of reasons as genuinely "out there" (having existence somehow apart from just scorekeeping), thereby allowing ourselves to get some traction on the idea that we are therefore proposing claims or entitlements *as* reasons. A form of life amounts to more than just keeping score.[5] This suggestion, however, raises

2. The most notable exception being J. M. Bernstein, *Adorno: Disenchantment and Ethics* (Cambridge: Cambridge University Press, 2001).

3. Robert Brandom, *Making It Explicit: Reasoning, Representing, and Discursive Commitment* (Cambridge, MA: Harvard University Press, 1998), 172.

4. I take this to be a chief point in John McDowell, "Autonomy and Community: Some Remarks on the Second Movement of Brandom's Sonata" (unpublished manuscript).

5. I take this point to be developed against Brandom in J. M. Bernstein, "Mimetic Rationality and Material Inference: Adorno and Brandom," *Revue Internationale de Philosophie* 58, no. 227 (2004): 7–25

new worries, especially in that it begins to look like a sort of Platonism. I took Adorno's implicit view of the space of reasons, which I reconstructed in chapter 3, to be best understood through analogy to mathematics,[6] where once established, such a space exists—in a deep sense—"apart from us" but is nonetheless also *constructed*, socially and historically. What comes to matter, then, is how and to what extent we are initiated into a form of life (and what that form of life looks like, whether it has mathematics or morality or whatever else as its component parts, and in turn what those parts look like).

Adorno's suggestion thereby overlaps, at least in part, with the way contemporary Hegelians respond to this issue (see chapter 3). I have pushed this overlap by presenting a reading of Hegel that is congruent with Adorno's own understanding of history in terms that exclude theodicy. In my opinion, the standoff between the beautiful soul and the evil consciousness demonstrates that modern forms of life, or moments within them, reach stalemates and do not necessitate (although also do not bar) a resolution. Such stalemates, in turn, are not helped by the suggestion that what really matters is that reasons come to be seen as reasons, for the issue with the beautiful soul and the evil consciousness is that the *only* reason for moving forward appears to be an intuition (*Anschauung*) of things. (Although, again, *given* the rich spiritual nature of this shape, such an intuition is permeated in a robust way with conceptual capacities, and thereby reason.) That is, it may be that we *do* see reasons as reasons but cannot come to agree. Without denying irrationality in modern life, it may be that segments of it are simply irreconcilable without being irrational (being struck by this point is one way to understand Cavell's presence in this book).

This is when Adorno becomes a particularly interesting interlocutor, and there are two issues to stress here. First, all of this suggests that an account of our historical situation must be given anew, again and again; this is what it means, as Hegel suggested, to "grasp one's own time in thoughts."[7] It is in this register that I would take Adorno's suggestion that an essential element of contemporary education might be taking students to "commercially produced films" and examining "morning broadcasts" and even "Sunday mornings cheerful music."[8] Cultural criticism is an essential part of philosophy

6. See section 8 of chapter 3, especially note 108.

7. Something Hegel *also* believed; cf. Terry Pinkard, *Hegel's Naturalism: Mind, Nature, and the Final Ends of Life* (Oxford: Oxford University Press, 2012), 202n65.

8. Theodor W. Adorno and Helmut Becker, "Education for Maturity and Responsibility," *History of the Human Sciences* 12, no. 3 (1999): 31.

(without implying that philosophy is just cultural criticism). This suggests, in turn, that the scope of any critical inquiry or mapping of a "shape of spirit" has to be strikingly robust, in part because it must account for a wide *variety* of spiritual objects (from art to religion to philosophy and beyond—and we cannot underestimate how all these spheres have ineluctably become more complex since Hegel's time),[9] and in another part, because the space of reasons is constantly expanding through our interactions and creations, all worked through, parsed, and actualized in a variety of domains and registers. (And I must stress, with Adorno, that not all of them are beneficent.)

The second reason Adorno is especially interesting in this context is that he shows how any space of reasons might become rigid because of certain seemingly innocuous assumptions within that space of reasons (as, for example, with the dialectic of enlightenment and Kantian autonomy). In response, through a dialogue with Cavell, we can see how Adorno stresses our somatic capacities, manifest in pursuits of happiness, impulses toward utopia, and a wide variety of other imaginative and aesthetic drives. These desires are important because they can spark the space of reasons, expanding the range of reflective attitudes we can take *upon* that space, thereby exactly making it more likely that we *come to take* reasons as reasons and do so in qualitatively rich and thick ways.[10] In this way such somatic impulses have an essential role in actualizing our freedom. We can see this if we imagine a case where someone *does* reflect on what he is doing, thereby taking himself to be acting autonomously (or maturely, to return to Kant's phrasing from "What Is Enlightenment?"). What guarantee is there that such reflection is not conducted under conditions of conceptual paucity? Perhaps the qualitative conditions of our agent's social space are so warped or thin that such reflection is little more than a rubber stamp on what comes before it. It is here that such somatic impulses serve an important task: they expand our conceptual capacities (returning the favor, we might say, in the same way that it also possible for our conceptual capacities to expand our somatic impulses).[11] I take this to be the upshot of chapter 3, especially with Adorno's theory of action and morality.

9. This point is stated eloquently in Robert B. Pippin, *Hegel's Practical Philosophy: Rational Agency as Ethical Life* (Cambridge: Cambridge University Press, 2008), 280–81.

10. We might cite in this context the work of Charles Taylor, especially "Self-Interpreting Animals," in *Human Agency and Language* (Cambridge: Cambridge University Press, 1985), 1:45–76.

11. There is here a potentially fruitful overlap with Arendt's stress on an "enlarged mentality." See Hannah Arendt, *Lectures on Kant's Political Philosophy* (Chicago: University of Chicago Press, 1982).

We can illustrate all this especially well by reference to Adorno's notion of a "model."[12] For Adorno, models are closely related to "constellations" (HF 184). Both are ways of approaching items within the space of
reasons, that is, concepts. Adorno points out that constellations spring
from "the determinate failure of all concepts" and the necessary "citation
of others" (ND 53/6:62; translation modified).[13] He continues by suggesting
that language itself might be used as an example for constellations, since
it offers "no mere system of signs for cognitive functions" (ND 162/6:164).
Instead, language allows concepts to obtain "their objectivity through the
relationship in which it puts [setzen] the concepts, centered on a thing (ND
162/6:164; translation modified and emphasis added). Here a useful analogy can be drawn to Austin's description of his method as a "linguistic
phenomenology" in "A Plea for Excuses" (1956): "When we examine what
we should say when, what words we should use in what situations, we
are looking again not *merely* at words (or "meanings," whatever they may
be) *but also at the realities we use the words to talk about*: we are using a
sharpened awareness of words to sharpen our perception of, though not as
the final arbiter of, *the phenomena*."[14]

Although writing in starkly different contexts, both Adorno and Austin are suggesting that our language and concepts acquire sedimentation
around fixed notions, imparting a certain "slovenliness" and "grotesque
crudity and fatuousness" to our perception of things (inspired by Adorno,
we might also add "danger").[15]

In employing constellations, we might come to forge alternative paths.
As Adorno puts it, "By gathering around the thing to be cognized, the concepts potentially determine its inner core, thinking to attain what thinking
necessarily stamped out of itself" (ND 162/6:164–65; translation modified).
Constellations are a way of hanging together a "cluster of related" concepts
"without implying that the concepts used are identical" with the thing in
question.[16] The idea is that by arranging them in this way, we might sharpen

---

12. The best discussion of this notion in Adorno is still Fredric Jameson, *Late Marxism:
Adorno, or The Persistence of the Dialectic* (London: Verso, 1990), 59–63.

13. This is also a key step into Adorno's religious thought; see David Kaufmann, "Correlations, Constellations and the Truth: Adorno's Ontology of Redemption," *Philosophy and Social
Criticism* 26, no. 5 (2000): 62–80.

14. J. L. Austin, "A Plea for Excuses," in *Philosophical Papers* (Oxford: Oxford University
Press, 1979), 182.

15. Stanley Cavell, "Austin at Criticism," in *Must We Mean What We Say?* (Cambridge,
MA: Harvard University Press, 2002), 103.

16. Gillian Rose, *The Melancholy Science: An Introduction to the Thought of Theodor W.
Adorno* (New York: Columbia University Press, 1978), 90.

our understanding of the thing in question—an understanding that could appear only *in light of* that constellation. Adorno will use the metaphor of the precise combination that opens a safe (ND 163/6:165). A "model" is a distinct type of "constellation"; we know that Adorno's notion of a "model" is based on that of Arnold Schönberg, for whom the notion designated "the raw material of a specific composition . . . which is to say, for twelve-tone music, the specific row itself."[17] In this way a model is a sort of exercise. It is in this *practical* sense, then, that we ought to understand the models within *Negative Dialectics*, especially the last one, "Meditations on Metaphysics." (And as Fredric Jameson rightly points out, the Schönberg connection is tightly stressed here, with exactly twelve segments.)

This is significant for two reasons. First, it suggests that not only might the contents of these models be alternatively arranged (and this is certainly true, as any reader of Adorno's nondiscursive style quickly realizes), but that it is also important to find and undertake *additional* models. Second, and perhaps more important, it suggests that we ought to take seriously the last model's being labeled a *meditation*, for it is meant to serve a practical purpose as much as a theoretical one. Developing this point in full is still a necessary task, and I can only gesture toward it here, but its contours should have some plausibility given the picture of morality sketched in chapter 3. If Adorno and Cavell are as close as I have suggested, then not only is it proper to call Adorno a perfectionist thinker,[18] but he might even be profitably viewed as standing within a broader tradition of "spiritual exercises."[19]

But essential to such "models," and to their efficacy as exercises used to trigger greater self-reflection, is the possibility of inserting into the constellation items that might otherwise not appear there, even *after* reflection. These are items that do not at present exist, that are only immanently embedded within our concepts or that can arise from them (and not necessarily or predictably—they are genuinely novel). Such insertions are creatively pulled into constellations, and such creativity should be seen as originating in the speculative surplus elaborated in chapter 3. This "somatic" dimension of the space of reasons is more than a mere "normative" surplus, for it

17. Jameson, *Late Marxism*, 61.

18. Cf. Ståle Finke, "Adorno and the Experience of Metaphysics," *Philosophy and Social Criticism* 25, no. 6 (1999): 107ff. See also Martin Shuster, "'Nothing to Know': Framing Adorno's Moral Perfectionism" (unpublished manuscript).

19. See especially Pierre Hadot, "What Is Ethics?" in *The Present Alone Is Our Happiness: Conversations with Jeanine Carlier and Arnold I. Davidson*, ed. Arnold I. Davidson (Palo Alto, CA: Stanford University Press, 2011), 182–83.

implies that its basis might be in no *particular* norm, but might emerge only from a somatic impulse characterized by the imperative to *find* the norm in question. It is in this sense that such impulses represent the "innermost cells of thought, which are not the same as the latter" (ND 408/6:400; translation modified). Similarly, this is how such impulses ought to be understood to be in solidarity "with metaphysics at the moment of its fall" (ND 408/6:400; translation modified). They are in solidarity with metaphysics because, like metaphysics, they suggest more than what simply is. One of Adorno's contributions to discussions about the space of reasons, then, might be the idea that this space can be seen to be governed as much by concepts or norms that at present do exist as by ones that do not, and that might not even be *imaginable* at present (see especially the discussion in section 7 of chapter 3).[20] And all without suggesting that such future norms cannot thereby also be understood only *from* within the spaces of reasons (i.e., without falling into the myth of the given, or without recourse to any talk of merely banal logical possibility or any extreme form of modal realism). As an example we might cite elements of "modern art, where a work can challenge what counts as art and potentially redefine the entire field of what art can be."[21] In this way I take *Autonomy After Auschwitz* to have reconstructed a formal model for understanding ourselves as agents. The actualization and the contours of that agency, however, remain a practical task (and this includes possible modifications to the formal account).

In *Minima Moralia* there is an aphorism that somehow captures these points and strikes me as an appropriate way to end this book. Adorno recounts that in his childhood he derived great happiness from a song about two rabbits gunned down by a hunter as they rested in a field. After the shots, surprised, the rabbits realized they were still alive and could get up and run away (MM §128). Adorno writes about his understanding of the song:

> But only later did I understand the moral of this: reason [*Vernunft*] can only endure in despair and exuberance; it needs absurdity in order not to be consumed [*erliegen*] by objective madness [*Wahnsinn*]. One should be like the two hares: when the shot comes, madly fall down, and if one still has breath, gather oneself, recollect, and then run. The capacity for

20. There is much more to be said about this. For an excellent discussion, see Iain Macdonald, " 'What Is, Is More Than It Is': Adorno and Heidegger on the Priority of Possibility," *International Journal of Philosophical Studies* 19, no. 1 (2011) 31–57.

21. Ibid., 44. Macdonald's discussion of Rosa Parks is also very apt.

fear and happiness is the same—the boundless openness to experience amounting to increased self-disclosure [*Selbstpreisgabe*], in which the consumed [*Erliegende*] retrieves itself. What would happiness be, which is not measured by the immeasurable sorrow of what is? For the course of the world is unsettling [*verstört*]. He who precariously conforms to it, by this very act has a part in its madness, while the eccentric alone resists [*standhielte*] and demands it stop its folly. (MM §128, 200/4:226; translation modified)

WORKS CITED

Adorno, Theodor W. *Aesthetic Theory*. Edited by Gretel Adorno and Rolf Tiedemann. Translated by Robert Hullot-Kentor. Minneapolis: University of Minnesota Press, 1997.

———. *Against Epistemology: A Metacritique*. Translated by Willis Domingo. Cambridge, MA: MIT Press, 1983.

———. *Beethoven: The Philosophy of Music*. Translated by Edmund Jephcott. Stanford, CA: Stanford University Press, 1993.

———. *Can One Live After Auschwitz? A Philosophical Reader*. Edited by Rolf Tiedemann. Stanford, CA: Stanford University Press, 2003.

———. *Critical Models: Interventions and Catchwords*. Translated by Henry W. Pickford. New York: Columbia University Press, 1998.

———. *Dialectic of Enlightenment: Philosophical Fragments*. Translated by Edmund Jephcott. Palo Alto, CA: Stanford University Press, 2002.

———. "The Essay as Form." *New German Critique* 32 (1984): 151–71.

———. *Gesammelte Schriften*. 20 vols. Frankfurt am Main: Suhrkamp, 1984.

———. *Hegel: Three Studies*. Cambridge, MA: MIT Press, 1993.

———. *History and Freedom*. Edited by Rolf Tiedemann. Translated by Rodney Livingstone. Cambridge: Polity Press, 2006.

———. *Kant's "Critique of Pure Reason."* Edited by Rolf Tiedemann. Translated by Rodney Livingstone. Cambridge: Polity Press, 2001.

———. *Lectures on Negative Dialectics*. Edited by Rolf Tiedemann. Translated by Rodney Livingstone. Cambridge: Polity Press, 2008.

———. *Metaphysics*. Edited by Rolf Tiedemann. Translated by Edmund Jephcott. Stanford, CA: Stanford University Press, 2000.

———. *Metaphysik: Begriff und Probleme*. Edited by Rolf Tiedemann. Frankfurt am Main: Suhrkamp, 2006.

———. *Minima Moralia*. Translated by Edmund Jephcott. London: Verso, 2005.

———. *Negative Dialectics*. Translated by E. B. Ashton. New York: Continuum, 1973.

———. *Probleme der Moralphilosophie*. Edited by Thomas Schröder. Frankfurt am Main: Suhrkamp, 1996.

———. *Problems of Moral Philosophy*. Translated by Rodney Livingstone. Stanford, CA: Stanford University Press, 2000.

———. "Society." *Salmagundi* 10/11 (1969/1970): 144–53.

———. "Sociology and Psychology 1." *New Left Review* 46 (1967): 67–80.

———. "Sociology and Psychology 2." *New Left Review* 47 (1967): 79–99.

———. *Vorlesung über Negative Dialektik*. Edited by Rolf Tiedemann. Frankfurt am Main: Suhrkamp, 2003.

———. "Theses on the Language of the Philosopher." In *Adorno and the Need in Thinking: Critical Essays*, ed. Donald A. Burke, Colin J. Campbell, Kathy Kiloh, Michael K. Palamarek, and Jonathan Short, 35–39. Toronto: University of Toronto Press, 2007.

———. *Zur Lehre von der Geschichte und von der Freiheit*. Edited by Rolf Tiedemann. Frankfurt am Main: Suhrkamp, 2001.

Adorno, Theodor W., and Helmut Becker. "Education for Maturity and Responsibility." *History of the Human Sciences* 12, no. 3 (1999): 21–34.

Allison, Henry E. *The Kant-Eberhard Controversy*. Baltimore: Johns Hopkins University Press, 1973.

———. *Kant's Theory of Freedom*. Cambridge: Cambridge University Press, 1990.

———. *Kant's Transcendental Idealism*. 2nd ed. New Haven, CT: Yale University Press, 2004.

Ameriks, Karl. "Kant's Deduction of Freedom and Morality." In *Interpreting Kant's Critiques*, 161–93. Oxford: Oxford University Press, 2003.

Anderson, Elizabeth. *Value in Ethics and Economics*. Cambridge, MA: Harvard University Press, 1995.

Anderson-Gold, Sharon. "The Good Disposition and the Highest Good." In *Akten des Siebenten Internationalen Kant-Kongresses*, edited by Gerhard Funke, 2:2.229–37. Berlin: Bouvier, 1991.

———. *Unnecessary Evil: History and Moral Progress in the Philosophy of Immanuel Kant*. New York: State University of New York Press, 2001.

Anscombe, G. E. M. *Intention*. Cambridge, MA: Harvard University Press, 2000.

———. "Modern Moral Philosophy." *Philosophy* 33, no. 124 (1958): 1–19.

———. "Practical Inference." In *Virtues and Reasons: Philippa Foot and Moral Theory*, edited by Rosalind Hursthouse, Gavin Lawrence and Warren Quinn, 1–35. Oxford: Oxford University Press, 1995.

Arendt, Hannah. *Eichmann in Jerusalem*. New York: Viking Press, 1963.

———. *The Human Condition*. Chicago: University of Chicago Press, 1958.

———. *Lectures on Kant's Political Philosophy*. Chicago: University of Chicago Press, 1982.

———. *The Origins of Totalitarianism*. London: André Deutsch, 1986.

Auld, A. Grame. "Cities of Refuge in Israelite Tradition." *Journal for the Study of the Old Testament* 4, no. 10 (1979): 26–40.

Aune, Bruce. *Kant's Theory of Morals*. Princeton, NJ: Princeton University Press, 1979.

Austin, J. L. "A Plea for Excuses." In *Philosophical Papers*, 175–204. Oxford: Oxford University Press, 1979.

Auxter, Thomas. "The Unimportance of Kant's Highest Good." *Journal of the History of Philosophy* 17, no. 2 (1979): 121–34.

Baz, Avner. "On When Words Are Called For: Cavell, McDowell, and the Wording of the World." *Inquiry* 46 (2003): 473–500.

———. *When Words Are Called For: A Defense of Ordinary Language Philosophy*. Cambridge, MA: Harvard University Press, 2012.

Beck, Lewis White. *A Commentary on Kant's "Critique of Practical Reason."* Chicago: University of Chicago Press, 1960.

———. *Early German Philosophy: Kant and His Predecessors*. Cambridge, MA: Harvard University Press, 1969.

Beiser, Frederick. *The Fate of Reason: German Philosophy from Kant to Fichte*. Cambridge, MA: Harvard University Press, 2006.

———. "Moral Faith and the Highest Good." In *The Cambridge Companion to Kant and Modern Philosophy*, edited by Paul Guyer. Cambridge: Cambridge University Press, 2006.

Benjamin, Walter. *Illuminations*. New York: Schocken Books, 1968.

Bernasconi, Robert. "Hegel and Levinas: The Possibility of Forgiveness and Reconciliation." *Archivio di Filosofia* 1, no. 3 (1986): 325–46.

Bernstein, J. M. *Adorno: Disenchantment and Ethics*. Cambridge: Cambridge University Press, 2001.

———. "Confession and Forgiveness: Hegel's Poetics of Action." In *Beyond Representation: Philosophy and Poetic Imagination*, edited by Richard Eldridge, 34–66. Cambridge: Cambridge University Press, 1996.

———. "Conscience and Transgression: The Persistence of Misrecognition." *Bulletin of the Hegel Society of Great Britain* 29 (1994): 55–70.

———. "Mimetic Rationality and Material Inference: Adorno and Brandom." *Revue Internationale de Philosophie* 58, no. 227 (2004): 7–25.

———. "Negative Dialectic as Fate: Adorno and Hegel." In *The Cambridge Companion to Adorno*, edited by Tom Huhn. Cambridge: Cambridge University Press, 2004.

———. "Re-enchanting Nature." In *Reading McDowell: On Mind and World*, edited by Nicholas H. Smith, 217–46. London: Routledge, 2002.

Bernstein, Richard J. *Radical Evil: A Philosophical Interrogation*. Cambridge: Polity Press, 2002.

Bittner, Rüdiger, and Konrad Cramer, eds. *Materialien zu Kants "Kritik der praktischen Vernunft."* Frankfurt am Main: Suhrkamp, 1975.

Bloxham, Donald. *The Final Solution: A Genocide*. Oxford: Oxford University Press, 2009.

———. *Genocide, the World Wars and the Unweaving of Europe*. Middlesex, UK: Mitchell Vallentine, 2008.

Bowie, Andrew. "Adorno, Pragmatism, and Aesthetic Relativism." *Revue Internationale de Philosophie*, no. 227 (2004): 25–45.

Brandom, Robert. "Action, Norms, and Practical Reasoning." *Noûs* 32, no. S12 (1998): 127–39.

———. "Freedom and Constraint by Norms." *American Philosophical Quarterly* 16, no. 3 (1979): 187–96.

———. *Making It Explicit: Reasoning, Representing, and Discursive Commitment*. Cambridge, MA: Harvard University Press, 1998.

Brandt, Reinhard. "Analytic/Dialectic." In *Reading Kant: New Perspectives on Transcendental Arguments and Critical Philosophy*, edited by Eva Schaper and Wilhelm Vossenkuhl, 179–96. Oxford: Blackwell, 1989.

Brandt, Reinhard, and Werner Stark, eds. *Neue Autographen und Dokumenten zu Kants Leben, Schriften und Vorlesungen, Kant Forschungen.* Hamburg: Felix Meiner, 1987.

Bristow, William. *Hegel and the Transformation of Philosophical Critique.* Oxford: Oxford University Press, 2007.

Brunkhorst, Hauke. "Dialectical Positivism of Happiness." In *On Max Horkheimer: New Perspectives*, edited by Seyla Benhabib, Wolfgang Bonss, and John McCole, 67–99. Cambridge, MA: MIT Press, 1993.

———. "The Enlightenment of Rationality: Remarks on Horkheimer's and Adorno's *Dialectic of Enlightenment.*" *Constellations* 7 (2000): 133–40.

Buber, Martin. *I and Thou.* Translated by Walter Kaufmann. New York: Scribner's, 1970.

Buck-Morss, Susan. *The Origin of Negative Dialectics: Theodor W. Adorno, Walter Benjamin, and the Frankfurt Insitute.* New York: Free Press, 1977.

Burke, Donald A., Colin J. Campbell, Kathy Kiloh, Michael K. Palamarek, and Jonathan Short, eds. *Adorno and the Need in Thinking: Critical Essays.* Toronto: University of Toronto Press, 2007.

Butler, Judith. "Adorno on Becoming Human." In *Giving an Account of Oneself*, 101–11. New York: Fordham University Press, 2005.

Castañeda, Hector-Neri. "Conditional Intentions, Intentional Action and Aristotelian Practical Syllogisms." *Erkenntnis* 18, no. 2 (1982): 239–60.

Caswell, Matthew. "Kant's Conception of the Highest Good, the *Gesinnung*, and the Theory of Radical Evil." *Kant Studien* 97 (2006): 184–209.

Cavell, Stanley. "Austin at Criticism." In *Must We Mean What We Say?* 97–114. Cambridge, MA: Harvard University Press, 2002.

———. "The Availability of Wittgenstein's Later Philosophy." In *Must We Mean What We Say?* 44–73. Cambridge, MA: Harvard University Press, 2002.

———. *Cities of Words: Pedagogical Letters on a Register of the Moral Life.* Cambridge, MA: Harvard University Press, 2004.

———. *The Claim of Reason: Wittgenstein, Skepticism, Morality, and Tragedy.* Oxford: Oxford University Press, 1979.

———. *Conditions Handsome and Unhandsome.* Chicago: University of Chicago Press, 1990.

———. *In Quest of the Ordinary: Lines of Skepticism and Romanticism.* Chicago: University of Chicago Press, 1994.

———. "Knowing and Acknowledging." In *Must We Mean What We Say?* 238–66. Cambridge, MA: Harvard University Press, 2002.

———. "A Matter of Meaning It." In *Must We Mean What We Say?* 213–37. Cambridge, MA: Harvard University Press, 2002.

———. *Must We Mean What We Say? A Book of Essays*: Cambridge, MA: Harvard University Press, 2002.

———. *This New Yet Unapproachable America: Lectures after Emerson after Wittgenstein.* Albuquerque, NM: Living Batch Press, 1989.

Chisholm, Roderick. "Freedom and Action." In *Freedom and Determinism*, edited by Keith Lehrer, 11–44. New York: Random House, 1966.

Cook, Deborah. *The Culture Industry Revisited: Theodor W. Adorno on Mass Culture.* Lanham, MD: Rowman and Littlefield, 1996.

———. "From the Actual to the Possible: Nonidentity Thinking." *Constellations* 12, no. 1 (2005): 21–35.

Cornelius, Hans. *Kommentar zu Kants "Kritik der Reinen Vernunft."* Erlangen, Germany: Verlag der Philosophischen Akademie, 1926.

Crary, Alice. *Beyond Moral Judgment*. Cambridge, MA: Harvard University Press, 2007.

Dallmayr, Fred R. *Life-World, Modernity and Critique: Paths between Heidegger and the Frankfurt School.* Cambridge: Polity Press, 1991.

Danto, Arthur. *Analytical Philosophy of Action.* Cambridge: Cambridge University Press, 1973.

Davidson, Donald. "Actions, Reasons, and Causes." In *Essays on Actions and Events*, 3–21. Oxford: Clarendon Press, 2001.

———. "Agency." In *Essays on Actions and Events*, 43–63. Oxford: Clarendon Press, 2001.

———. "Freedom to Act." In *Essays on Actions and Events*, 63–83. Oxford: Clarendon Press, 2001.

Deleuze, Gilles. *Difference and Repetition.* Translated by Paul Patton. New York: Columbia University Press, 1994.

———. *Kant's Critical Philosophy: The Doctrine of the Faculties.* Translated by Hugh Tomlinson and Barbara Habberjam. Minneapolis: University of Minnesota Press, 1983.

Derrida, Jacques. *On Cosmopolitanism and Forgiveness.* Translated by Michael Hughes and Mark Dooley. London: Routledge, 2001.

de Vries, Hent. *Minimal Theologies: Critiques of Secular Reason in Adorno and Levinas.* Translated by Geoffrey Hale. Baltimore: Johns Hopkins University Press, 2005.

———. *Philosophy and the Turn to Religion.* Baltimore: Johns Hopkins University Press, 1999.

DeVries, Willem. "Hegel on Reference and Knowledge." *Journal of the History of Philosophy* 26, no. 2 (2008): 297–307.

Dewey, John. *The Later Works, 1925–1953.* Edited by Jo Ann Boydston. Carbondale: Southern Illinois University Press, 1988.

Dretske, Fred. *Explaining Behavior: Reasons in a World of Causes.* Cambridge, MA: MIT Press, 1991.

Dreyfus, Hubert L. *Being-in-the-World: A Commentary on Heidegger's "Being and Time," Division I.* Cambridge, MA: MIT Press, 1991.

———. "Detachment, Involvement, and Rationality: Are We Essentially Rational Animals?" *Human Affairs* 17 (2007): 101–9.

———. "Overcoming the Myth of the Mental: How Philosophers Can Profit from the Phenomenology of Everyday Expertise." *Proceedings and Addresses of the American Philosophical Association* 79, no. 2 (2005): 47–65.

———. "The Return of the Myth of the Mental." *Inquiry* 50, no. 4 (2007): 352–65.

Düsing, Klaus. "Das Problem des höchsten Gutes in Kants praktischer Philosophie."
    Kant Studien 62 (1971): 5–42.
Düttmann, Alexander García. *The Memory of Thought: An Essay on Heidegger and
    Adorno*. Translated by Nicholas Walker. London: Continuum, 1991.
Eldridge, Richard. "The Normal and the Normative: Wittgenstein's Legacy, Kripke, and
    Cavell." *Philosophy and Phenomenological Research* 46, no. 4 (1986): 555–75.
Engstrom, Stephen. "The Concept of the Highest Good in Kant's Moral Theory." *Philoso-
    phy and Phenomenological Research* 52, no. 4 (1992): 747–80.
Enoch, David. "Agency, Shmagency: Why Normativity Won't Come from What Is Consti-
    tutive of Action." *Philosophical Review* 115, no. 2 (2006): 169–98.
Falkenstein, Lorne. *Kant's Intuitionism: A Commentary on the Transcendental Aes-
    thetic*. Toronto: University of Toronto Press, 2004.
Ferrero, Luca. "Constitutivism and the Inescapability of Agency." *Oxford Studies in
    Metaethics* 4 (2009): 303–33.
Finke, Ståle. "Adorno and the Experience of Metaphysics." *Philosophy and Social Criti-
    cism* 25, no. 6 (1999): 105–26.
———. "Between Ontology and Epistemology." In *Adorno: Key Concepts*, edited by
    Deborah Cook, 88–99. Stocksfield, UK: Acumen, 2008.
———. "Concepts and Intuitions: Adorno After the Linguistic Turn." *Inquiry* 44 (2001):
    171–200.
Finlayson, James Gordon. "Adorno on the Ethical and the Ineffable." *European Journal of
    Philosophy* 10, no. 1 (2002): 1–25.
———. "Morality and Critical Theory: On the Normative Problem of Frankfurt School
    Social Criticism." *Telos* 2009, no. 146 (2009): 7–41.
Ford, Anton. "Action and Generality." In *Essays on Anscombe's Intention*, edited by
    Anton Ford, Jennifer Hornsby, and Frederick Stoutland, 76–104. Cambridge, MA:
    Harvard University Press, 2011.
Förster, Eckart. "Hegels 'Entdeckungsreisen': Entstehung und Aufbau der '*Phänomenolo-
    gie des Geistes.*'" In *Hegels "Phänomenologie des Geistes": Ein kooperativer Kom-
    mentar zu einem Schlüsselwerk der Moderne*, edited by Klaus Vieweg and Wolfgang
    Welsch, 37–57. Frankfurt am Main: Suhrkamp, 2008.
———. *Kant's Final Synthesis*. Cambridge, MA: Harvard University Press, 2000.
———. "Reply to Friedman and Guyer." *Inquiry* 46 (2003): 228–38.
———. *The Twenty-Five Years of Philosophy: A Systematic Reconstruction*. Cambridge,
    MA: Harvard University Press, 2012.
Foster, Roger. *Adorno: The Recovery of Experience*. Albany: State University of New
    York Press, 2007.
Frankfurt, Harry. "Freedom of the Will and the Concept of a Person." *Journal of Philoso-
    phy* 68, no. 1 (1971): 5–20.
———. *Necessity, Volition, and Love*. Cambridge: Cambridge University Press, 1999.
Franks, Paul W. *All or Nothing: Systematicity, Transcendental Arguments, and Skepti-
    cism in German Idealism*. Cambridge, MA: Harvard University Press, 2005.
———. "The Discovery of the Other: Cavell, Fichte, and Skepticism." *Common Knowl-
    edge* 5, no. 2 (1996): 72–105.

Freyenhagen, Fabian. "Adorno's Ethics without the Ineffable." *Telos* 2011, no. 155 (2011): 127–49.

———. "Moral Philosophy." In *Adorno: Key Concepts*, edited by Deborah Cook, 99–114. Stocksfield, UK: Acumen, 2008.

———. "No Easy Way Out: Adorno's Negativism and the Problem of Normativity." In *Nostalgia for a Redeemed Future: Critical Theory*, edited by Stefano Giacchetti Ludovisi, 39–50. Rome: John Cabot University Press, 2009.

Friedman, R. Z. "The Importance and Function of Kant's Highest Good." *Journal of the History of Philosophy* 22, no. 3 (1984): 325–42.

Geuss, Raymond. "Art and Theodicy." In *Morality, Culture, and History: Essays on German Philosophy*, 78–116. Cambridge: Cambridge University Press, 1999.

———. "Suffering and Knowledge in Adorno." *Constellations* 12, no. 1 (2005): 3–20.

Gibson, James J. *The Ecological Approach to Visual Perception*. Boston: Houghton Mifflin, 1986.

Gibson, John. *Fiction and the Weave of Life*. Oxford: Oxford University Press, 2008.

Godlove, Terry F., Jr. "Moral Actions, Moral Lives: Kant on Intending the Highest Good." *Southern Journal of Philosophy* 25, no. 1 (1987): 49–65.

Goebel, Eckart. "Das Hinzutretende: Ein Kommentar zu Seiten 226–230 der '*Negativen Dialektik*.'" In *Frankfurter Adorno Blatter*, edited by Theodor W. Adorno Archiv, 4:109–16. Munich, 1992.

Greenberg, Sean. "From Canon to Dialectic to Antinomy: Giving Inclinations Their Due." *Inquiry* 48, no. 3 (2005): 232–48.

Grier, Michelle. *Kant's Doctrine of Transcendental Illusion*. Cambridge: Cambridge University Press, 2001.

Grimm, Jacob, and Wilhelm Grimm. *Deutsches Wörterbuch*. Leipzig: Hirzel, 1885.

Guyer, Paul. "Beauty, Systematicity, and the Highest Good." *Inquiry* 46 (2003): 195–214.

———, ed. *The Cambridge Companion to Kant*. Cambridge: Cambridge University Press, 1992.

———. "Moral Faith and the Highest Good." In *The Cambridge Companion to Kant and Modern Philosophy*, edited by Paul Guyer, 588–630. Cambridge: Cambridge University Press, 2006.

———. "Naturalistic and Transcendental Moments in Kant's Moral Philosophy." *Inquiry* 50, no. 5 (2007): 444–64.

Habermas, Jürgen. *The Philosophical Discourse of Modernity*. Cambridge, MA: MIT Press, 1987.

———. *Philosophical Political Profiles*. Translated by Frederick G. Lawrence. Cambridge, MA: MIT Press, 1983.

Hadot, Pierre. "What Is Ethics?" In *The Present Alone Is Our Happiness: Conversations with Jeanine Carlier and Arnold I. Davidson*, edited by Arnold I. Davidson, 175–86. Palo Alto, CA: Stanford University Press, 2011.

Hamann, Johann Georg. *Briefwechsel*. Wiesbaden, Germany: Insel, 1994.

Hammer, Espen. "Adorno and Extreme Evil." *Philosophy and Social Criticism* 26, no. 4 (2000): 75–93.

———. *Adorno and the Political*. London: Routledge, 2006.

———. "Minding the World: Adorno's Critique of Idealism." *Philosophy and Social Criticism* 26, no. 1 (2000): 71–92.

———. *Philosophy and Temporality from Kant to Critical Theory.* Cambridge: Cambridge University Press, 2011.

———. "Review of *Adorno: Disenchantment and Ethics.*" *Notre Dame Philosophical Reviews* (2002). http://ndpr.nd.edu/news/23372/?id=1247.

Hare, John E. *The Moral Gap: Kantian Ethics, Human Limits, and God's Assistance.* Oxford: Oxford University Press, 1996.

Harris, H. S. *Hegel's Ladder.* Indianapolis, IN: Hackett, 1997.

Hausius, Karl Gottlob. *Materialien zur Geschichte der critischen Philosophie.* Leipzig: Breitkopf, 1793.

Haym, Rudolf. *Hegel und seine Zeit: Vorlesungen über Entstehung und Entwicklung, Wesen und Werth der Hegel'schen Philosophie.* Berlin: Rudolph Gaertner, 1857.

Hegel, G. W. F. *The Encyclopedia Logic.* Translated by T. F. Geraets, W. A. Suchting and H. S. Harris. Indianapolis, IN: Hackett, 1991.

———. *Elements of the Philosophy of Right.* Translated by H. B. Nisbet. Cambridge: Cambridge University Press, 1991.

———. *Gesammelte Werke.* Edited by Rheinisch-Westfälischen Akademie der Wissenschaften. Hamburg: Felix Meiner, 1968.

———. *Hegel's Aesthetics: Lectures on Fine Art.* Translated by T. M. Knox. Oxford: Oxford University Press, 1975.

———. *Hegels Philosophie des subjektiven Geistes/Hegel's Philosophy of Subjective Spirit.* Translated by Michael Petry. Dordrecht: Riedel, 1978.

———. *Hegel's Philosophy of Mind.* Translated by William Wallace. Oxford: Oxford University Press, 2007.

———. *Phänomenologie des Geistes.* Frankfurt am Main: Suhrkamp, 1970.

———. *Phenomenology of Spirit.* Translated by A. V. Miller. Oxford: Oxford University Press, 1977.

———. *Philosophie des Rechts: Die Vorlesung von 1819/1820.* Edited by Dieter Henrich. Frankfurt am Main: Suhrkamp, 1983.

———. *Science of Logic.* London: Routledge, 2004.

———. *Werke.* Frankfurt am Main: Suhrkamp, 1970.

Heine, Heinrich. *On the History of Religion and Philosophy in Germany and Other Writings.* Edited by Terry Pinkard. Cambridge: Cambridge University Press, 2007.

Henrich, Dieter. "The Concept of Moral Insight." In *The Unity of Reason,* edited by Richard L. Velkley. Cambridge, MA: Harvard University Press, 1994.

———. "The Moral Image of the World." In *Aesthetic Judgment and the Moral Image of the World.* Palo Alto, CA: Stanford University Press, 1994.

Herman, Barbara. *The Practice of Moral Judgment.* Cambridge, MA: Harvard University Press, 1993.

Höffe, Otfried. *Ethik und Politik: Grundmodelle und Probleme der praktischen Philosophie.* Frankfurt am Main: Suhrkamp, 1979.

Hoffmeister, Johannes, ed. *Briefe von und an Hegel.* Hamburg: Felix Meiner, 1952.

Honneth, Axel. *The Critique of Power: Reflective Stages in a Critical Social Theory.* Translated by Kenneth Baynes. Cambridge, MA: MIT Press, 1991.

———. *Pathologies of Reason: On the Legacy of Critical Theory.* New York: Columbia University Press, 2009.

Horkheimer, Max. *Between Philosophy and Social Science.* Translated by G. Frederick Hunter, Matthew S. Kramer, and John Torpey. Cambridge, MA: MIT Press, 1993.

———. *Eclipse of Reason.* New York: Oxford University Press, 1947.

———. *Gesammelte Schriften.* 19 vols. Frankfurt am Main: S. Fischer, 1987.

———. "Traditional and Critical Theory." In *Critical Theory: Selected Essays*, 188–243. New York: Seabury, 1972.

Hullot-Kentor, Robert. "Back to Adorno." *Telos* 81 (1989): 5–29.

———. "The Idea of Natural History." *Telos* 60 (1984): 111–24.

———. "The Problem of Natural History in the Philosophy of Theodor W. Adorno." PhD diss., University of Massachusetts, 1985.

———. *Things Beyond Resemblance: Collected Essays on Theodor W. Adorno.* New York: Columbia University Press, 2006.

Hyppolite, Jean. *Genesis and Structure of Hegel's "Phenomenology of Spirit."* Evanston, IL: Northwestern University Press, 1979.

Jaeggi, Rahel. "'No Individual Can Resist': *Minima Moralia* as Critique of Forms of Life." *Constellations* 12, no. 1 (2005): 65–82.

James, William. "What Pragmatism Means." In *Essays in Pragmatism*, edited by Alburey Castell, 141–59. New York: Free Press, 1948.

———. "What Pragmatism Means." In *Pragmatism*, 43–85. New York: Longmans, Green, 1949.

Jameson, Fredric. *The Hegel Variations: On the "Phenomenology of Spirit."* London: Verso, 2010.

———. *Late Marxism: Adorno, or The Persistence of the Dialectic.* London: Verso, 1990.

———. *Marxism and Form.* Princeton, NJ: Princeton University Press, 1971.

Janack, Marianne. *What We Mean by Experience.* Palo Alto, CA: Stanford University Press, 2012.

Jarvis, Simon. *Adorno: A Critical Introduction.* Cambridge: Polity Press, 1998.

———. "Adorno, Marx, Materialism." In *The Cambridge Companion to Adorno*, 79–99. Cambridge: Cambridge University Press, 2004.

———. "What Is Speculative Thinking?" *Revue Internationale de Philosophie* 58, no. 227 (2004): 69–83.

Jauss, Hans Robert. "Der literarische Prozess des Modernismus von Rousseau bis Adorno." In *Adorno-Konferenz*, edited by Ludwig von Friedeburg and Jürgen Habermas. Frankfurt am Main: Suhrkamp, 1983.

Jay, Martin. *The Dialectical Imagination: A History of the Frankfurt School and the Institute of Social Research, 1923–1950.* Berkeley: University of California Press, 1973.

Jütten, Timo. "Adorno on Kant, Freedom and Determinism." *European Journal of Philosophy* 20, no. 4 (2010): 548–74.

Kaan, André. "L'honnêteté et l'imposture dans la société civile (à propos du chapitre V.C. de la *Phénoménologie*: La règne animal de l'esprit)." *Hegel Jahrbuch*, 1971, 45–49.

Kane, Robert. *The Significance of Free Will.* Oxford: Oxford University Press, 1996.

Kant, Immanuel. *Critique of Practical Reason.* Translated by Lewis White Beck. Indianapolis, IN: Bobbs-Merrill, 1956.

———. *Critique of Pure Reason*. Translated by Paul Guyer and Allen W. Wood. Cambridge: Cambridge University Press, 1998.

———. *Critique of the Power of Judgment*. Translated by Paul Guyer and Eric Matthews. Cambridge: Cambridge University Press, 2000.

———. *"Foundations of the Metaphysics of Morals" and "What Is Enlightenment?"* Translated by Lewis White Beck. 2nd ed. Upper Saddle River, NJ: Prentice Hall, 1997.

———. *Gesammelte Schriften*. Edited by Preussischen Akademie der Wissenschaften. 29 vols. Berlin: Walter de Gruyter, 1912.

———. *Lectures on Ethics*. Translated by Peter Heath. Cambridge: Cambridge University Press, 1997.

———. *Lectures on Logic*. Translated by J. Michael Young. Cambridge: Cambridge University Press, 2004.

———. *On History*. Edited by Lewis White Beck. *Neue Autographen und Dokumenten zu Kants Leben, Schriften und Vorlesungen*. Translated by Lewis White Beck, Robert E. Anchor, and Emil L. Fackenheim. New York: Bobbs-Merrill, 1963.

———. *Practical Philosophy*. Edited and translated by Mary J. Gregor. Cambridge: Cambridge University Press, 1996.

———. *Prolegomena zu einer jeden künftigen Metaphysik, die als Wissenschaft wird auftreten könne*. Edited by Rudolf Malter. Stuttgart: Reclam, 1989.

———. *Religion within the Boundaries of Mere Reason*. Edited by Allen Wood and George di Giovanni. Cambridge: Cambridge University Press, 1998.

———. *Theoretical Philosophy, 1775–1770*. Cambridge: Cambridge University Press, 1992.

Kaufmann, David. "Correlations, Constellations and the Truth: Adorno's Ontology of Redemption." *Philosophy and Social Criticism* 26, no. 5 (2000): 62–80.

Kierkegaard, Søren. *The Kierkegaard Reader*. Translated by Jonathan Rèe and Jane Chamberlain. London: Blackwell, 2001.

Kleingeld, Pauline. "The Conative Character of Reason in Kant's Philosophy." *Journal of the History of Philosophy* 36, no. 1 (1998): 77–97.

———. "What Do the Virtuous Hope For? Re-reading Kant's Doctrine of the Highest Good." In *Proceedings of the Eighth International Kant Congress*. Milwaukee, WI: Marquette University Press, 1995.

Knoll, Manuel. *Theodor W. Adorno, Ethik als erste Philosophie*. Munich: Wilhelm Fink, 2002.

Kolakowski, Leszek. *Main Currents of Marxism: Its Rise, Growth and Dissolution*. Translated by P. S. Falla. 3 vols. Oxford: Oxford University Press, 1978.

Korsgaard, Christine M. *Creating the Kingdom of Ends*. Cambridge: Cambridge University Press, 1996.

———. *Self-Constitution: Agency, Identity, and Integrity*. Oxford: Oxford University Press, 2009.

———. *The Sources of Normativity*. Cambridge: Cambridge University Press, 1996.

Kosch, Michelle. *Freedom and Reason in Kant, Schelling, and Kierkegaard*. Oxford: Oxford University Press, 2006.

Kreines, James. "The Inexplicability of Kant's *Naturzweck*: Kant on Teleology, Explanation and Biology." *Archiv für Geschichte der Philosophie* 87, no. 3 (2005): 270–311.

Kuehn, Manfred. *Kant: A Biography*. Cambridge: Cambridge University Press, 2001.

Laitinen, Arto. "Hegel on Intersubjective and Retrospective Determination of Intention." *Bulletin of the Hegel Society of Great Britain*, no. 49/50 (2004): 54–72.

Larmore, Charles. *The Morals of Modernity*. Cambridge: Cambridge University Press, 1996.

Lear, Jonathan. "Transcendental Anthropology." In *Open Minded: Working Out the Logic of the Soul*, 247–82. Cambridge, MA: Harvard University Press, 1998.

Lee, Lisa Yun. *Dialectics of the Body: Corporeality in the Philosophy of Theodor Adorno*. London: Routledge, 2004.

Leibniz, G. W. *Philosophical Essays*. Indianapolis, IN: Hackett, 1989.

Levene, Mark. *Genocide in the Age of the Nation State*. 4 vols. London: I. B. Tauris, 2005.

Levinas, Emmanuel. "Language and Proximity." In *Collected Philosophical Papers*, 109–26. Dordrecht: Martinus Nijhoff, 1987.

———. *Totality and Infinity: An Essay on Exteriority*. Translated by Alphonso Lingis. Pittsburgh, PA: Duquesne University Press, 1980.

Linden, Henry van der. *Kantian Ethics and Socialism*. Indianapolis, IN: Hackett, 1988.

Longuenesse, Béatrice. *Kant and the Capacity to Judge*. Princeton, NJ: Princeton University Press, 1998.

———. *Kant on the Human Standpoint*. Cambridge: Cambridge University Press, 2005.

Lovibond, Sabina. *Realism and Imagination in Ethics*. Minneapolis: University of Minnesota Press, 1983.

Macdonald, Iain. "Cold, Cold, Warm: Autonomy, Intimacy and Maturity in Adorno." *Philosophy and Social Criticism* 37, no. 6 (2011): 669–89.

———. "Un utopisme modal? Possibilité et actualité chez Hegel et Adorno." In *Les normes et le possible: Héritage et perspectives de l'École de Francfort*, edited by Pierre-François Noppen, Gérard Raulet, and Iain Macdonald, 343–57. Paris: Maison des Sciences de l'Homme, 2013.

———. "'What Is, Is More Than It Is': Adorno and Heidegger on the Priority of Possibility." *International Journal of Philosophical Studies* 19, no. 1 (2011): 31–57.

MacIntyre, Alasdair. *After Virtue: A Study in Moral Theory*. Notre Dame, IN: University of Notre Dame Press, 1981.

Mann, Michael. *The Dark Side of Democracy: Explaining Ethnic Cleansing*. Cambridge: Cambridge University Press, 2005.

Marcel, Anthony. "The Sense of Agency: Awareness and Ownership of Action." In *Agency and Self-Awareness*, edited by Johannes Roessler and Naomi Eilan, 48–94. Oxford: Oxford University Press, 2003.

Marder, Michael. "*Minima Patientia*: Reflections on the Subject of Suffering." *New German Critique* 33, no. 1 (2006): 53–72.

Marrati, Paola. "Political Emotions: Stanley Cavell on Democracy." *Revue Internationale de Philosophie* 2, no. 256 (2011): 167–82.

Martin, Wayne. *Theories of Judgment: Psychology, Logic, Phenomenology*. Cambridge: Cambridge University Press, 2006.

McDowell, John. "Autonomy and Community: Some Remarks on the Second Movement of Brandom's Sonata." http://cas.uchicago.edu/workshops/germanphilosophy/files/2011/04/Autonomy-and-Community.pdf.

———. "Autonomy and Its Burdens." *Harvard Review of Philosophy* 17 (2010): 1–15.

———. "Conceptual Capacities in Perception." In *Having the World in View: Essays on Kant, Hegel, and Sellars*, 127–47. Cambridge, MA: Harvard University Press, 2009.

———. "Might There Be External Reasons?" In *Mind, Value, and Reality*, 95–111. Cambridge, MA: Harvard University Press, 1998.

———. *Mind, Value, and Reality*. Cambridge, MA: Harvard University Press, 1998.

———. "Response to Dreyfus." *Inquiry* 50, no. 4 (2007): 366–70.

———. "Self-Determining Subjectivity and External Constraint." In *Having the World in View: Essays on Kant, Hegel, and Sellars*, 90–107. Cambridge, MA: Harvard University Press, 2009.

———. "Virtue and Reason." In *Mind, Value, and Reality*, 50–73. Cambridge, MA: Harvard University Press, 1998.

———. "What Myth?" *Inquiry* 50, no. 4 (2007): 338–51.

———. "Wittgenstein on Following a Rule." In *Mind, Value, and Reality*, 221–63. Cambridge: Cambridge University Press, 1998.

Menke, Christoph. "Critical Theory and Tragic Knowledge." In *Handbook of Critical Theory*, edited by David M. Rasmussen, 78–119. Oxford: Blackwell, 1996.

———. "Virtue and Reflection: The 'Antinomies of Moral Philosophy.'" *Constellations* 12, no. 1 (2005): 36–49.

Merleau-Ponty, Maurice. *Phenomenology of Perception*. Translated by Colin Smith. London: Routledge, 2002.

Mill, John Stuart. *Essays on Politics and Society*. Edited by J. M. Robson. Vol. 8 of *Collected Works of John Stuart Mill*. Toronto: University of Toronto Press, 1977.

Milne, Drew. "The Beautiful Soul: From Hegel to Beckett." *Diacritics* 32, no. 1 (2002): 63–82.

Moran, Richard. *Authority and Estrangement: An Essay on Self-Knowledge*. Princeton, NJ: Princeton University Press, 2001.

Mörchen, Hermann. *Adorno und Heidegger: Untersuchung einer philosophischen Kommunikationsverweigerung*. Stuttgart: Klett Cotta, 1981.

———. *Macht und Herrschaft im Denken von Adorno und Heidegger*. Stuttgart: Klett Cotta, 1980.

Morgan, Michael. *Discovering Levinas*. Cambridge: Cambridge University Press, 2007.

Moses, A. Dirk. *Empire, Colony, Genocide: Conquest, Occupation, and Subaltern Resistance in World History*. London: Berghahn Books, 2008.

Moyar, Dean. *Hegel's Conscience*. Oxford: Oxford University Press, 2011.

Müller-Doohm, Stefan. *Adorno: A Biography*. Cambridge: Polity Press, 2005.

Munzel, G. Felicitas. *Kant's Conception of Moral Character*. Chicago: University of Chicago Press, 1999.

Murdoch, Iris. "Vision and Choice in Morality." In *Existentialists and Mystics*, 76–99. New York: Penguin, 1997.

Murphy, Jeffrie. "The Highest Good as Content for Kant's Ethical Formalism." *Kant Studien* 56 (1965): 102–10.

Nagel, Thomas. "Moral Luck." In *Mortal Questions*, 24–38. Cambridge: Cambridge University Press, 1979.

Neuhouser, Frederick. *Foundations of Hegel's Social Theory: Actualizing Freedom*. Cambridge, MA: Harvard University Press, 2003.

Noerr, Gunzelin Schmid. "Die Stellung der 'Dialektik der Aufklärung' in der Entwicklung der Kritischen Theorie." In Max Horkheimer, *Gesammelte Schriften*, 5:423–52. Frankfurt am Main: S. Fischer, 1987.

Noppen, Pierre-François. "Reflective Rationality and the Claim of *Dialectic of Enlightenment*." *European Journal of Philosophy*, forthcoming.

Norton, Robert. *The Beautiful Soul: Aesthetic Morality in the Eighteenth Century*. Ithaca, NY: Cornell University Press, 1995.

O'Connor, Brian. "Adorno and the Rediscovery of Autonomy." In *Nostalgia for a Redeemed Future: Critical Theory*, edited by Stefano Giacchetti Ludovisi, 51–61. Rome: John Cabot University Press, 2009.

———. "The Concept of Mediation in Hegel and Adorno." *Bulletin of the Hegel Society of Great Britain* 39/40 (1999): 84–96.

O'Neill, Onora. *Constructions of Reason: Explorations of Kant's Practical Philosophy*. Cambridge: Cambridge University Press, 1989.

———. "Kant on Reason and Religion." In *The Tanner Lectures on Human Values*, edited by Grethe B. Peterson. Salt Lake City: University of Utah Press, 1996.

———. "Reason and Autonomy in *Grundlegung* III." In *Constructions of Reason: Explorations of Kant's Practical Philosophy*, 51–66. Cambridge: Cambridge University Press, 1989.

———. "Vindicating Reason." In *The Cambridge Companion to Kant*, edited by Paul Guyer. Cambridge: Cambridge University Press, 1992.

Parry, David M. *Hegel's Phenomenology of the "We."* New York: Peter Lang, 1988.

Pinkard, Terry. *German Philosophy, 1760–1780: The Legacy of Idealism*. Cambridge: Cambridge University Press, 2002.

———. *Hegel: A Biography*. Cambridge: Cambridge University Press, 2001.

———. *Hegel's Naturalism: Mind, Nature, and the Final Ends of Life*. Oxford: Oxford University Press, 2012.

———. *Hegel's Phenomenology: The Sociality of Reason*. Cambridge: Cambridge University Press, 1996.

———. "Innen, Aussen und Lebensformen: Hegel und Wittgenstein." In *Hegels Erbe*, 254–92. Frankfurt am Main: Suhrkamp, 2004.

———. "Sellars the Post Kantian?" In *The Self-Correcting Enterprise: Essays on Wilfrid Sellars*, edited by Michael P. Wolf and Mark Norris Lance, 21–52. New York: Editions Rodopi, 2007.

———. "What Is a Shape of Spirit?" In *"The Phenomenology of Spirit": A Critical Guide*, edited by Dean Moyar and Michael Quante, 112–30. Cambridge: Cambridge University Press, 2008.

Pippin, Robert B. "The Actualization of Freedom." In *The Cambridge Companion to German Idealism*, edited by Karl Ameriks, 92–118. Cambridge: Cambridge University Press, 2000.

———. "Concept and Intuition: On Distinguishability and Separability." *Hegel-Studien* 40 (2005): 25–39.

———. *Hegel on Self-Consciousness: Desire and Death in the "Phenomenology of Spirit."* Princeton, NJ: Princeton University Press, 2011.

——. *Hegel's Practical Philosophy: Rational Agency as Ethical Life.* Cambridge: Cambridge University Press, 2008.

——. "Kant's Theory of Value: On Allen Wood's '*Kant's Ethical Thought.*'" *Inquiry* 43, no. 2 (2000): 239–65.

——. *Modernism as a Philosophical Problem: On the Dissatisfaction of European High Culture.* 2nd ed. Oxford: Blackwell, 1999.

——. "Natural and Normative." *Daedalus* 138, no. 3 (2009): 35–43.

——. "Naturalness and Mindedness: Hegel's Compatibilism." *European Journal of Philosophy* 7, no. 2 (1999): 194–212.

——. "Negative Ethics: Adorno on the Falseness of Bourgeois Life." In *The Persistence of Subjectivity,* 98–121. Cambridge: Cambridge University Press, 2005.

——. *The Persistence of Subjectivity: On the Kantian Aftermath.* Cambridge: Cambridge University Press, 2005.

——. "What Is the Question for Which Hegel's Theory of Recognition Is the Answer?" *European Journal of Philosophy* 8, no. 2 (2000): 155–72.

Pöggeler, Otto. *Hegels Idee einer Phänomenologie des Geistes.* Munich: Karl Alber, 1993.

——. "Die Komposition der '*Phänomenologie des Geistes.*'" In *Materialien zu Hegels "Phänomenologie des Geistes,"* edited by Dieter Henrich and Hans Friedrich Fulda. Frankfurt am Main: Suhrkamp, 1973.

Protevi, John. *Political Affect: Connecting the Social and the Somatic.* Minneapolis: University of Minnesota Press, 2009.

Quante, Michael. *Hegel's Concept of Action.* Translated by Dean Moyar. Cambridge: Cambridge University Press, 2004.

Quine, W. V. O. *Word and Object.* Cambridge, MA: MIT Press, 1960.

Rabinbach, Anson. *In the Shadow of Catastrophe.* Berkeley: University of California Press, 1997.

Railton, Peter. "On the Hypothetical and Non-hypothetical in Reasoning about Belief and Action." In *Ethics and Practical Reason,* edited by Garrett Cullity and Berys Gaut, 53–79. Oxford: Oxford University Press, 1997.

Ramberg, Bjørn. "Post-ontological Philosophy of Mind: Rorty versus Davidson." In *Rorty and His Critics,* edited by Robert B. Brandom, 351–70. Oxford: Blackwell, 2000.

Rand, Sebastian. "The Importance and Relevance of Hegel's Philosophy of Nature." *Review of Metaphysics* 61, no. 2 (2007): 379.

Rawls, John. *Lectures on the History of Moral Philosophy.* Edited by Barbara Herman. Cambridge, MA: Harvard University Press, 2000.

——. *A Theory of Justice.* Cambridge. MA: Harvard University Press, 1971.

Reath, Andrews. "Two Conceptions of the Highest Good in Kant." *Journal of the History of Philosophy* 26, no. 4 (1988): 593–619.

Reich, Klaus. "Kant and Greek Ethics (II)." *Mind* 48 (1939): 446–63.

Reijen, Willem van. *Adorno: An Introduction.* Translated by Dieter Engelbrecht. Philadelphia: Pennbridge, 1992.

Rensmann, Lars, and Samir Gandesha. "Understanding Political Modernity: Rereading Arendt and Adorno in Comparative Perspective." In *Arendt and Adorno: Political and Philosophical Investigations*, edited by Lars Rensmann and Samir Gandesha, 1–31. Palo Alto, CA: Stanford University Press, 2012.

Rhees, Rush. "'What Is Language?'" In *Wittgenstein and the Possibility of Discourse*, edited by D. Z. Phillips, 21–33. Oxford: Blackwell, 2006.

Richter, Gerhard. "Aesthetic Theory and Nonpropositional Truth Content in Adorno." *New German Critique* 33, no. 1 (2006): 119–35.

Ricouer, Paul. "Freedom in the Light of Hope." In *The Conflict of Interpretations: Essays in Hermeneutics*, 398–421. Evanston, IL: Northwestern University Press, 1974.

Rocco, Christopher. "Between Modernity and Postmodernity: Reading *Dialectic of Enlightenment* against the Grain." *Political Theory* 22, no. 1 (1994): 71–97.

Romdenh-Romluc, Komarine. "Merleau-Ponty and the Power to Reckon with the Possible." In *Reading Merleau-Ponty: On "Phenomenology of Perception,"* edited by Thomas Baldwin, 44–58. London: Routledge, 2007.

Rorty, Richard. *Contingency, Irony, and Solidarity*. Cambridge: Cambridge University Press, 1989.

———. "The Overphilosophication of Politics." *Constellations* 7, no. 1 (2000): 128–32.

Rorty, Richard, and Eduardo Mendieta. *Take Care of Freedom and Truth Will Take Care of Itself: Interviews with Richard Rorty*. Stanford, CA: Stanford University Press, 2006.

Rose, Gillian. "How Is Critical Theory Possible? Theodor W. Adorno and Concept Formation in Sociology." *Political Studies* 24, no. 1 (1976): 69–85.

———. *The Melancholy Science: An Introduction to the Thought of Theodor W. Adorno*. New York: Columbia University Press, 1978.

Rosenberg, Jay F. *The Thinking Self*. Philadelphia: Temple University Press, 1986.

Roth, Abraham S. "Reasons Explanations of Actions: Causal, Singular, and Situational." *Philosophical and Phenomenological Research* 59, no. 4 (1999): 839–74.

Rousseau, Jean-Jacques. *The Social Contract*. Translated by Maurice Cranston. New York: Penguin, 1968.

Rutter, Benjamin. *Hegel on the Modern Arts*. Cambridge: Cambridge University Press, 2010.

Schmidt, James. "The *Eclipse of Reason* and the End of the Frankfurt School in America." *New German Critique* 34, no. 1 (2007): 47–76.

———. "Genocide and the Limits of Enlightenment: Horkheimer and Adorno Revisited." In *Enlightenment and Genocide, Contradictions of Modernity*, edited by Bo Strath. Brussels: Peter Lang, 2000.

———. "Language, Mythology, and Enlightenment: Historical Notes on Horkheimer and Adorno's *Dialectic of Enlightenment*." *Social Research* 65, no. 4 (1998): 807–38.

———. "What Enlightenment Project?" *Political Theory* 28, no. 6 (2000): 734–57.

Schmucker, Josef. *Die Ursprünge der Ethik Kants in seinem vorkritischen Schriften und Reflektionen*. Meisenheim am Glan, Germany: Anton Hain, 1961.

Schoolman, Morton. *Reason and Horror: Critical Theory, Democracy, and Aesthetic Rationality*. London: Routledge, 2001.

Schopenhauer, Arthur. *The World as Will and Representation*. 2 vols. New York: Dover, 1958.

Searle, John. *Intentionality*. Cambridge: Cambridge University Press, 1983.

Sellars, Wilfrid. *Empiricism and the Philosophy of Mind*. Cambridge, MA: Harvard University Press, 1997.

Shapiro, Gary. "Notes on the Animal Kingdom of the Spirit." In *The "Phenomenology of Spirit" Reader*, edited by Jon Stewart, 225–43. New York: State University of New York Press, 1998.

Shell, Susan Meld. *Kant and the Limits of Autonomy*. Cambridge, MA: Harvard University Press, 2009.

Sherman, Nancy. *Making a Necessity of Virtue: Aristotle and Kant on Virtue*. Cambridge: Cambridge University Press, 1997.

Sherratt, Yvonne. *Adorno's Positive Dialectic*. Cambridge: Cambridge University Press, 2002.

Short, Jonathan. "Experience and Aura: Adorno, McDowell, and 'Second Nature.'" In *Adorno and the Need in Thinking: Critical Essays*, edited by Donald A. Burke, Colin J. Campbell, Kathy Kiloh, Michael K. Palamarek, and Jonathan Short, 181–203. Toronto: University of Toronto Press, 2007.

Shuster, Martin. "Adorno and Anscombe on the Final Ends of Life." Unpublished manuscript.

———. "Loneliness and Language: Arendt, Cavell, and Modernity." *International Journal of Philosophical Studies* 20, no. 4 (2012): 473–97.

———. "'Nothing to Know': Framing Adorno's Moral Perfectionism." Unpublished manuscript.

———. "Philosophy and Genocide." In *The Oxford Handbook of Genocide Studies*, edited by Donald Bloxham and A. Dirk Moses, 217–35. Oxford: Oxford University Press, 2010.

Shusterman, Richard. *Body Consciousness: A Philosophy of Mindfulness and Somaesthetics*. Cambridge: Cambridge University Press, 2008.

Siep, Ludwig. *Anerkennung als Prinzip der praktischen Philosophie: Untersuchungen zu Hegels Jenaer Philosophie des Geistes*. Freiburg: Alber, 1979.

Silber, John R. "The Copernican Revolution in Ethics: The Good Re-examined." *Kant-Studien* 51 (1951): 85–101.

———. "The Importance of the Highest Good in Kant's Ethics." *Ethics* 73 (1963): 179–97.

———. "Kant's Conception of the Highest Good as Immanent and Transcendent." *Philosophical Review* 68 (1959): 469–92.

Smith, Nick. "Making Adorno's Ethics and Politics Explicit." *Social Theory and Practice* 29, no. 3 (2003): 487–98.

Smith, Steven G. "Worthiness to Be Happy and Kant's Concept of the Highest Good." *Kant Studien* 75 (1984): 168–90.

Speight, Allen. *Hegel, Literature, and the Problem of Agency*. Cambridge: Cambridge University Press, 2001.

Stewart, Jon. *The Hegel Myths and Legends*. Evanston, IL: Northwestern University Press, 1996.

———. "Hegel's Doctrine of Determinate Negation: An Example from Sense-Certainty and Perception." *Idealistic Studies* 26, no. 1 (1996): 57–78.

———. *The Unity of Hegel's "Phenomenology of Spirit": A Systematic Interpretation*. Evanston, IL: Northwestern University Press, 2000.

Tassone, Giuseppe. "Amoral Adorno: Negative Dialectics outside Ethics." *European Journal of Social Theory* 8, no. 3 (2005): 251–67.

Taylor, Charles. "Hegel's Philosophy of Mind." In *Human Agency and Language: Philosophical Papers*, 1:77–97. Cambridge: Cambridge University Press, 1985.

———. "The Opening Arguments of the *Phenomenology*." In *Hegel: A Collection of Critical Essays*, edited by Alasdair MacIntyre, 151–87. Garden City, NY: Doubleday, 1972.

———. *A Secular Age*. Cambridge, MA: Harvard University Press, 2007.

———. "Self-Interpreting Animals." In *Human Agency and Language*, 1:45–76. Cambridge: Cambridge University Press, 1985.

———. "What Is Human Agency?" In *Human Agency and Language*, 1:15–44. Cambridge: Cambridge University Press, 1985.

Taylor, Robert S. "Kant's Political Religion: The Transparency of Perpetual Peace and the Highest Good." *Review of Politics* 72 (2010): 1–24.

Thompson, Michael. *Life and Action: Elementary Structures of Practice and Practical Thought*. Cambridge, MA: Harvard University Press, 2008.

Thyen, Anke. *Negative Dialektik und Erfahrung: zur Rationalität des Nichtidentischen bei Adorno*. Frankfurt am Main: Suhrkamp, 1989.

Todd, Charles Norman. "Life Interrupted: Akrasia, Action, and Active Irrationality." PhD diss., University of Chicago, 2011.

Velkley, Richard L. *Freedom and the End of Reason: On the Moral Foundation of Kant's Critical Philosophy*. Chicago: University of Chicago Press, 1989.

Velleman, J. David. *The Possibility of Practical Reason*. Oxford: Oxford University Press, 2000.

Verene, Donald Phillip. "Hegel's Spiritual Zoo and the Modern Condition." *Owl of Minerva* 25 (1994): 235–40.

Voeller, Carol W. *The Metaphysics of the Moral Law: Kant's Deduction of Freedom*. New York: Garland, 2001.

Vogel, Steven. *Against Nature: The Concept of Nature in Critical Theory*. Albany: State University of New York, 1996.

Vogler, Candace. "Anscombe on Practical Inference." In *Varieties of Practical Reasoning*, edited by Elijah Milgram, 453–62. Cambridge, MA: MIT Press, 2001.

———. "The Moral of the Story." *Critical Inquiry*, no. 34 (2007): 5–35.

———. *Reasonably Vicious*. Cambridge, MA: Harvard University Press, 2002.

Walker, Arthur. "The Problem of Weakness of Will." *Noûs* 23, no. 5 (1989): 653–76.

Watkins, Eric. *Kant and the Metaphysics of Causality*. Cambridge: Cambridge University Press, 2005.

Wellmer, Albrecht. "Ludwig Wittgenstein: On the Difficulties of Receiving His Philosophy and Its Relation to the Philosophy of Adorno." In *Endgames: The Irreconcilable Nature of Modernity, Essays and Lectures*, 239–51. Cambridge, MA: MIT Press, 1988.

Wiggerhaus, Rolf. *Adorno und Wittgenstein: Zwei Spielarten modernen Philosophierens*. Göttingen: Wallstein, 2000.

———. *The Frankfurt School*. Translated by Michael Robertson. Cambridge, MA: MIT Press, 1994.

Wiggins, David. *Needs, Values, Truth: Essays in the Philosophy of Value*. Oxford: Blackwell, 1987.

———. "Truth as Predicated of Moral Judgments." In *Needs, Values, Truth: Essays in the Philosophy of Value*, 139–84. Oxford: Blackwell, 1987.

———. "Truth, Invention, and the Meaning of Life." In *Needs, Values, Truth: Essays in the Philosophy of Value*, 87–137. Oxford: Blackwell, 1987.

Wike, Victoria S. *Kant on Happiness in Ethics*. Albany: State University of New York Press, 1994.

Williams, Bernard. *Ethics and the Limits of Philosophy*. London: Routledge, 1993.

———. "Internal and External Reasons." In *Moral Luck*, 101–14. Cambridge: Cambridge University Press, 1981.

———. "Moral Luck." In *Moral Luck*, 20–40. Cambridge: Cambridge University Press, 1981.

———. *Shame and Necessity*. Berkley: University of California Press, 2008.

Williams, Robert. *Recognition: Fichte and Hegel on the Other*. Buffalo: State University of New York Press, 1992.

Wittgenstein, Ludwig. *On Certainty*. New York: Harper and Row, 1969.

———. *Philosophical Investigations*. Translated by G. E. M. Anscombe. Upper Saddle River, NJ: Prentice Hall, 1973.

Wood, Allen W. *Hegel's Ethical Thought*. Cambridge: Cambridge University Press, 1990.

———. *Kant's Ethical Thought*. Cambridge: Cambridge University Press, 1999.

———. *Kant's Moral Religion*. Ithaca, NY: Cornell University Press, 1970.

Yack, Bernard. *The Longing for Total Revolution: Philosophic Sources of Social Discontent from Rousseau to Marx and Nietzsche*. Princeton, NJ: Princeton University Press, 1986.

Yeomans, Christopher. "Hegel and Analytic Philosophy of Action." *Owl of Minerva* 42, no. 1/2 (2011): 41–62.

Yovel, Yirmiyahu. *Kant and the Philosophy of History*. Princeton, NJ: Princeton University Press, 1980.

Zahavi, Dan. "Subjectivity and the First-Person Perspective." *Southern Journal of Philosophy* 45, no. S1 (2007): 66–84.

Zuidervaart, Lambert. *Social Philosophy After Adorno*. Cambridge: Cambridge University Press, 2007.

———. "Truth and Authentication: Heidegger and Adorno in Reverse." In *Adorno and Heidegger*, edited by Iain Macdonald and Krzysztof Ziarek, 22–47. Stanford, CA: Stanford University Press, 2008.

INDEX

Absolute Knowing. *See* Absolute Knowledge
Absolute Knowledge, 143, 152, 155–56, 164, 166
acknowledgment, 122–23; as an interpretation of knowledge, 122n115
action: Adorno's philosophy of, 73–79, 85–99; and affordances, 84n22, 87–88, 98, 100, 103, 99, 134–35; and *akrasia*, 91n40, 95n55; as best explained by other actions, 86, 89; and desire, 106–14, 130–33; and inner and outer distinction, 79–81, 81n17, 94, 96, 122, 157; and intention, 36, 61, 81–83, 94–97, 117, 137, 159; and irrationality, 73, 78–79, 81–82, 86–87, 91, 93, 98, 106, 133–35, 154, 170; morally practical bases for action, 73–79, 99–102, 103, 119; morally practical bases for action in Kant, 67; rationalization of, 81–82, 89–90; rational necessity of, 5, 77, 87–88; in relationship to reflection, 133–35; and self-ascription requirement, 78–79; social understanding of, 75, 75n8, 94–96; structure of, 90–99; technically practical bases for action in Kant, 67; and time, 87–99, 96, 96n58 (*see also* intentions-in-action)
addendum: alleged irrationality of, 73, 78–79, 81–82, 86–87, 91, 93, 98, 106; as involved in action, 85–86; moral, 72–73, 100; normative elements to, 76, 79–85, 92–99; somatic aspect of, 74, 76, 79, 81–84, 86, 88, 96, 113, 121, 125, 127–28, 173–74; two components to, 74, 81
administration, 103–4
Adorno, Gretel, 10, 122n113

Adorno, Theodor W.: and bourgeois coldness, 123, 132; criticism of subjectivity in the work of, 13–32, 75–76, 82–84, 87, 97–98; criticism of transcendental philosophy in the work of, 79–85; critique of autonomy in the work of, 21–41; critique of modernity, 32–39, 102–23; *Dialectic of Enlightenment*, as author of, 9–11; elitism of, 115, 117–20; importance of notion of experience for, 102–23; and links to the thought of Stanley Cavell, 4, 36–37, 84–85, 107–23, 127, 173; as a moral perfectionist thinker, 173n18; "Meditations on Metaphysics" of, 172–73; and *Minima Moralia*, 38, 72, 76, 80, 174; moral philosophy of, 73–79, 99–128; negativism of, 72, 75, 104; normativity in the work of, 79–85; and notion of autonomy in the work of, 2, 33–39, 71n1; and notion of freedom, 85–99, 102–28; and notion of a model in the work of, 173–74; philosophy of action in the work of, 85–99; relationship of work of to Hegel, 134–37, 166–68; relationship to Marxism, 13n28; role of concept of expression in the work of, 105–23; view of practical reason in the work of, 85–102, 123–28
affordances. *See* action, and affordances
agency: dissolution of (*see* subjectivity, dissolution of); embodied, 75, 78, 83–84, 86–88, 92–93, 96, 112, 128, 133, 136; as expression, 105–23; in Kant (*see* Kant, Immanuel, notion of a maxim for)
akrasia. See action, and *akrasia*
Alien Hand. *See* Hemisomatoagnosia